Teaching, Responsibility, and the Corruption of Youth

Educational Futures

RETHINKING THEORY AND PRACTICE

Series Editor

Michael A. Peters (*Beijing Normal University, P.R. China*)

Editorial Board

Michael Apple (*University of Wisconsin-Madison, USA*)
Miriam David (*UCL Institute of Education, London, UK*)
Cushla Kapitzke (*Queensland University of Technology, Australia*)
Simon Marginson (*UCL Institute of Education, London, UK*)
Mark Olssen (*Auckland University of Technology, New Zealand*)
Fazal Rizvi (*University of Melbourne, Australia*)
Susan Robertson (*University of Cambridge, UK*)
Linda Tuhiwai Smith (*University of Waikato, New Zealand*)
Arun Kumar Tripathi (*Indian Institute of Technology, Mandi, Himachal Pradesh, India*)

VOLUME 71

The titles published in this series are listed at *brill.com/edfu*

Teaching, Responsibility, and the Corruption of Youth

By

Tina (A.C.) Besley and Michael A. Peters

BRILL
SENSE

LEIDEN | BOSTON

All chapters in this book have undergone peer review.

Library of Congress Cataloging-in-Publication Data

Names: Besley, Tina A.C., author. | Peters, Michael A., author.
Title: Teaching, responsibility, and the corruption of youth / by Tina (A.C.)
   Besley, Michael A. Peters.
Description: Leiden, The Netherlands ; Boston : Brill Sense, [2019] | Series:
   Educational futures : rethinking theory and practice ; volume 71 |
   Includes bibliographical references.
Identifiers: LCCN 2018047124 (print) | LCCN 2018055551 (ebook) | ISBN
   9789004380776 (ebook) | ISBN 9789004380769 (hardback : alk. paper) | ISBN
   9789004380752 (pbk. : alk. paper)
Subjects: LCSH: Educational accountability. | Teaching--Moral and ethical
   aspects. | In loco parentis. | School discipline. | Behavior modification.
   | Education and globalization.
Classification: LCC LB2806.22 (ebook) | LCC LB2806.22 .B48 2018 (print) | DDC
   371.102--dc23
LC record available at https://lccn.loc.gov/2018047124

Typeface for the Latin, Greek, and Cyrillic scripts: "Brill". See and download: brill.com/brill-typeface.

ISSN 2214-9864
ISBN 978-90-04-38075-2 (paperback)
ISBN 978-90-04-38076-9 (hardback)
ISBN 978-90-04-38077-6 (e-book)

Copyright 2019 by Koninklijke Brill NV, Leiden, The Netherlands, except where stated otherwise.
Koninklijke Brill NV incorporates the imprints Brill, Brill Hes & De Graaf, Brill Nijhoff, Brill Rodopi,
Brill Sense, Hotei Publishing, mentis Verlag, Verlag Ferdinand Schöningh and Wilhelm Fink Verlag.
All rights reserved. No part of this publication may be reproduced, translated, stored in a retrieval system,
or transmitted in any form or by any means, electronic, mechanical, photocopying, recording or otherwise,
without prior written permission from the publisher.
Authorization to photocopy items for internal or personal use is granted by Koninklijke Brill NV provided
that the appropriate fees are paid directly to The Copyright Clearance Center, 222 Rosewood Drive, Suite
910, Danvers, MA 01923, USA. Fees are subject to change.

Brill has made all reasonable efforts to trace all rights holders to any copyrighted material used in this
work. In cases where these efforts have not been successful the publisher welcomes communications from
copyright holders, so that the appropriate acknowledgements can be made in future editions, and to settle
other permission matters.

This book is printed on acid-free paper and produced in a sustainable manner.

Contents

Preface IX
Acknowledgements XIII
Introduction: Teachers, Responsibility and the Resistance of Youth XIV

1 Philosophy, Education and the Corruption of Youth
   From Socrates to Islamic Extremists 1
   Introduction 1
   Youth, Moral Development and Indoctrination 2
   The Case of Socrates – A Teacher Accused of Corrupting Youth 4
   Education, Dissent, Indoctrination and Corrupting Youth –
       Contemporary Exemplars 11
   Conclusion 15

2 Heidegger, De-Nazification and the Art of Teaching 19
   Introduction 19
   Heidegger as Teacher 19
   Heidegger's Comportment and the Art of Teaching 22

3 Truth-Telling as an Educational Practice of the Self
   Foucault, Parrhesia and the Ethics of Subjectivity 25
   Introduction 25
   Foucault on the Truth: From Regimes to Games of Truth 28
   Parrhesia, Education and Practices of Truth-Telling 32
   Conclusion: Foucault and the Prospects for *Parrhesiastical* Education 39

4 Interculturalism, Ethnocentrism and Dialogue 46
   Introduction: Interculturalism and Ethnocentrism 46
   Dialogue 49
   Conclusion 60

5 Understanding the Sources of Anti-Westernism
   A Dialogue between Michael A. Peters and Jan Nederveen Pieterse 63

6 Islam and the End of European Multiculturalism?
   From Multiculturalism to Civic Integration 81
   Introduction 81

From Multiculturalism to the Crisis of Civic Integration   82
David Cameron's 2011 Speech at the Munich Security Conference   85
Education and the Rise of Terrorism Studies   88
Reactions to Islamic Extremism: Hate Preachers and 'Poisonous Narratives'   94
'Radicalization' as 'Education'   95
The 'Crisis of Integration'   97

7 **'Western Education Is Sinful'**
Boko Haram and the Abduction of Chibok Schoolgirls   102
Introduction   102

8 **Global Citizenship Education**
Politics, Problems and Prospects   109
Introduction   109

9 **The Refugee Crisis and the Right to Political Asylum**   116
Introduction   116

10 **The Refugee Crisis in Europe**
Words without Borders   126
Introduction   126
'Refugee Blues', by W.H. Auden   126
From 'A Mother in a Refugee Camp', by Chinua Achebe   127
From 'Home', by Warsan Shire   128
From 'When I am Overcome by Weakness', by Najat Abdul Samad   129
From 'I am a Refugee', by Mohamed Raouf Bachir   130

11 **From State Responsibility for Education and Welfare to Self-Responsibilisation in the Market**   133
Introduction   133

12 **Pedagogies of the Walking Dead**
Diminishing Responsibility for Social Justice in a Neoliberal World   143
Introduction: Zombie Theory   143
Responsibilizing Teachers: The International Agencies   149
Neoliberalism and Teachers   151

Conclusion: Education for Ecological Democracy   157
Democracy, Yet Again   157
Ecological Democracy   158

Origins and Possibilities   161
Education for Ecological Democracy   162

Postscript: The End of Neoliberal Globalization and the Rise of Authoritarian Populism   167

Preface

We left the shores of New Zealand in 2000, after nearly a decade at the University of Auckland and headed for the University of Glasgow. It was a very different political and ideological environment. Radical Islam Al-Qaeda and the Islamic State posed a global threat although less so for Scotland than England. However, Glasgow was not immune to the Jihadist threat as the attack on Glasgow Airport in 2007 indicated. It was the first terrorist attack on Scottish soil since the Lockerbie bombing in 1988 and took place only 36 hours after the London car bomb attacks. While five members of the public were injured, some severely, fortunately there were no deaths of civilians. In New Zealand at Canterbury and Auckland Universities we had been closely connected with the so-called Māori political and cultural renaissance, being part of both teaching and research on Māori education and supporting Māori scholars in their efforts to establish *kura kaupapa* Māori schooling.

In Scotland, we were exposed first hand to the radicalization of young British Muslims although Scotland's experience differed greatly from that of England that was exposed through more extreme attitudes toward immigration and an aggressive foreign policy. The then British Prime Minister Tony Blair had fallen in with Bush's war in Iraq. We arrived in 2000 when Scotland was little concerned with the effects of religious intolerance and racism experienced by Muslim communities. It was a time when the threat of radical Islam issued in statements by politicians and commentators about the end of European multiculturalism. We were interested in what philosophy of education could tell us about these issues and conceived a book about the corruption of youth that examined questions of education from a philosophical point of view about education, teaching, and ethnocentrism. We wanted to go back to those labelled 'corruptors' of youth at the time – Socrates, Heidegger, Foucault – to see what light they could shed on contemporary matters. Indeed, rather than corrupting youth these philosophers enlightened us with notions of dialogue, truth, criticism and truth-telling that it seemed to us were essential tools of the teaching profession if we were to tackle problems of globalization in a non-ideological way. Of course, we did not claim that any of these philosophers themselves were free from criticism, especially Heidegger whose sullied past implicated him in the very kind of European racism that we were examining. The orientation of the book soon shifted from a philosophical book concerned with philosophers to contemporary issues of teaching and the responsibility for youth, and specifically the difficulties of teaching responsibility in a conflicted world. We also wanted to examine the sources of anti-Westernism and the prospects for interculturalism in what became the agenda for global citizenship (Besley & Peters, 2012). It was in 2014 that Boko Haram, the West African Islamic State, abducted 276 Chinok schoolgirls in a campaign of violence claiming 'Western education is sinful'.

These matters were exacerbated when what was referred to as the 'refugee problem in Europe' began in 2015 and reached its peak soon after with over 1.8 million Syrians, Afghani, Iraqi and others since 2014 migrating to Europe, sparking illiberal policies in hard-line eastern and central European states like Hungary and Poland. Since then the number of migrants to Europe has subsided although the problems have multiplied leading to the rise of Alt-Right parties in Europe since 2010 with fascist and neo-Nazi parties, alongside far-right parties gaining ground in countries where national culture and white identity is perceived to be under threat. How does one teach in this environment? What are the responsibilities for teachers? We don't mean to reduce responsibility to a narrow neoliberal accountability but to view it in the wider ethical sense of responsibility for Others and to enjoin a notion of responsibility that has a collective and generational dimension tied to action. How else are we to proceed in the Anthropocene?

In 2005 we were invited to the University of Illinois at Urbana-Champaign and joined the new program in Global Studies in Education set up by Fazal Rizvi. The program seemed well timed and we taught various courses around the kinds of issues raised in the chapters of this book. Events in Europe, while not exactly the same, had some resonance in the USA. We arrived in time to spend a day campaigning for Obama in his first term. Of course, there is nothing in Europe that approaches the history of US Civil Rights, or the issues and problems of Black and Latino education that plague the US. That was in part the subject for the book *Obama and the End of the American Dream* (Peters, 2012).

In 2011 we departed the USA to return to New Zealand and the University of Waikato located in Hamilton. We had been away from our homeland for over a decade, and we were amazed at how things had changed! After forty years of neoliberalism, New Zealand, the historic home of the welfare state, was in extreme social disorder with some estimated 290,000 children living on the poverty line, and young couples and families shut out of the speculative housing market in Auckland (Peters, 2011). We were appalled and held several conferences on poverty and Freirean education to try to bring interested scholars together. Neoliberalism had also affected the universities and Waikato was no exception, with strong line management systems that eroded academic culture and collegiality, while accruing power to administrators and managers. We had one line manager who didn't have a research degree and had been in the institution thirty-five years producing one peer reviewed paper in that time.

The last couple of chapters recognize the prevalence of this political change that makes schools and universities instruments of the marketized and manergerialist state, and inhibits criticism, truth and social justice (Peters et al., 2016). In Chapter 11 we use the Foucaultian term 'responsibilization' to indicate the massive changes in political economy that took place with the shift from state welfare to the market. After neoliberalism or alongside it we have seen the rise of the so-called Alt-Right and return of the racism of white supremacist ideology. What does education become in a post-truth world and how do teachers deal with the rise of authoritarian populism? Education in the age of Trump is a very different era from either welfare state or neoliberal market education.

In 2017 Jacinda Ardern, the darling of the Labour Party, with the help of Winston Peters became Prime Minister of New Zealand, leading a Coalition Government including NZ First and NZ Green parties. Just seven weeks before the 2017 general election Ardern assumed leadership of the Labour Party following the resignation of Andrew Little. She became the third female prime minister and the youngest at 37 to lead New Zealand. Immediately she identified child poverty and homelessness as priorities, blaming the 'blatant failure' of neoliberal capitalism. She has been identified by more than one commentator as the hero of the global left.

In the years since 2011 we had established the Centre for Global Studies in Education at Waikato but funding for it soon dried up and the University and the Faculty seemed uninterested in such global matters or approaches in philosophy of education. In mid 2018 we were offered positions at Beijing Normal University, having travelled and worked with colleagues there in various capacities for many years, with strong links to Sociology, Philosophy and Education. In September 2018 we took up full time posts as Distinguished Professors and look forward to working with our new Chinese colleagues.

We would like also to acknowledge our colleagues at Waikato University who worked with us in Global Studies including Jayne White, Sonja Arndt, and Carl Mika and a number of PhD students including Richard Heraud, Lynley Tulloch, Maggie Lyall, Robert Stratford, Barnaby Pace, Rene Novak, Shamaila Noreen, Nachia Muthiamal, Thanh Dao, Sally Kim, and Lilien Skudder. These students and staff in Global Studies of Education made our return to New Zealand worthwhile, as did our friends and colleagues of the Philosophy of Education Society of Australasia who have not given up on the critical project.

References

Besley, T., & Peters, M. (2012). *Interculturalism, education and dialogue*. New York, NY: Peter Lang.

Peters, M. (2011). *Neoliberalism and after? Education, social policy and the crisis of western capitalism.* New York, NY: Peter Lang.

Peters, M. (2012). *Obama and the end of the American dream.* Rotterdam, The Netherlands: Sense Publishers.

Peters, M., Rider, S., Hyvönen, M., & Besley, T. (Eds.). (2018). *Post-truth and fake news: Viral modernity and higher education.* Singapore: Springer.

Acknowledgements

We wish to acknowledge and thank the copyright holders for permission to publish our work in this collection. We also wish to thank Jolanda Karada and the editorial team at Brill | Sense for their suggestions and support in producing this book.

- Chapter 1, 'Philosophy, Education and the Corruption of Youth', *Educational Philosophy and Theory*, 45(1), 2013, 6–19.
- Chapter 2, 'Heidegger, De-Nazification and the Art of Teaching' is based on a paper presented to the European Conference on Educational Research (ECER), Lisbon, 2002: Philosophy of Education Symposia on 'Good Teaching'.
- Chapter 3, 'Truth-Telling as an Educational Practice of the Self', *Oxford Review of Education*, 29(2), 2003, 207–223.
- Chapter 4, 'Interculturalism, Ethnocentrism and Dialogue', *Policy Futures in Education*, 9(1), 2011, 1–12.
- Chapter 5, 'Understanding the Sources of Anti-Westernism', *Policy Futures in Education*, 10(1), 2012, 59–69.
- Chapter 6, 'Islam and the End of European Multiculturalism? From Multiculturalism to Civic Integration', *Policy Futures in Education*, 12(1), 2014, 1–15.
- Chapter 7, 'Western Education is Sinful': Boko Haram and the Abduction of Chibok Schoolgirls', *Policy Futures in Education*, 12(2), 2014, 1–5.
- Chapter 8, 'Global Citizenship Education: Politics, Problems and Prospects', *Citizenship, Social and Economics Education*, 9(1), 2010, 43–47.
- Chapter 9, 'The Refugee Crisis and the Right to Political Asylum', *Educational Philosophy and Theory*, 47(13–14), 2015, 1367–1374.
- Chapter 10, 'The Refugee Crisis in Europe: Words without Borders', in Peter McLaren & Suzi Soohoo (Eds.), *Radical Imagine-Nation*, 2017, pp. 191–198, Peter Lang, New York.
- Chapter 11, 'From State Responsibility for Education and Welfare to Self-Responsibilization in the Market', *Discourse: Studies in the Cultural Politics of Education*, 38, 2017, 138–145.
- Chapter 12, revised 2018, following the article 'Pedagogics of the Walking Dead: Diminishing responsibility for social justice in a neoliberal world', *Artículo de Reflexión Pedagogía y Saberes*, No. 43 Universidad Pedagógica Nacional Facultad de Educación, 2015, 49–57.
- Conclusion. 'Education for Ecological Democracy', *Educational Philosophy and Theory*, 49(10), 2017: 941–945.
- Postscript, 'The End of Neoliberal Globalization and the Rise of Authoritarian Populism', *Educational Philosophy and Theory*, 50, 2018, 323–325.

INTRODUCTION

Teachers, Responsibility and the Resistance of Youth

Responsibility is a key concept in our lives with moral, social, financial and political aspects. It embraces two main forms – legal and moral – and takes different forms in relation to personal, professional, corporate and social dimensions. The concept refers to the state of *being accountable* or *answerable* for one's actions and can also imply a sense of obligation or duty normally associated with being in a position of authority such as a parent, teacher or guardian being in authority over children. *Loco parentis,* a Latin phrase that means in place of the parent and originally derived from English Common Law, gives teachers, educational institutions and guardians legal responsibilities for specific functions as a parent to act in the best interests of students without infringing on the civil rights of students.

The concept was first adopted as a motto by the Manchester Warehousemen and Clerks' Orphan Schools in 1855 and was applied for wards of the state. Its legal meaning in U.S. education was only tested during the 1960s when student conduct especially when materially affecting the rights of other students was not considered immune by constitutional guarantees of freedom. Teachers administering discipline were seen not merely as acting as parents but as representatives of the state. First amendment rights of students in public schools are not generally seen as coextensive with those of adults in other settings. The concept is still being refined: dress codes and lockers, cell phones or computer searches have not yet been tested in court. Student freedom of expression is considered by some judicial authorities to be significantly limited by *loco parentis*. Private institutions by contrast are generally given more authority over their student charges. Prior to the 1960s even students in higher education experienced many restrictions on their private lives including curfews', and dress codes especially for women. The Student Free Speech Movement at Berkeley challenged many of these restrictions in the mid-1960s based on the students' rights to free speech and academic freedom especially in relation to campus political activities. Generally, as the decades rolled on *loco parentis* has become more of an anachronism. The question of pastoral care is now open to greater scrutiny as the main agencies for the care of children, students and teenagers, both public and private, have been exposed as being based on a range of unacceptable punishments including solitary confinement, violence, and physical, sexual and emotional abuse.[1]

In this brief initial analysis already we can see that the concept of responsibility implies a notion of moral agency and accountability for one's actions, often attached to a particular role. The etymology of the word suggests that it surfaces around the 1590s in French and Latin with the meaning of being answerable to someone or for something (from the Latin *respons*), and later in the 1640s for being accountable for one's actions: two senses often conflated in modern discussions.

In terms of our moral vocabulary it is a concept that it relatively recent and one that springs from two quite different traditions. Garreth Williams (n.d.) maintains that the word only finds a home in the political debates on representative government in the eighteenth century and only later in twentieth century philosophy does it establish its own language game when the concept is introduced based on debates concerning free will, causation and determinism. This etymology suggests that the concept came into being at the same time that notions of autonomy, the individual and the subject began to form within the liberal network of rights and the citizen.

Professional responsibility emerged much later again with the development of professional ethics that while its origins date from the adoption of the Hippocratic oath by medical practitioners in the fifth century really only came in widespread use and adoption in the twentieth century. Increasingly when professionals utilize specialist knowledge and skills in the service of the public they are required to adhere to the norms of confidentiality, transparency, integrity, and honesty as formulated and regulated by a professional code of practice. It probably began in earnest with moral rules of professional conduct governing the conduct of lawyers in the court although the word professional has roots to 'profess' and is associated with the concept of confession made by a person entering a religious order and is therefore connected to the idea of a *calling*.

Official accounts of teacher responsibility tend to emphasise the behaviours that teachers ought to exhibit or model – 'The teacher as a person' – with an accent on vocational qualities like empathy, trust, confidence, high student expectations, equal treatment, good communication skills, 'a professional manner', 'a sense of humour'. This constitutes a 'personalogical' approach to teacher responsibility and often involves the mere statement of these qualities as though they were self-evident and require no theoretical interpretation of justification. In other approaches teachers are seen as being responsible for 'classroom management and organization' with an accent on the 'well-ordered' classroom that is nevertheless arranged or 'grouped' in order to promote interaction and discussion with fair access to instruction and classroom teaching materials.

Another feature of teacher responsibility is responsibility for determining content of lessons under curriculum guidelines to promote high-quality instruction that progressively develops a syllabus and observes the national curriculum guidelines. This is surely an aspect of teacher professionalism that is based on subject knowledge on the one hand and teaching experience and understanding on the other. It is a form of professional preparation and preparedness that leads on naturally to teaching itself and to the act of instruction including all the criteria concerning logical structuring of material that encourages higher thinking skills, student questioning, assessment and different forms of learning. Sometimes teacher education programs lay down subject specific responsibilities such as that of the English teacher who for instance should provide good listening behaviours, or offer opportunities for different kinds of speech acts, class discussion or experience of written genres. A science teacher might be reminded about special lab safety conditions, or the means of progressing in science through 'discoveries' and 'investigations' that highlights the collection and analysis of facts. Assessment in particular has become a large part of professional responsibility of teachers including all aspects of monitoring and managing student progress and its effective record often in relation to national standards. These can be regarded as 'compliance' forms of responsibility where the teacher is required to abide by standards laid down by statutory authority.

In addition to these tasks focused on the act of teaching, authorities often specify certain administrative, community, and parental responsibilities as well as the capacity to respond to certain groups of students labelled as 'at-risk' or 'high-ability' students. Many accounts of teacher responsibilities highlight the relationship and treatment of learners such as the need to '[t]reat learners fairly, respectfully, and without bias related to their age, race, gender, sexual orientation, disability, religion, or national origin'.[2] Many authorities also discuss 'Responsibility in Professional Relationships' and 'Responsibility in Relationships with Patients and Families'. In addition, not only do teacher authorities mention teacher responsibilities in relation to different groups of students including increasingly those with disabilities, or those with special health needs, or 'drug problems' but they also differentiate among the teaching profession to emphasise different responsibilities of the 'classroom teacher', 'curriculum team leader', 'head of department' or 'head teacher'.

Seen in this light teaching is considered a 'calling' that implies a commitment of care. This includes responsibilities, duties and obligations often to minors and to children on whose behalf teachers, as professionals, must act, but also to those adults who are deemed incapable or unable to act in their own self interests. Professionals in this sense are seen as occupying a place between the state and the public based on a relationship of trust and good faith. They are presumed to act in the service of the public for the common good on behalf of the community to undertake specific functions based on their knowledge and skills.

Fani Lauermann (2013, p. 1) in her thesis 'Teacher Responsibility: Its Meaning, Measure, and Educational Implications' writes:

> Teachers' personal sense of responsibility potentially influences their instructional practices, psychological well-being, and ultimately their students' learning and performance. Various conceptualizations of teacher responsibility have been linked to such outcomes as positive attitudes toward teaching and professional dedication (Halvorsen, Lee, & Andrade, 2009), job satisfaction (Winter, Brenner, & Petrosko, 2006), positive affect toward teaching (Guskey, 1984), teachers' beliefs in their ability to influence students, teachers' willingness to implement new instructional practices (Guskey, 1988), and with student achievement (Lee & Smith, 1996, 1997). Furthermore, the assumption that teachers are personally responsible, or that they should assume personal responsibility for their students' educational outcomes – primarily test performance – is at the core of high-impact educational policies such as the implementation of accountability systems in American schools. (Linn, 2006, 2010; Schraw, 2010)

Her analysis of the extant literature on teacher responsibility demonstrates conceptual and operational ambiguity: 'the term responsibility has been used interchangeably with related constructs such as internal locus of control and teacher efficacy, measurement instruments have incorporated items originally designed to assess other constructs such as efficacy, and have generally failed to acknowledge the multidimensional nature of teacher responsibility, and the literature lacks a comprehensive and consistent definition of the term' (Lauerman, 2013, p. 1). She adopts Lenk's (1992) six-component framework of teacher responsibility: (a) Who is responsible? (b) For what? (c) For/to whom? (d) Who is the judge? (e) In relation to what criteria? and (f) In what realm? Her analysis of different conceptualizations of responsibility suggests that it reflects 'a sense of internal obligation and commitment to produce or prevent designated outcomes or that these outcomes should have been produced or prevented' (p. 42). But this is a literature based analysis and synthesis from an educational psychological view rather than a philosophical, political or historical analysis of a changing concept.

We argue that the conceptual and operational ambiguity is the result of a profound change in the concept of responsibility that reflects the shift of a notion from liberalism based in individual and professional autonomy and moral agency to neoliberalism based on a thin concept of market accountability. Increasingly this shift has resulted in the collapse of moral and legal responsibility and the promotion of a form of regulation under accountability. In the analytic tradition responsibility is defined as a duty or obligation to fulfil or complete a task related to a profession, to universally accepted moral obligation or to a majority or group of people as a form of political accountability. Accountability and the rise of audit cultures have accompanied neoliberalism and new managerialism in the public sector. As Michael Power (1994, p. 47) argues: 'Audit is an emerging principle of social organization [that] ... constitutes a major shift of power: from the public to the professional, and from teachers, engineers and managers to overseers'.

There are, roughly speaking four different contemporary forms that 'accountability' takes. We might call them *accountability regimes*. They are not mutually exclusive and may exist as hybrids. First, there is the state-mandated agency form that regulates activity or performance according to standards or criteria laid down at state or federal level. Typically, this form is often associated with devolution of management (though not necessarily governance) and the development of parallel privatization and/or the quasi market in the delivery of public services. Second, there is professional accountability which tends to operate through the control of entry and codes of practice that are struck by professional associations, most often in occupations like law, accountancy, dentistry, doctoring. This professional self regulation often does not include occupations like teaching and nursing, although it may include counselling. Third, there is consumer accountability, that is, accountability through the market, especially where consumer organizations have been strengthened in relation to the development of public services delivered through markets or market-like arrangements. Fourth, there is a form of democratic accountability that has its home in democratic theory and is premised on the demand for both internal and external accountability, that is, typically accountability of a politician to parliament or governing organization and accountability to his/her electorate. The second form or professional accountability may be seen, in reality, to be a form of the fourth or democratic form. Both proceed from Kantian-like assumptions about autonomy, self-regulation, duty and responsibility for one's actions whether this be considered in institutional (e.g., parliament, university) or individual terms.

There has been an observable tendency in Western liberal states to emphasize both agency and consumer forms at the expense of professional and democratic forms, especially where countries are involved in large-scale shifts from traditional Keynesian welfare state regimes to more market-oriented and consumer-driven systems. Indeed, it could be argued that there are natural affinities by way of shared concepts, understandings and operational procedures between these two couplets. One of the main criticisms to have emerged is that the agency/consumer couplet instrumentalizes, individualizes, standardizes, marketizes and externalizes accountability relationships at the expense of democratic values such as participation, self-regulation, collegiality, and collective deliberation that are said to enhance and thicken the relationships involved.

We would argue also in a society where power is no longer based on prohibitions but is normalised then teachers ought to teach students how to be free based on the distinction between the 'account-ability' demanded by neoliberals and the 'response-ability' based on an ethics of caring for others – the response-ability towards others. One is a thin narrow accounting notion and the other is expansive and ecological. The first is to be associated with a passive project of the subject, and 'subjectification' in relation to social institutions; the other, is an account of self in critical relations to others and the environment based on *ethike* or 'care of the self' extended to others. These are two different forms of fashioning the self: the first observes power in a process of normalization; the second provides a potential basis for resistance to power that is inherent in Foucault's later works *The Hermeneutics of the Subject* (2005), *The Government of the Self and Others* (2010) and *The Courage of the Truth* (2011) that together sketch a subject of responsibility for others.

Since Ancient Greek times, citizens, political leaders and philosophers have argued about the wellbeing of youth, their education, their morality and how best to mould youth as responsible citizens. At the same time, education has been identified with a range of different ways of enhancing or inflaming youth passions – as a means to incite or prevent revolution, violence and terrorism. Education may be considered a form of indoctrination or political socialization especially when particular regimes set out to politicize notions of culture, religion and national identity. Moreover, teachers and their ideas can have considerable impact on student attitudes and actions as exemplified by the famous charges of corrupting youth and impiety against Socrates in Ancient Greece.

Charges of the corruption of youth and incitement to rebellion have been levelled at teachers in the context of Nazism, the Cold War, the Vietnam era, Christian fundamentalism and Jihadism. One of the principal concerns of this book is the question of teacher responsibility and student action in relation to this history and these examples. It asks the question: Are teachers responsible for their students' actions? And it provides a political context in which to deliberate on this question by investigation the Western tradition of pedagogy, politics and philosophy, the history of free speech, and the development of citizenship and human rights education.

At the same time, the question of teacher responsibility has been narrowed as a professional concept closely related to a duty of care in an increasingly legally complex environment that reflects historically the growing involvement of parents and parental organizations, teacher associations, state agencies, and the raft of new private and public sector organizations like business roundtables that make pronouncement on the role and responsibilities of teachers. It is also the case that the movement of students' rights has advanced considerably in the last half century. Student constitutional and civil rights developed during the 1960s especially after the free speech movement at Berkeley. The 1960s was the decade of the growth of student power and student protest not only associated with an emphasis on greater democratization of universities and schools but also the growth of civil rights, the New Left, feminism and variously motivated new political groups based around anti-Vietnam and anti-war movements. Much of the action in the U.S. was against segregation in education and for the Black student constitutional right to a basic education.

By comparison today there has been narrowing to consumer rights as the user-pays policies and forms of privatization in education have been established by neoliberals. In a consumer-driven system the emphasis has changed to consumer sovereignty and consumer rights with increasing shifts to issues of security and privacy. The question of access and equality has dropped off the political agenda and now across the Western world the issue of student poverty has become a huge problem along with student indebtedness. Securitization has led to the expression of freedom of expression and freedom of movement. The history of student rights is a relatively recent phenomenon.[3] Traditionally children were not regarded as bearers of rights because they were not considered adults and parents were held to act in their self-interest while teachers acted in *loco parentis*. Paradoxically, *loco parentis* permitted and justified the legal administration of corporal punishment until the 1980s and while most of the West no longer accepts corporal punishment in schools, it is still permitted in Singapore, some Australian and U.S. states, where the corporal punishment legacy lives on in the institutional ethos.

Today many countries hold teachers responsible for providing appropriate moral training and education. Increasingly, accountability extends beyond achievement results to questions of moral and political influence. As a social activity, depending on many factors including the degree of relationship between teacher and student, the teachers charisma, intelligence, knowledge, powers of persuasion, and other influences on a young person (e.g. family, politics, religion), the teacher can have a profound and influential effect on the ethical and political self-constitution of youth for good or for bad.

This book explores the intersection of philosophy, education and the influence of teaching on youth, beginning with the Ancient Athenian democracy, reviewing historical evidence about the intersection between a teachers influence and how Socrates' contemporary Athenians might have viewed him and his students' actions. Philosophy so often presents a de-contextualized and ahistorical picture. Socrates and his teachings must be seen within the historical and political context of his time, when his teachings can be seen as subversively anti-democratic and implicated in three uprisings led by his students against Athenian democracy for which he accepted little or no responsibility. This re-evaluation runs somewhat against the dominant philosophical account of Socrates as one of the great teachers in the Western tradition.

The book then brings the issue of teaching, dissent and democracies into the current era by briefly examining Foucault on free speech (*parrhesia*), education for democracy, citizenship education, the famous case of Heidegger and Nazism, McCarthyism and free speech in the Cold War, student protests of the Vietnam era, and threats from Islamist jihadists. The concern from ancient times to the present about the influence of teachers, education and indoctrination on youth poses a vital question: to what extent is it reasonable to hold a teacher responsible for a student's subsequent actions?

The book also investigates and poses problems for teacher responsibility over contentious issues concerning a range of issues that demonstrate problems of interculturalism, globalization, Jihadism, terrorism, the massive growth of refugees worldwide, and environmentalism in the period that bridges the end of liberal internationalism under Obama and the beginning of national populism and the rise of the alt-right under Trump. In general the books focuses on the new complexity of responsibility of teachers in an era when intercultural issues challenge traditional liberal policies and disrupts borders of the nation state. To the issues of classism, racism and sexism we can add a welter of new questions concerning mass immigration and the movement of peoples across borders as a result of conflict, war and poverty. The paradigm of the migrant as the Other highlights anew problems and paradoxes of ethnocentrism that beset the liberal state with many European nations and the U.S. turning their back on the plight of migrants to reinforce borders, erect fences, and rekindle forms of national populism that acerbate 'we-they' prejudices.

Notes

1 See, for instance, the Australian Royal Commission into the Institutional Responses to Child Sexual Abuse, https://www.hildabuseroyalcommission.gov.au/. See also "The prevalence of child abuse and neglect" (2017), https://aifs.gov.au/cfca/ publications/prevalence-child-abuse-and-neglect
2 See https://hms.harvard.edu/departments/office-registrar/student-handbook/4-student-conduct-and-responsibility/401-responsibilities-teachers-and-learners
3 http://psych.fullerton.edu/mbirnbaum/psych466/LG/academicinterestspage.htm

References

Burchell, G., Davidson, A., & Foucault, M. (2010). *The government of the self and others: Lectures at the Collège de France 1982–1983*. London: Palgrave Macmillan.

Eshleman, A. (2009). Moral responsibility. In Edward N. Zalta (Ed.), *The Stanford encyclopedia of philosophy*. Stanford, CA: Stanford University Press. Retrieved from http://plato.stanford.edu/archives/sum2014/entries/moral-responsibility/

Foucault, M. (2005). *The hermeneutics of the subject: Lectures at the College de France 1981–1982*. New York, NY: Palgrave Macmillan.

Foucault, M. (2011). *The courage of the truth*. London: Palgrave Macmillan.

Guskey, T. R. (1984). The influence of change in instructional effectiveness upon the affective characteristics of teachers. *American Educational Research Journal, 21*(2), 245–259. doi:10.2307/1162442

Guskey, T. R. (1988). Teacher efficacy, self-concept, and attitudes toward the implementation of instructional innovation. *Teaching and Teacher Education, 4*(1), 63–69.

Halvorsen, A.-L., Lee, V. E., & Andrade, F. H. (2009). A mixed-method study of teachers attitudes about teaching in urban and low-income schools. *Urban Education, 44*(2), 181–224.

Lauermann, F. (2013). *Teacher responsibility: Its meaning, measure, and educational implications* (Unpublished PhD dissertation). University of Michigan, Ann Arbor, MI.

Lee, V. E., & Smith, J. B. (1996). Collective responsibility for learning and its effects on gains in achievement for early secondary school students. *American Journal of Education, 104*(2), 103–147.

Lee, V. E., & Smith, J. B. (1997). High school size: Which works best and for whom? *Educational Evaluation and Policy Analysis, 19*(3), 205–227.

Lenk, H. (Ed.). (1992). *Zwischen Wissenschaft und Ethik*. Frankfurt am Main: Suhrkamp Verlag.

Linn, R. L. (2006). *Educational accountability systems*. Los Angeles, CA: CRESST.

Linn, R. L. (2010). A new era of test-based educational accountability. *Measurement: Interdisciplinary Research and Perspectives, 8*(2–3), 145–149.

Schraw, G. (2010). No school left behind. *Educational Psychologist, 45*(2), 71–75.

Williams, G. (n.d.). Responsibility. *The Internet Encyclopedia of Philosophy*. Retrieved from http://www.iep.utm.edu/responsi/

Winter, P. A., Brenner, D. B., & Petrosko, J. M. (2006). Teacher job satisfaction in a reform state: The influence of teacher characteristics, job dimensions, and psychological states. *Journal of School Leadership, 16*(4), 416–437.

CHAPTER 1

Philosophy, Education and the Corruption of Youth
From Socrates to Islamic Extremists

Introduction

Since Ancient Greek times, citizens, political leaders and philosophers have argued about youth wellbeing, education, morality and how best to mould youth as responsible citizens. Education has been identified with a range of different ways of enhancing or inflaming youth passions, as a means to incite or prevent revolution, violence and terrorism. Education may be considered a form of indoctrination or political socialization especially when particular regimes set out to politicize notions of culture, religion and national identity. Moreover, teachers and their ideas can have considerable impact on student attitudes and actions as exemplified by the famous charges of corrupting youth and impiety against Socrates in Ancient Greece. Today many countries hold teachers responsible for providing appropriate moral training directly or indirectly. As a social activity, depending on many factors including the degree of relationship between teacher and student, the teacher's charisma, intelligence, knowledge, powers of persuasion, and other influences on a young person (e.g. family, politics, religion), teaching can have either a profound or a limited effect on youth.

This chapter explores the intersection of philosophy, education and the influence of teaching on youth beginning with the Ancient Athenian democracy, reviewing historical evidence about the intersection between a teacher's influence and how Socrates' contemporary Athenians might have viewed him and his students' actions. Socrates and his teachings must be seen within the historical and political context of his time, when his teachings became seen as subversively anti-democratic and were implicated in three uprisings led by his students against Athenian democracy for which he accepted little or no responsibility. This re-evaluation runs somewhat against the dominant philosophical account of Socrates as one of the great teachers in the Western tradition, whereby philosophy so often presents a de-contextualized and a historical picture.

The chapter then brings the issue of teaching, dissent and democracies into the current era by briefly examining reactions to threats from Islamist jihadists. The concern from ancient times to the present about the influence of teachers, education and indoctrination on youth poses a vital question: to what extent is it reasonable to hold a teacher responsible for a student's subsequent actions?

Youth, Moral Development and Indoctrination

In *Rhetoric*, Book II, Chapters 12–13, Aristotle (1941) clearly identifies three life stages (omitting childhood). He distinguishes youth, from men in the prime of life (adults), to those in old age (aged). Aristotle eloquently describes the character of young men of Ancient Greece in terms of their 'emotions' – 'anger, desire and the like' and 'moral qualities' – 'virtues and vices'. He describes 'the Youthful type of character' – its passions, sexual desires, tempers, emotions, idealism, nobility, friendship and recognized that youth are susceptible to ideology because of their heightened passions, idealism and willingness to take risks. His description of youth – a category which today includes females – holds much that seems to resonate with how youth are viewed today, especially the negative press they receive from the media and ensuing moral panics (see Besley, 2002, 2010). In identifying life stages he paves the way for a philosophy of youth as a category distinct from other stages of life, and for later work on stage theories of development by the likes of Freud, Piaget, Kohlberg and many others.

Philosophers of education have critically examined the notion of indoctrination by focussing on important conceptual differences between the terms 'education' and 'indoctrination' (e.g. see Snook, 1972; Siegel, 1991; Spiecker, 1991).

> To indoctrinate is to imbue one, via teaching, with a doctrine or set of beliefs that involves intentionality on the part of the teacher. It is inherently ideological and suggests that someone is taking advantage of a privileged role to influence those under his charge in a manner which is likely to distort their ability to assess the evidence on its own merit. (Snook, 1972, p. 66)

In contrast, the liberal theory of education promoted by the likes of John Dewey and R. S. Peters, is concerned with broadening the mind and developing rationality and a critical world view which is epitomized in terms of problem-solving, decision-making or the employment of scientific method.

Moral or values education and civic education are contemporary areas of education where indoctrination is most likely to occur because informed people differ in how they perceive these and how and what they believe young people should be taught. It can be difficult for educators to balance the conceptual issues between indoctrination and education as they seek to imbue mainstream societal values and morality in young people in order that they know and appreciate what is good while still respecting their potential or actual rationality. At one extreme, some would argue (following Rousseau, 1979) that all moral and social training should be avoided until the child has developed sufficient rationality to assess, evaluate and form reasonable conclusions about various moral ideas. This may ensure a negative freedom, that is, a freedom from something, but it does not ensure a positive freedom, a freedom to do something. It makes the erroneous assumption that rationality is something that a child acquires at a certain age, denying that rationality is the result of the child experiencing and working through their reactions to a range of social and moral situations and dilemmas. Denying a child such experiences is likely to stunt his or her rationality and moral development. Yet how can education transmit the cultural values and traditions in which rationality itself is defined, without indoctrination and without stunting the rationality of the child in the process? The question then becomes one of the form that education should take once the child is considered educable and what form it should take prior to this. If a programme of moral education is designed to encourage children to weigh evidence and consider the consequences of their actions it becomes the opposite of how indoctrination has been defined.

Just as people in the 21st century are so often concerned about the link between youth, their moral development and the type of education required for them to become responsible citizens, such concerns were predominant in Ancient Greece. With no formal schooling in pre-Socratic Athens, the travelling bands of Sophists who taught rhetoric, oratory and the art of persuasion to the sons of citizens, provided vital skills for debating in the Assembly and the Council of Five Hundred – i.e. for partaking in the democratic process. The Sophist emphasis was on argumentation, on proving a position regardless of truth and on relativity as summed up by Protagoras' famous

> Man is the measure of all things: of things which are, that they are, and of things which are not, that they are not emphasizing that importance of the individual man. (c.485–c.411 BCE in Plato's *Theaetetus*, section 152a [http://classics.mit.edu/ Plato/theatu.html])

Subsequently Plato's dialogue, *Sophist*, is highly critical of them, regarding them as not seekers of truth whose only concern was making money and teaching their students' success in argument by whatever means. Aristotle said that a Sophist was "one who made money by sham wisdom" (*Sophist* [http://classics.mit.edu/Plato/sophist.html]).

The notion of *parrhesia* goes a large way to address this sham wisdom (Foucault, 2001). Foucault's work in *Fearless Speech* (2001), six lectures given at Berkeley in 1985, takes up Plato's and Socrates' attack on the Sophists and its part in the crisis of democratic institutions in 4th century BCE Athens. He discusses how *parrhesia* (usually translated as free speech) or truth-telling speech activities evolved to take various forms – political, philosophical and personal (Foucault, 2001, p. 11). Foucault's intention was not to deal with the problem of truth, but with the problem of truth-teller or truth-telling as an activity (Foucault, 2001, p. 169). Central to his analysis is the importance of the education of youth, how it was central to care of the self, public life and the crisis of democratic institutions. The five major criteria of *parrhesia* that Foucault identifies are:

> *Parrhesia* is a kind of verbal activity where the speaker has a specific relation to truth through frankness, a certain relationship to his own life through danger, a certain relation to himself or other people through criticism ..., and a specific relation to moral law through freedom and duty. More precisely, *parrhesia* is a verbal activity in which a speaker expresses his personal relationship to truth, and risks his life because he recognizes truth-telling as a duty to improve or help other people (as well as himself). In *parrhesia*, the speaker uses his freedom and chooses frankness instead of persuasion, truth instead of falsehood or silence, the risk of death instead of life and security, criticism instead of flat- tery, and moral duty instead of self-interest and moral apathy. (Foucault, 2001, pp. 19–20)

Subjectivity and Truth (Besley & Peters, 2007) elaborates on the notion, discussing Socrates as exemplifying a form of *parrhesia* and providing modern day exemplars. Although Plato uses the word several times, he never refers to Socrates in the role of the *parrhesiastes*. Yet, Socrates appears in the *parrhesiastic* role in both the *Apology* (http://classics.mit.edu/Plato/apology.html) and *Alcibiades Major* (http://www.ancienttexts.org/library/greek/plato/alcibiades1.html) where he demonstrates his care for others in their concern for truth and the perfection of their souls. This omission seems strange since he assigns various positive moral qualities to Socrates, but may be accounted for when we historicize Socrates' trial.

The Case of Socrates – A Teacher Accused of Corrupting Youth

Doug Linder (2002) poses a key question that generally seems to be ignored when philosophers consider Socrates' trial and Plato's *Apology*: Why would a jury of 500 Athenians sentence to death a 70-year-old philosopher who was probably close to the end of his natural lifespan; had taught many of aristocratic youth all his adult life without apparent threat from authorities, despite obviously annoying some people (the old informal charges): What could he have said or done that prompted this?

Was this a political trial or martyrdom by democracy? Was it the tyranny of the majority, the trampling of the voice of reason and individual con- science by mass rule, of the common mans hatred of the man of genius ... as suggested by Gooch (in Rowe, 1999). Strangely, our present day notion of trial by jury is exactly this (but not by so many, so maybe we are less democratic in this respect) – trial by a group of peers – a democratic decision, so why should the trial of Socrates be held up as some sort of aberration and unreasonable event? How did his Athenian peers view him?

Socrates leaves no written record, but Plato, his student and supporter, writes about him in the *Apology* after his death. Subsequent Platonists and even Foucault (2010) have tended to deify Socrates as a *parrhesiastic* hero – as one who showed all the characteristics of *parrhesia* when facing the full force of the Athenian law as he was tried before a jury – the Assembly of 500 Athenians – for "corrupting the young, and by not believing in the gods in whom the city believes, but in other *daimonia* that are novel" (*Apology*, 24b). Foucault (2010) maintained that Socrates took the position that as a philosopher he ignored (or was above) politics, yet the argument set out here largely rebuts that viewpoint. He was found guilty by 280 to 220 votes and famously condemned to death by drinking hemlock. Requiring a majority decision from the 500 *dikasts* (Athenian citizens chosen by lot to serve as jurors), 30 more in his favour would have found him innocent.

Plato and many philosophers subsequently focus on Socrates' words, style and arguments, ignoring the difficult political times facing Athens. However, separating speeches from the context gives only a limited picture of the Athenian Assembly decision. It is important to historicize the famous trial of Socrates, for here we have the intersection of philosophy, democracy, youth and education. Debra Nails (2009) provides a useful timeline in 'A Chronology of the Historical Socrates in the Context of Athenian History and the Dramatic Dates of Plato's Dialogues' but barely touches on the wars, battles, defeats, threats and criticisms of the Athenian democracy (https://plato.stanford.edu/entries/socrates/#ChrHisSocConAthHisDraDatPlaDia).

Following the Golden Age of Pericles in 430, Athens became embroiled in the disastrous Peloponnesian War (431–404 BCE). Socrates' trial was in 399 BCE, shortly after Athens' defeat by Sparta, a time when Athenians were defeated, demoralized, concerned about the safety, wellbeing, right-thinking, education and democracy of its youth. Socrates was not alone in his criticisms for democracy. He was not egalitarian nor in favor of democracy, instead believing that people needed the guidance of a wise shepherd. He denied that citizens had basic virtue necessary to nurture a good society, instead equating virtue with a knowledge unattainable by ordinary people. Striking at the heart of Athenian democracy, he contemptuously criticized the right of every citizen to speak in the Athenian assembly (Linder, 2002) and as shown in Plato's *Republic* (http://classics.mit.edu/Plato/republic.html), generally praises Sparta not Athens. That free speech (*parrhesia*) and space for criticism of the state's systems should be possible are hallmarks of a democracy – notions that Western democracies cherish today, and which date from the days of Ancient Athens (see Besley & Peters, 2007). Foucault identifies such other critics as the aristocratic Pseudo-Xenophon and Isocrates who worried that "Athenians listen to the most depraved orators; they are not even willing to hear truly good speaker, for they deny them the possibility of being heard by driving them off the platform if they don't support what they wish" (Foucault, 2001, p. 81). But attitudes to democracy then and today differ considerably. Many Athenian critics like Xenophon were the elite class to whom:

> … giving poor and uneducated people power over their betters seemed a reversal of the proper, rational order of society. For them the demos in democracy meant not the whole people, but the people as opposed to the elite. Instead of seeing it as a fair system under which everyone has equal rights, they saw it as the numerically preponderant poor tyrannizing over the rich. They viewed society like a modern stock company: democracy is like a company where all shareholders have an equal say regardless of the scale of their holding; one share or ten thousand, it makes no difference. They regarded this as manifestly unjust. (http://en.wikipedia.org/wiki/Athenian_democracy)

It seems clear that Socrates held such a position.

The Peloponnese Wars between Sparta and Athens involved militarist city-states with opposing political systems. Athens as an open society espoused democracy for male citizens. Sparta was a closed society – a kingdom totally focused on militarism – but whose women had a totally different role, more equal to men. Aristotle describes the kingship at Sparta as 'a kind of unlimited and perpetual generalship' (Pol. iii. 1285a) while Isocrates refers to the Spartans as 'subject to an oligarchy at home, to a kingship on campaign' (iii. 24) (http://en.wikipedia.org/wiki/Sparta). Linder points out a revealing reference to Socrates in Aristophanes' *The Birds*, written six years after *The Clouds*, when he labels a gang of pro-Sparta aristocratic youths as 'Socratified', suggesting that considering the enmity between Sparta and Athens, Socrates' teaching may have already started to be seen as subversive by 417 BCE (Linder, 2002). Yet many Athenians, especially Platonists, admired its rival Sparta as an ideal state, strong, brave, and free from the corruptions of commerce and money. Some, like the aristocratic general Xenophon, sent their sons as foreign students' *trophimoi* (foster sons) to be educated in the *agoge*, the rigorous education and training regimen mandated for all male Spartan citizens (http://en.wikipedia.org/wiki/Sparta).

Concerns about Socrates' ideas, influence and teaching, must have increased after 415 BCE. The Athenian fleet led by Socrates' student Alcibiades, Nicias and Lamachus was due to sail to invade Sicily, when the *herms*, statues of the face and phallus of Hermes, god of travel, that marked the city boundary, were mutilated overnight. Such a sacrilegious act was a bad omen and fearing a conspiracy against it, the city formed a commission:

> ... to investigate not only the herm-smashing, but all crimes of irreverence (*asebeia*) that could be discovered, offering rewards for information. In a climate of near-hysteria over three months, accusations led to executions (including summary executions), exile, torture, and imprisonment affecting hundreds of people, some of whom were close to Socrates (Alcibiades, Phaedrus, Charmides, Critias, Eryximachus, and others). The actual herm-mutilators turned out to be a young men's drinking club, and some of the accusers ultimately admitted to lying; although death penalties imposed in absentia were rescinded, nothing could bring back the innocent dead. (Nails, 2009)

Athenians had a legal obligation to publicly participate in religious festivals, and with *asebeia* or irreverence a capital crime, it was not surprising that Alcibiades fled. But defecting to Sparta and proposing ways to help Sparta defeat Athens was viewed as treachery by many Athenians. Yet, criticism of belief in gods occurred in the democracy. For example, Xenophanes chastised the human vices of the gods as well as their anthropomorphic depiction. Rather than polytheism, Plato, speaking through Socrates in *The Republic*, believed in one supreme god – the 'Form of the Good' – as the emanation of perfection in the universe. Aristotle also disagreed that polytheistic deities existed, because he could not find enough empirical evidence for it. He was a pantheist believing in a deity called the 'Prime Mover', which had set creation going, but was not connected or interested in the universe (http://en.wikipedia.org/wiki/ Religion_in_ancient_Greece).

Two much more serious assaults on democracy occurred when Athens was betrayed to Sparta and the democracy briefly overthrown by two of Socrates' students. A third attempt in 401 BCE to overthrow, also involving his students, was unsuccessful.

The first coup, by Alcibiades, lasted four months in 411–410 BCE (http://www.britannica.com/EBchecked/topic/13306/Alcibiades). This coup was known as 'The 400' – the reduced number of people who now ruled Athens instead of the usual Council of 500. Concern about Socrates' ideas no doubt arose from the close relationship he had with Alcibiades, an aristocratic general whose political allegiance shifted several times. He defected to Sparta where he advised in campaigns against Athens, was forgiven and returned, but ended up leaving Athens again (see http://en.wikipedia.org/wiki/Alcibiades and Alcibiades, in Encylopedia Britannica http://www.britannica.com/EBchecked/ topic/13306/Alcibiades).

The second overthrow of democracy in 404–403 BCE for slightly longer was much more crucial in bringing about the trial. The Spartans defeated and entered Athens, established an oligarchy known as 'the Thirty" and also as the "Thirty Tyrants" led by Critias and including Charmides (both were relatives of Plato and Socrates' students). 'The Thirty' confiscated the estates of Athenian aristocrats, banished 5,000 women, children, and slaves, and summarily executed about 1,500 of Athens most prominent democrats. Many leading democratic citizens went into exile (including Anytus, who became one of Socrates' accusers along with Meletus and Lycon) where they organized a resistance movement. In the *Apology* Socrates relates an incident and criticizes the oligarchy that:

> ... sent for me and four others into the rotunda, and bade us bring Leon the Salaminian from Salamis, as they wanted to execute him. This was a specimen of the sort of commands which they were always giving with the view of implicating as many as possible in their crimes; and then I showed, not in words only, but in deed, that, if I may be allowed to use such an expression, I cared not a straw for death, and that my only fear was the fear of doing an unrighteous or unholy thing. For the strong arm of that oppressive power did not frighten me into doing wrong; and when we came out of the rotunda the other four went to Salamis and fetched Leon, but I went quietly home. For which I might have lost my life, had not the power of the Thirty shortly afterwards come to an end. And to this many will witness. (*Apology,* http://classics.mit.edu/Plato/apology.html)

He may have not followed the order in what is famously cited as an act of civil disobedience, but neither did he stand up to 'The Thirty' on behalf of Leon.. Further, Socrates refused to obey Critia's edict forbidding (unsuccessfully) Socrates in instruction in the art of words to men under thirty (i.e. youths and unmarried men, Xenophon, *Memorabilia* 1.2.31). Socrates responded sarcastically:

if someone was a herdsman and made his cattle fewer and more poor, would he not agree that he was a bad herdsman; yet it is a great wonder, if someone was a leader of a city and made his citizens fewer and poorer, that he would not be ashamed nor think himself a bad leader of a city (Xenophon, *Memorabilia* 1.2.32). Charicles threatens to punish Socrates if he does not stop making statements against the regime (Xenophon, *Memorabilia* 1.2.37–38). Critias makes only a withering remark about the philosophers' affinity for tanners, craftsmen, and bronze workers. (Xenophon, *Memorabilia* 1.2.37)

William Morison (2005), in *The Internet Encyclopedia of Philosophy*, notes: Xenophon characterized Critias as a ruthless, amoral tyrant, whose crimes would eventually be the cause of Socrates' death. Similarly, Philostratus called him 'the most evil ... of all men' (*Lives of the Sophists* 1.16). In contrast, Plato whitewashes his second cousin in four dialogues (Lysis, Charmides, Critias, and Timaeus) presents Critias as a refined and well-educated member of one of Athens oldest and most distinguished aristocratic families and as a regular participant in Athenian philosophical culture (http://www.iep.utm.edu/critias/).

That Socrates chose to remain in Athens rather than go to Thebes like many exiles and Pythagoreans associates further suggests his tacit support for the regime, even if he refused to partake in their violence (Waterfield, 2009). So why even though invited, did he not join the exiles who plotted to overthrow 'the Thirty'? The question remains hanging.

Once democracy was restored in 404 BCE after the violence of the Thirty, Athenians must have wondered why this had happened again and must have looked at influences on the ringleaders – Alcibiades, Critias, and Charmides – all Socrates' students. Were his teachings responsible for the overthrow of the democracy? Was he responsible for their actions? Were his expressions of disdain for the constitution at least partly responsible for the death and suffering during the tyranny? His criticisms may well have been tolerated and even admired by many in the past, but times had changed and following these coups, his teaching and influence could scarcely be seen as harmless or eccentric; rather his criticisms, alternative ideas, powerful oratory skills and interlocutions, and his "icy logic – came to be seen as a dangerous and corrupting influence, a breeder of tyrants and enemy of the common man" (Linder, 2002, http://www.law.umkc.edu/faculty/projects/ftrials/socrates/socratesaccount.html).

Characteristically, Socrates spent time with the city youth and after democracy was restored in 403 BCE, students again started flocking to him. Many Athenians must have feared that his influence and teaching might again inspire willful and violent youth to attempt to overthrow democracy. However, even if citizens had wanted to bring charges against him they could not because Eucleides' amnesty of 403 BCE meant that no one who committed a crime before or during the rule of The Thirty could be prosecuted. Any charges had to relate to the years after the amnesty – the four years prior to his trial. The final straw may well have been another antidemocratic uprising – this one unsuccessful – in 401. Athens finally had enough of 'Socratified' youth (Linder, 2002, http://www.law.umkc.edu/faculty/projects/ftrials/socrates/socratesaccount.html). Furthermore, Linder considers it significant that the earliest surviving reference to the trial of Socrates that does not come from one of his disciples. In 345 BCE, the famous orator Aechines told a jury: "Men of Athens, you executed Socrates, the sophist, because he was clearly responsible for the education of Critias, one of the thirty anti-democratic leaders" (Linder, 2002, http://www.law.umkc.edu/faculty/projects/ftrials/socrates/socratesaccount.html).

Plato's *Apology* presents Socrates' reasons for his bad reputation but omits the political context. Socrates' defence is well known, so will only briefly be addressed here. Socrates argued that his reputation followed his actions from when he was a youth after a visit to the oracle at Delphi with Chaerephon who was told that no one is wiser than Socrates. Subsequently from his youth, Socrates' goal was to test the wisdom of politicians, poets, and theologians against his own wisdom, finding that "In my investigation in the service of the god I found that those who had the highest reputation were nearly the most deficient, while those who were thought to be inferior were more knowledgeable" (*Apology*, 26). He then addresses the issue of corrupting youth which seems to be at the heart of the charges that he corrupted youth, arguing that no one would intentionally corrupt another person (because they stand to be harmed by him at a later date) http://classics.mit.edu/Plato/apology.html. Meletus (*Euthyphro* 3c–d) claimed there were two forms of irreverence:

> Socrates did not believe in the gods of the Athenians (indeed, he had said on many occasions that the gods do not lie or do other wicked things, whereas the Olympian gods of the poets and the city were quarrelsome and vindictive); Socrates introduced new divinities (indeed, he insisted that his *daimonion* had spoken to him since childhood). (Nails, 2009, http://plato.stanford.edu/entries/socrates/)

In the *Apology*, Socrates turned the tables, arguing that if he is convicted, it will be because Aristophanes play *The Clouds* – (which was produced approximately twenty-four years earlier and mocked Socrates) corrupted the minds of his accusers when they were young. Nails points out that:

Aristophanes genuinely objected to what he saw as social instability brought on by the freedom Athenian youths enjoyed to study with professional rhetoricians, sophists and natural philosophers, e.g., those who, like the pre-Socratics, studied the cosmos or nature. That Socrates eschewed any earning potential in philosophy does not seem to have been significant to the comic playwright. Aristophanes' depiction is important because Plato's Socrates says at his trial (*Apology* 18a–b, 19c) that most of his jurors have grown up believing the falsehoods spread about him in the play. Socrates calls Aristophanes more dangerous than the three men who brought charges against him in 399 because Aristophanes had poisoned men's minds while they were young. Aristophanes did not stop accusing Socrates in 423 when *Clouds* placed third behind another play in which Socrates was mentioned as barefoot; rather, he soon began writing a revision, which he published but never produced. Aristophanes appears to have given up on reviving *Clouds* in about 416, but his attacks on Socrates continued. Again in 414 with *Birds*, and in 405 with *Frogs*, Aristophanes complained of Socrates' deleterious effect on the youths of the city, including Socrates' neglect of the poets. (Nails, 2009, http://plato.stanford.edu/entries/socrates/)

The case of Socrates is still contentious 2000 years later, but rather than simply focus on his philosophy and defence, historicizing and contextualizing gives us a more nuanced picture of the social and political fabric of Athens at the time when it finally had enough of this 70-year-old gadfly who still poses a dilemma for us today. With such superb oratory skills couldn't he have easily swayed the jury and defeated his accusers? Why did he taunt his accusers? Why did he not take advantage of opportunities to escape – as many expected and encouraged him to do? At age 70, probably near the end of his lifetime, had he had enough of living, was he becoming infirm? Was this an early form of 'suicide by cop'? Did he know or expect that Plato would promote his ideas? ...

Education, Dissent, Indoctrination and Corrupting Youth – Contemporary Exemplars

Concern about the type of education and the ability of teachers to influence, indoctrinate or corrupt youth has by no means dissipated over time. In the West, from the 1950s until the collapse of the Soviet Union, fears of indoctrination were related to the Cold War especially fears about communism and Marxism. Since 9/11, the fear has primarily related to Islamic fundamentalism and terrorism, to the way some youth have been radicalized by Islamist educators, be they in formal educational institutions or in religious settings, and encouraged to adopt either unacceptable positions or attitudes or transnational jihadist extremism and even undertake suicide-bombing missions. Consequently several countries – not all democracies – have made efforts to control this as the following four exemplars from Austria, Kenya, Saudi Arabia and the U.K. indicate.

In February 2009, the Austrian Ministry of Education began implementing measures against extremist Muslim educators when it withdrew the teaching licence of an anti-Semitic Islam religion teacher. Austria had become alarmed at the state of religious education now that it has approximately 400,000 Muslims – almost 5% of the population (mostly from Turkey or the former Yugoslavia) and a study in January 2009 found that 21.9 percent of them opposed democracy on religious grounds. The Minister of Education (Claudia Schmied) made it clear that the Muslim community must revoke teaching licences to those 'who have proved to disassociate themselves from democratic values or human rights'. Religious education has its limits where the constitution, democracy and the rule of law are affected (12 February 2009, *Earth Times*, http://www.earthtimes.org/articles/ news/255471,austria-starts-to-crack-down-on-extremist-islam-teachers.html).

In Kenya, Sudarsan Raghavan reported in *The Washington Post* on 22 August 2010, that the Eastleigh, Nairobi district Somali immigrant neighborhood is an incubator for jihad where moderate Islamic Imams who now compete with hard-line preachers pushing a strict interpretation of Islam are fearful at the inroads being made by extremist groups in schools and mosques an area that has lived peacefully in the predominantly Christian country. Anti-Western literature is sold in bookstores and some locals are fearful of militant youth spies who are taught to praise al-Shabab, an Al-Qaeda-linked militia, for waging jihad in Somalia against the U.S.-backed government. He also notes that the area has attracted U.S. funding this year with $96,000 for job creation, education and tolerance programs, mostly directed at youth, to bolster moderate views of Islam in Eastleigh (Raghavan, 2010, http://www.washingtonpost.com/wp-dyn/content/article/2010/08/21/AR2010082102682.html).

The U.K. Muslim population of approximately 1.5 million (2.7% of the total population) is predominantly peaceful and law abiding (Demography of the U.K., 2010, http://en.wikipedia.org/wiki/Demography_of_the_United_Kingdom). However, U.K. universities have been aware for some time that some students are being radicalised. For example: Omar Saeed Sheikh, convicted in 2002 in Pakistan for his part in the kidnap and murder of American journalist Daniel Pearl, was first exposed to Islamist ideology at the London

PHILOSOPHY, EDUCATION AND THE CORRUPTION OF YOUTH 13

School of Economics (O'Neill, 2006). British suicide bombers, Omar Khan Sharif and Asif Muhammad Hanif attacked a café in Tel Aviv in April 2003. Sharif (who escaped but drowned; Hanif was killed) was radicalized partly by Hizb ut-Tahrir activists at Kings College, London (http://news.bbc.co.uk/2/hi/middle_east/2990061.stm; http://www.newstatesman.com/200604240017).

Hizb ut-Tahrir (The Liberation Party, U.K.), an Islamic organization, promotes an Islamic Caliphate system that is dictatorial, non-democratic, excludes non-Muslims, and promotes Sharia law. It regards integration of Muslims as dangerous, and orders all Muslims to keep apart from non-believers; Muslims who believe in democracy are Kafir, or apostates (for details see http://en.wikipedia.org/wiki/Hizb_ut-Tahrir; http://www.hizb.org.uk/).

Omar Bakri Muhammad, who founded Hizb ut-Tahrir in London, then left in 1996 and set up al-Muhajiroun, was one of the last to talk to Sharif before his terrorist attack stated:

> The last six months, for sure he was attending my circuits but he wasn't at all asking about jihad issues. He was debating issues, theological issues. Two weeks before he left for Israel, Sharif was seen leafleting on Derby streets for Bakris' organisation. He also attended Islamic theology sessions that Bakri travelled up from London to deliver, the last of them on 14 April. So, did Bakri have anything to do with the attack? It was no conspiracy. There was no plan from Britain. He just went by himself, on his own. (O'Neill, 2006)

According to O'Neill,

> Student unions and vice-chancellors have made various attempts to tackle the problem but have trodden carefully for fear of being accused of Islamophobia. The radical groups have continued to organise and indoctrinate, often under false names, and have found the process increasingly easy in the climate of anger surrounding the Iraq war. (O'Neill, 2006)

Following jihadist terrorist attacks in London in July 2005 and Glasgow in 2007, serious concerns were expressed in popular media about threats from the teachings of several extremist Islamic organizations including al-Muhajiroun and Hizb ut-Tahrir. Yet in *The Telegraph*, July 2010, Andrew Gilligan, reported that a Whitehall Report claimed that Hizb ut-Tahrir is not a gateway to terrorism, rather that some of these organizations can be an important safety valve for Muslim youth, as indicated by a memorandum from Robert Mason to Eric Pickles, the Communities Secretary, the papers present 'a clear assessment that individuals do not progress through non-violent extremist groups to violent groups' ... Extreme groups may also provide a legal "safety valve" for extreme views. Yet then Prime Minister David Cameron agreed to do more to tackle non-violent extremism, including extremist views such as Hizb ut-Tahrir's. Gilligan challenged the report by pointing out the attitudes teaching and influences of al-Muhajiroun (subsequently banned under the Labour Government but re-grouped under different names) and Hizb ut-Tahrir:

> At least 19 terrorists convicted in Britain have had links with al-Muhajiroun, including Omar Khayam, sentenced to life imprisonment as leader of the fertiliser bomb plot, and Abdullah Ahmed Ali, the ringleader of the airliner liquid bomb plot, who is also serving life.
> Al-Muhajiroun provided backing to Abu Hamza, the extremist cleric, whose Finsbury Park mosque was a forming-ground for other terrorists. Advertising a conference held in the mosque in 2002, al-Muhajiroun leaflets described the 9/11 hijackers as the magnificent 19.
> Former al-Muhajiroun activists demonstrated against a parade by British troops through Luton and threatened to do the same against the coffins of dead soldiers passing through the Wiltshire town of Wootton Basset.
> Hizb-ut-Tahrir says it opposes terrorism and condemned the 9/11 and 7/7 attacks. However, it regards integration as dangerous, orders all Muslims to keep apart from non-believers and says that those [Muslims] who believe in democracy are Kafir, or apostates. (Gilligan, 2010)

The Whitehall documents note:

> ... a minority of terrorists have been involved with non-violent extremist groups such as al-Muhajiroun, and state that such groups can foster a sense of Muslim isolationism from wider U.K. society, which may increase vulnerability to radicalization. (Gilligan, 2010)

The reports cited illustrate the power of people teaching ideas that are radically different to views that the democratic state holds and how youth can be incited to violent acts. It also highlights several aspects of the difficult relationship between democracy and Islam. Some Muslims view democracy as a foreign concept imposed by Westernizers and secular reformers. Some believe that popular sovereignty is a form of idolatry because it denies the fundamental

Islamic affirmation of the sovereignty of God. Others argue that democracy is a requirement of Islam. The separation of religion and politics, which is usually seen as an essential part of democracy, runs counter to some Islamic viewpoints. Others argue that Islamist groups only advocate democracy as a tactic to gain political power.

It is not only Western democracies that are concerned about the influence of teachers inciting youth to violence. In 2010, both the Gulf News and the Saudi Gazette reported that Saudi Arabia moved more than 2,000 teachers who tried to teach students about al-Qaeda into administrative positions over the past two years (15 July 2010, *Gulf News*). On 17 September, 2010, The Saudi Gazette elaborated further with Al-Hadlaq saying they had been promoting extremist ideology (Al-Awwad, 2010), which aimed to remove the monarchy. Abdul Rahman al-Hadlaq, an adviser to Prince Muhammad bin Nayef, the assistant Interior Minister for Security Affairs said that the decision reflects the kingdoms commitment to fighting Al-Qaeda and militant Islam (Al-Awwad, 2010).

Conclusion

There are many more examples, but these contemporary exemplars indicate how governments still struggle to deal with perceived threats to the state from issues of youth radicalization and violence; with indoctrination of youth by teachers, be they religious and/or politically motivated. They highlight that in a democracy free speech is acceptable, with limitations regarding lying (slander, libel, defamation and hate speech) but not advocacy of violence. Practices linking truth-telling and education are important in shaping our contemporary subjectivities, in understanding the exercise of power and control and of contemporary citizenship, especially in sit- uations where there is some risk for a person in telling the truth to a superior – a case of *parrhesia* – that clearly can occur in schools, in the student-teacher relationship and which certainly occurred for some U.K. youth in their anti-Iraq war activities in 2003 and for whistle-blowers (see Besley, 2006).While corrupt and oppressive societies stand to be changed or overthrown, the democratic way is by election not revolution or terrorism. Clearly, education and persuasive teachers can influence youth in ways that society does not deem to be for the better, but in ways that go against its value and cherished ideals. So a vital question for education in a democracy is: how can we support free speech, but prevent teachers from inciting youth passions to translate into violence?

Acknowledgement

This chapter was previously published as Besley, A. C. (Tina), 'Philosophy, Education and the Corruption of Youth', *Educational Philosophy and Theory*, 45(1), 2013, 6–19, © Philosophy of Education Society of Australasia, reprinted by permission of Taylor & Francis Ltd., http://www.tandfonline.com on behalf of Philosophy of Education Society of Australasia.

Notes

1 Pseudo-Xenophon, *The Constitution of the Athenians*, H. Frisch, trans. pp. 6–9; and Isocrates, On the Peace. G. Norlin, trans. p. 113. Work described by Foucault as an ultra-conservative, ultra-aristocratic lampooning of democratic Athenian constitution, probably written during the second half of the 5th century was formerly attributed to Xenophon, but scholars now think that this is incorrect so have re-named it as Pseudo-Xenophon (Foucault, 2001, p. 78).
2 *The Encyclopædia Britannica: A Dictionary of Arts, Sciences, Literature and General Information*, p. 611 (primary source); secondary source (http://en.wikipedia.org/wiki/Sparta).
3 There were three political bodies where citizens gathered in numbers running into the hundreds or thousands. These are the assembly (in some cases with a quorum of 6000), the council of 500 (*boule*) and the courts (a minimum of 200 people, but running at least on some occasions up to 6000). Of these three bodies it is the assembly and the courts that were the true sites of power – although courts, unlike the assembly, were never simply called the demos (the People) as they were manned by a subset of the citizen body, those over thirty. But crucially citizens voting in both were not subject to review and prosecution as were council members and all other officeholders. In the 5th century BC we often hear of the assembly sitting as a court of judgment itself for trials of political importance and it is not a coincidence that 6000 is the number both for the full quorum for the assembly and for the annual pool from which jurors were picked for particular trials. By the mid-4th century however the assemblys judicial functions were largely curtailed, though it always kept a role in the initiation of various kinds of political trial (http://en.wikipedia.org/wiki/Athenian_democracy).

References

Al-Awwad, M. (2010, July 13). 2,000 extremist teachers removed. *Saudi Gazette*. Retrieved from http://www.saudigazette.com.sa/index.cfm?method=home.regcon&contentID=2010071377917

Aristotle. (1941). *Rhetoric* (W. R. Roberts, Trans.). In R. Mckeon (Ed.), *The basic works of Aristotle* (pp. 1403–1406). New York, NY: Random House. Retrieved from http://libertyonline.hypermall.com/Aristotle/Rhetoric/Rhetoric-Bk2.html

Besley, A. C. (2002). *Counseling youth: Foucault, power and the ethics of subjectivity* (2nd ed.). Rotterdam, The Netherlands: Sense Publishers.

Besley, A. C. (2006). Technologies of the self and parrhesia: Education, globalization and the politicization of youth in response to the Iraq war 2003. In M. A. Peters (Ed.), *Education, globalisation and citizenship in an age of terrorism* (pp. 111–144). Boulder, CO: Paradigm Publishers.

Besley, A. C. (2010). Governmentality of youth: Managing risky subjects. *Policy Futures in Education, 8*(5), 528–547.

Besley, A. C., & Peters, M. A. (2007). *Subjectivity and truth: Foucault, education and the culture of self*. New York, NY: Peter Lang.

Foucault, M. (2001). *Fearless speech* (J. Pearson, Ed.). Los Angeles, CA: Semiotext(e).

Foucault, M. (2010). *The government of self and others: Lectures at the collège de France, 1982–1983* (G. Burchell, Trans.). New York, NY: Palgrave Macmillan.

Gilligan, A. (2010, July 25). Hizb ut Tahrir is not a gateway to terrorism, claims whitehall report. *The Telegraph*. Retrieved from http://www.telegraph.co.uk/journalists/andrew-gilligan/7908262/Hizb-ut-Tahrir-is-not-a-gateway-to-terrorism-claims-Whitehall-report.html

Linder, D. (2002). *The trial of Socrates*. Retrieved from http://www.law.umkc.edu/faculty/projects/ftrials/socrates/socratesaccount.html

Morison, W. (2005). Critias (460–403 BC). *The Internet Encyclopedia of Philosophy*. Retrieved from http://www.iep.utm.edu/critias/

Nails, D. (2009). Socrates. *Stanford Encyclopedia of Philosophy*. Retrieved from http://plato.stanford.edu/entries/socrates/

O'Neill, S. (2006, November 18). How radical preachers turned a young man into a suicide bomber. *The Times*. Retrieved from http://www.timesonline.co.uk/tol/life_and_style/education/student/news/article640346.ece

Plato. (1970). *Alcibiades 1* (B. Jowett, Trans.). Retrieved from http://www.ac-nice.fr/philo/textes/Plato-Works/07-Alcibiades.htm

Plato. *Apology* (B. Jowett, Trans.). Retrieved September, 2010, from http://classics.mit.edu/Plato/apology.html

Plato. *Sophist* (B. Jowett, Trans.). Retrieved September, 2010, from http://classics.mit.edu/Plato/sophist.html

Plato. *Theaetetus* (B. Jowett, Trans.). Retrieved September, 2010, from http://classics.mit.edu/Plato/theatu.html

Plato. *The republic* (B. Jowett, Trans.). Retrieved September, 2010, from http://classics.mit.edu/Plato/republic.html

Protagoras. (c.485–c.411 BCE). In Plato (360 BCE), *Theaetetus*. Retrieved September, 2010, from http://classics.mit.edu/Plato/theatu.html

Raghavan, S. (2010, August 24). Islamic extremism foments in Kenya or across Somalias border, an incubator for Islamic extremism. *The Washington Post.* Retrieved from http://www.washingtonpost.com/wp-dyn/content/article/2010/08/21/AR2010082102682.html

Rousseau, J.-J. (1979). *Émile, or on education* (A. Bloom, Trans.). New York, NY: Basic Books.

Rowe, C. (1999). *The uses and disadvantages of Socrates.* Retrieved September, 2010, from http://www.dur.ac.uk/Classics/histos/1998/rowe.html

Siegel, H. (1991). Indoctrination and education. In B. Spiecker & R. Straughan (Eds.), *Freedom and indoctrination in education: International perspectives.* London: Cassell.

Snook, I. A. (1972). *Indoctrination and education.* London: Routledge and Kegan Paul.

Spiecker, B. (1991). Indoctrination: The suppression of critical dispositions. In B. Spiecker & R. Straughan (Eds.), *Freedom and indoctrination in education: International perspectives.* London: Cassell.

Waterfield, R. (2009). *Why Socrates died: Dispelling the myths.* New York, NY: W.W. Norton & Company.

Websites

Alcibiades. *Encyclopedia Britannica.* Retrieved September, 2010, from http://www.britannica.com/EBchecked/topic/13306/Alcibiades

Athenian Democracy. Retrieved September, 2010, from http://en.wikipedia.org/wiki/Athenian_democracy

Demography of the U.K. Retrieved September, 2010, from http://en.wikipedia.org/wiki/Demography_of_the_United_Kingdom

Earth Times. (2009, February 12). *Austria starts to crack down on extremist Islam teachers.* Retrieved September, 2010, from http://www.earthtimes.org/articles/news/255471,austria-starts-to-crack-down-on-extremist-islam-teachers.html

Gulf News. (2010, July 15). *Saudi Arabia says extremist teachers transferred out of classrooms.* Retrieved September, 2010, from http://www.al-shorfa.com/cocoon/meii/xhtml/en_GB/newsbriefs/meii/newsbriefs/2010/07/15/newsbrief-01

Omar Saeed Sheikh – profile. Retrieved September, 2010, from http://news.bbc.co.uk/2/hi/uk_news/1804710.stm; http://en.wikipedia.org/wiki/Sparta

CHAPTER 2

Heidegger, De-Nazification and the Art of Teaching

Introduction

Rarely in the history of modern philosophy have the question of pedagogy and the ethics of teaching been so intimately tangled with politics and philosophy as in the case of Martin Heidegger. On July 23, 1945 Martin Heidegger appeared before the Committee on De-Nazification of Freiberg University which was charged with determining whether Heidegger should be debarred as a faculty member from the University for the nature and manner of his teaching, research and administration during the Nazi period. The inquiry focused on two charges against Heidegger: his alleged violation of academic freedom by turning the University into an instrument of Nazi propaganda and his alleged ideological corrupting influence on his students.

Perhaps, not since Socrates had such an influential philosopher been charged with corrupting youth and like Socrates, Heidegger's case places the question of pedagogy and the ethics of teaching center stage between philosophy and politics – the politics of philosophy and the philosophy of teaching. What constitutes good teaching? Is good teaching separable from the politics or ideology of the teacher? Is good teaching a neutral technology that we can get more or less right, technically speaking, or is it inherently bound up with ethics and politics? To what extent are teachers today complicit with the established order and to what extent is the teaching profession responsible for perpetuating a conception of teaching as a value-free, politically and ethically neutral activity? More specifically, we might ask of Heidegger, was his involvement with Nazism a temporary compromise or something more pervasive and intimately bound up with his philosophy?

Heidegger as Teacher

We should remember in attempting to answer these questions that, perhaps, no philosopher since Socrates, was so committed to questions of education and to good teaching as Heidegger. For instance, he begins a course of twenty-one lectures which he delivers to his students during 1951 and 1952, with the following words: 'We come to know what it means to think when we ourselves try to think. If the attempt is to be successful, we must be ready to learn thinking'.

Learning, in other words, is central to understanding thinking. He continues: 'In order to be capable of thinking, we need to learn it first. What is learning? Man learns when he disposes everything he does to him at any given moment. We learn to think by giving our mind to what there is to think about' (p. 4). Yet he suggests while there is an interest in philosophy there is no readiness to think. The fact is that, even though we live in the most thought- provoking age, 'we are still not thinking' (p. 4). In *What is Called Thinking?* Heidegger is immediately concerned with learning and construes the learner on the model of the apprentice, emphasizing the notion of relatedness – of the cabinetmakers apprentice to the different kinds of wood that sustain the craft. The relatedness of the learner-apprentice to his craft or subject, he determines will depend on the presence of a teacher. He continues:

> Teaching is even more difficult than learning. We know that; but we rarely think about it. And why is teaching more difficult than learning? Not because the teacher must have a larger store of information, and have it always ready. Teaching is more difficult than learning because what teaching call for is this: to let learn. The real teacher, in fact, lets nothing else be learned than – learning. His conduct, therefore, often produces the impressions that we properly learn nothing from him, if by learning we now suddenly understand merely the procurement of useful information. (Heidegger, 1968, p. 15)

The lectures that constitute *What is Called Thinking?* were the first course of public lectures Heidegger was permitted to give by the French occupying powers since 1944, the point at which the Nazis drafted him into the peoples' militia. Gray (1968, p. vi) explains: What this long interruption in his teaching activity must have cost him is not difficult to guess, for Heidegger is above all else a teacher. It is no accident that nearly all his publications since *Being and Time* (1927) were first lectures or seminar discussions. For him the spoken word is greatly superior to the written, as it was for Plato. In his book he names Socrates, a teacher not an author, 'the purest thinker of the West'.

Heidegger's contribution to philosophy of education – to teaching and learning – is now becoming more recognised (Peters, 2002). His critiques of humanism and modernity are considered central to post-humanist and poststructuralist conceptions of education. Furthermore, it could be said that many of his texts, especially those works that come to us as *lectures* to specific audiences, are specifically and self-consciously *pedagogical*, and that Heidegger was explicitly concerned with pedagogical matters, as is well evidenced his discussion of 'learning' in *What is Called Thinking?*

Heidegger submitted a deposition to the Committee in which he provides an extended and non-technical exposition of his views on teaching and university education in a sustained form not available in his extant works. While the Committee was predisposed to allow Heidegger to continue his faculty membership, under pressure from the Allied military government which viewed the reknowned philosophers' case as exemplary, he was suspended from teaching until 1951. This chapter provides an examination and critique of Heidegger's view on the art of teaching based upon a creative interpretation of what how Heidegger might have responded (Allen & Axiotis, 2002).

Specifically, this chapter examines his interpretation of the allegations against him, cast in terms of 'subversion of identities', the principal task he ascribes to the post-war German university ('understanding in ever more radical ways the notion of intentionality'), Heidegger's notion that 'the way of education leads today to a crossroads' which he describes historically in terms of the trivium (grammar, rhetoric, and dialectic), Heidegger's 'third way' which bypasses both liberal and vocational education to reclaim the figure of Socrates and to open new horizons with the compass of Greek *paideia*, and his comportment, which denies both the superordination of the theoretical over the practical and the notion that the 'contemplative point of view is prior to and independent of the background practices of involvement and concern with people and things'.

Allen and Axiotis (2002, p. 34) have Heidegger conclude his deposition with the words:

> Intentionality as comportment and truth as disclosure go hand in hand. Without radically rethinking intentionality, the university's attempts to lay claim to its much vaunted neutrality, to evade being the organ of the nation-state and of the market is quite futile. The religious particularity of the premodern university was eroded from two sides: nascent nationalism and economic utility. Despite the university's efforts to maintain a theoretical detachment from state and market interests, secularization does not result in independence from values but in replacement of one set of religious values with other, more abstract ones.

Allen and Axiotis (2002) have Heidegger ending his deposition, what he calls 'words of bequeathal', as he says 'however untimely, by a tragic educator, divided between a *not-yet* and a *no-longer*'. The chapter ends by making an assessment of Heidegger's view on pedagogy and education, and whether and to what extent, he answered the allegations against him.

This chapter is directly related to a topic of educational interest in that it examines Heidegger's views on the art of teaching. It constitutes an analytical inquiry based on exegesis and argument of Allen and Axiotis (2002) imagined and reconstructed excerpted transcript of Heidegger's deposition. The analysis and Heidegger's language (most unusually for Heidegger) is presented in clear and accessible language. The chapter is germane to the European and international context being concerned with Heidegger's views on pedagogy and the post-war university, at a point just after the war, with the Holocaust and Nazi crimes against humanity weighing on Europe and the world. Finally, it helps to establish a European dialogue on Heidegger's teaching and the importance of his thought for education by reference to an educational tradition.

Heidegger's Comportment and the Art of Teaching

In the Preface to his book *Heidegger's Crisis* Hans Sluga (1993, p. vii) writes of the relations between philosophy and politics as follows:

> If philosophy is simply understood as a search for truth and politics as the pursuit of power, the two appear to have little in common. In reality, however, both are concerned with the production, use, and control of truth, with generating, channeling, and manipulating streams of power – though admittedly in different ways – and from this comes their closeness and their conflict. Philosophy and politics are, in fact, inextricably tied together, but their relationship is also precarious and unstable.

If the interaction between the two is to be successful or productive, Sluga (1993) suggests that two conditions must be met: first, that the complex relations between truth and power should be persistently scrutinised; and, second, that both philosophy and politics be treated as evolving 'organic forms' so that we understand their relation as 'historical in character, not as determined once and for all' (p. viii). This is the fundamental insight that drives Sluga's historicist study of Heidegger's fateful entry into German politics in 1933. Sluga situates Heidegger's personal crisis within a more general account of the crisis of German philosophy. His argument, I believe, is salutary. Having told the story of Heidegger's crisis he concludes by suggesting that we must re-examine the question of philosophy's relation to politics:

> Philosophers, in my view, are not qualified to lay down authoritarian standards of political action. Whenever they have tried their hand at this, they have either described useless utopias or given dangerous

instructions. It might be more attractive to think of them as playing a critical role. But political critique is productive only if it is tempered by common sense and practical experience. Philosophical critics of politics, on the other hand, proceed all too often from supposedly absolute truths, and what they say then proves unhelpful and sometimes even destructive. Insofar as philosophy has any task to perform in politics, it is to map out new possibilities. By confronting actual political conditions with alternatives, it can help to undermine the belief that these conditions are inevitable. If the German philosophers of the 1930s had engaged in such reflection, they would not have surrendered so readily to the false certainties of Nazism. (pp. ix–x)

Sluga suggests that the debate over the relation between Heidegger's philosophy and his political commitment can be understood in terms of factionalism. One group – his detractors, including Pierre Bourdieu (1991), Tom Rockmore (1992, 1995) and Richard Wolin (1990) – have argued that Heidegger's philosophy of being is inherently political and that his politics emerge naturally as a consequence of his philosophy. The other group – his defenders, unnamed by Sluga – have tended to minimise such links. Thus, the debate suffers from 'factionalism', which 'already knows the answers to the questions it asks' (Sluga, 1993, p. 5). But the debate, in Sluga's view, involves two further difficulties: first, it is 'marred by useless moralizing' directed at ascertaining Heidegger's moral guilt or culpability; and, the second, is the 'psychologizing' tendencies of much of the debate where Heidegger's politics has been framed solely as a matter of biography and character. As regards this tendency, Sluga's study offers an historical corrective to these psychologising tendencies by locating Heidegger's politics within the broader spectrum of German philosophy and society. Heidegger's reluctance to speak of his support for the Nazi cause, his attempt to minimise his involvement with Nazis ideology, his omissions, denials and evasions of his complicity with Nazism, and his silence on the Holocaust, as Sluga (1993, p. 244) points out, were in fact characteristic of the whole of German society in the post-war years: 'An entire society had devoted itself to the task of forgetting, and the philosophers were only too willing to participate in the communal act of erasure'.

Sluga attempts to preserve the complexity of the connection between philosophy and politics, avoiding reductionist explanations characteristic of Marxist thinkers that treat consciousness as an epiphenomenon. By contrast, he adopts the view that there is 'no single model for describing this manifold of relations' and suggests that that "the relation between philosophy and politics cannot be described once and for all by means of any grand scheme, that their relation is intrinsically historical and understandable only in its narrative uniqueness" (p. 253).

Acknowledgement

This chapter is based on Michael A. Peters, 'Heidegger, De-Nazification and the Art of Teaching', a paper presented to the European Conference on Educational Research (ECER), Lisbon, 2002: Philosophy of Education Symposia on 'Good Teaching'.

References

Allen, V., & Axiotis, A. (2002). Heidegger's art of teaching. In M. A. Peters (Ed.), *Heidegger, education and modernity*. Boulder, CA: Rowman & Littlefield.

Heidegger, M. (1968). *What is called thinking?* New York, NY: Harper & Row.

Heidegger, M. (1977). *The question concerning technology, and other essays.* New York, NY: Garland Publishing.

Heidegger, M. (1985, March). "The self-affirmation of the German university", together with "the rectorate 1933/1934: Facts and thoughts". *Review of Metaphysics, 38*, 467–502.

Peters, M. A. (2000). Heidegger, Derrida, and the new humanities. In G. Biesta & D. Egea-Kuehne (Eds.), *Derrida and education*. London: Routledge.

Peters, M. A. (Ed.). (2002). *Heidegger, education and modernity*. Boulder, CA: Rowman & Littlefield.

Rockmore, T. (1992). *On Heidegger's nazism and philosophy*. London: Harvester Wheatsheaf.

Rockmore, T. (1995). *Heidegger and French philosophy: Humanism, antihumanism and being*. London: Routledge.

Sluga, H. (1993). *Heidegger's crisis: Philosophy and politics in Nazi Germany*. Cambridge, MA: Harvard University Press.

Wolin, R. (Ed.). (1993). *The Heidegger controversy: A critical reader*. Cambridge, MA: MIT Press.

Young, J. (1997). *Heidegger, philosophy, nazism*. Cambridge: Cambridge University Press.

CHAPTER 3

Truth-Telling as an Educational Practice of the Self
Foucault, Parrhesia and the Ethics of Subjectivity

> Of ourselves we are not knowers. ...
> FRIEDRICH NIETZSCHE, *The Genealogy of Morals* (1956), 149

∴

> My role – and that is too emphatic a word – is to show people that they are much freer than they feel, that people accept as truths, as evidence, some themes which have been built up at a certain moment in history, and that this so-called evidence can be criticized and destroyed. ... All my analyses are against the idea of universal necessities in human existence.
> R. MARTIN, Truth, Power, Self: An Interview with Michel Foucault, in:
> L. Martin et al. (Eds.) *Technologies of the self* (1988), 10–11

∴

> What is truth? A mobile army of metaphors, metonyms, anthropomorphisms, in short, a sum of human relations which were poetically and rhetorically heightened, transferred, and adorned, and after long use seem solid, canonical, and binding to a nation. Truths are illusions about which it has been forgotten that they are illusions, worn-out metaphors without sensory impact, coins that have lost their image and now can be used only as metal, and no longer as coins.
> FRIEDRICH NIETZSCHE, On Truth and Lie in an Extra-Moral Sense,
> *The Portable Nietzsche* (1974), 46–47

∴

Introduction

Michel Foucault, the iconoclast French philosopher-historian, was strongly influenced by his readings of both Friedrich Nietzsche and Martin Heidegger and indebted to them for ideas that led him to emphasise the close conceptual relations between the notions of truth, power and subjectivity in his genealogical investigations. He started reading these two philosophers in the early 1950s and while he wrote only one substantial paper on Nietzsche (Foucault, 1977) and nothing directly on Heidegger, it is clear that Foucault's works bear the unmistakable imprints of these two great thinkers.[1] Nietzsche's work, in particular, provided Foucault with novel ways to re-theorise and conceive anew the operation of power and desire in the constitution and self overcoming of human subjects. It enabled him to analyse the modes by which human beings become subjects without according either power or desire conceptual priority over the other, as had been the case in the discourses of Marxism (with its accent on power) and of Freudianism (with its accent on desire).

From Nietzsche, Foucault also intellectually inherited the concept and method of genealogy, a form of historical analysis that inquires into the formation and structure of value accorded Man, Reason, and Truth through a variety of techniques, including both etymological and linguistic inquiry alongside the investigation of the history of concepts.[2] For Foucault, as for Nietzsche, genealogy replaces ontology. Foucault's investigations into the modes by which human beings are made into subjects are, above all, historical investigations. For Foucault, as for Nietzsche, there are no essences of human beings and, therefore, also no possibility for universalist theories concerning the nature of human beings. Given that there is no human nature, fixed once and for all – no essential or universalisable nature – there is no question of a science of human nature (*a la* Hobbes or Hume) or the possibility of building other theories (of politics, of education, or of rights) on the basis of this alleged nature. All questions of ontology, in the hands of Nietzsche and Foucault, become radically historicised.[3] Thus, there is no sovereign individual or transcendental subject, but only human beings that have been historically constituted as subjects in different ways at different times.

In a late interview Foucault (1988, p. 251) once described himself as Nietzschean:

> I am simply Nietzschean, and I try to see, on a number of points, and to the extent that it is possible, with the aid of Nietzsche's texts ... what can be done in this domain.

Anyone who has read *Discipline and Punish* (Foucault, 1979) cannot help but be struck by the extent to which Nietzsche's discussion of punishment in the second essay of the *The Genealogy of Morals* (1956) its analysis of debt and its inscription on the body, permeates Foucault's method and investigations of discipline, power and knowledge in the institutions regulated by the emergent human sciences. It is also clear that Foucault broadly accepted Nietzsche's perspectival notion of truth, yet the degree to which we can properly ascribe him Nietzsche's view is fraught with difficulty, given the complexity and changing character of Nietzsche's own views, and the continuing development of Foucault's thought. It is clear that Foucault, at least toward the end of his life, neither denied the classical ideal of truth as correspondence to an independently existing world nor the analytics of truth, even though the early Nietzsche (1979) cast doubt precisely on this ideal. For Nietzsche, as an opening quotation demonstrates, truth is a convenient fiction, merely a belief about the possession of truth. Foucault's innovation was to historicise truth and materialise truth as discourse, first, in a conception of discourse as regimes of truth, and later, as practises in games of truth.

This chapter is devoted to an examination of Foucault's approach to truth-telling in relation to the changing practice of education. In the first section I examine briefly the notion of truth as Foucault uses it to investigate the socio-political sphere. The remainder of the chapter is given over to Foucault's six lectures entitled *Discourse and Truth: The Problematization of Parrhesia*, given at Berkeley during the months of October-November in 1983.[4] In these lectures, Foucault outlines the meanings and the evolution of the classical Greek word *parrhesia* and its cognates, as they enter into and exemplify the changing practices of truth-telling in Greek society. In particular, Foucault investigates the use of *parrhesia* in specific types of human relationships and the procedures and techniques employed in such relationships (34/66). Central to his analysis is the importance of education and its relations to care of the self, life and the crisis of democratic institutions.

The Berkeley lectures are to be seen, in part, as a continuation and elaboration of some of the themes concerning technologies of the self that Foucault gave as lectures at the University of Vermont a year earlier in 1982. The technology of the self is one of the four technologies described by Foucault, along with technologies of production (Marx), technologies of signs (Saussure), and technologies of domination. Foucault does not attempt to defend this fourfold typology or his indebtedness to Heidegger's conception of technology. Technologies of the self, for Foucault, is an approach to study the ethics of an individual whereby the individual can come to know himself as well as take care of himself – twin themes in the inherited Western ethical tradition associated with specific techniques of truth-telling practices that human beings apply to understand themselves. In his examination of classical Greek and early Christian texts Foucault distinguishes two models: the (defective) pedagogical Platonic model based on the art of dialogue between teacher and pupil which requires that the pupil know himself so that he can participate in dialogue;

and, the medical model which focuses on the presence of a continuous and permanent care of oneself. In terms of these two models analysed through various texts, Foucault demonstrates that the Senecan, Plutarchian and Pythagorean understanding of the self is different from the Platonic one. He later distinguishes ethical self-mastery of the Stoics based on askesis (a kind of training or exercise) from the self renunciation of the early Christians where techniques of the self were exercised through the imposition of conditions and rules for particular self-transformations leading to salvation through confession, penance, and obedience.[5]

There are now many good books on Foucault, which apply his methods to educational problems or issues, or directly address the relevance of his writings to the field of education (e.g., Ball, 1990; Marshall, 1996; Olssen, 1999; Baker, 2001). None of them, to my knowledge, focuses specifically on the question of truth in Foucault or refers to his Berkeley lectures. Yet these lectures demonstrate not only that Foucault did directly address education, but also that education was central to his elaboration of the theme of care of the self.

Foucault on the Truth: From *Regimes* to *Games* of Truth

In an interview a year before his death, Foucault confessed to Paul Rabinow and Hubert Dreyfus that his real quarry was not an investigation of power but rather the history of the ways in which human beings are constituted as subjects, a process that involved power relations as an integral aspect of the production of discourses involving truths. He writes:

> My objective ... has been to create a history of the different modes by which, in our culture, human beings are made subjects. My work has dealt with three modes of objectification which transform human beings into subjects .... The first is the modes of inquiry which try to give themselves the status of the sciences .... In the second part of my work, I have studied the objectivizating of the subject in what I shall call dividing practices .... Finally, I have sought to study – it is my current work – the way a human being turns himor herself into a subject. For example, I have chosen the domain of sexuality.... Thus it is not power, but the subject, that is the general theme of my research.
>
> It is true that I became quite involved with the question of power. It soon appeared to me that, while the human subject is placed in relations of production and of signification, he is equally placed in power relations that are very complex. (Foucault, 2001a, orig. 1983, pp. 326–327)

In his early work Foucault, treated truth as a product of the regimentation of statements within discourses that had progressed or were in the process of progressing to the stage of a scientific discipline. In this conception, the subject, historicised in relation to social practices, is denied its freedom or effective agency. This early conception of Foucault is to be contrasted with his later notion of the subject where freedom is seen to be an essential aspect of its constitution as in the concept of governmentality and in his studies of the history of sexuality. For the early Foucault (if I am permitted this biographical abbreviation), as he indicates:

> Truth is to be understood as a system of ordered procedures for the production, regulation, distribution, circulation and operation of statements. (Foucault, 1980, p. 133)

In the progress of a scientific discipline, studying how the human sciences emerged, Foucault (1972, pp. 186–187) proposed four stages through which a science must develop.[6] First, the discursive practices begin to exhibit individuality and autonomy from other discourses, although there is no attempt yet to systematise accumulated knowledge in the form of theory. Second, the emerging discipline begins to make claims of verification and coherence for some of its pronouncements, which are formulated as laws, as yet unproven or justified. Third, propositions are regulated in terms of formal criteria for the production of true statements and efforts are made to formalise the knowledge of the discipline into a systematic framework. Finally, the discipline moves beyond formalization to reach mature scientific status and is, accordingly, able to offer a proven methodology that demonstrates success in solving most problems exhibited by its domain. At this stage practitioners become professionals who provide valid solutions to a broad range of recognisable problems. With its institutional development and its own canon, the discipline becomes acceptable as a science also by those outside the discipline. It is at this stage that the discipline must question its own epistemological foundations, questioning both its own reasoning methods and how its reaches the truth, otherwise it will begin to repeat itself, lose its relevance, become useless and disappear, as other disciplines supersede it.

Thus, for Foucault (1972, pp. 182–183) knowledge is, first of all, a group of elements, formed in a regular manner by discursive practice and the field of coordination and subordination of statements in which concepts appear, and are defined and transformed. It is also, that of which one can speak in a discursive practice, and which is specified by that fact, emphasising that knowledge is not the sum of what is thought to be true, but rather the whole set of practices that are distinctive of a particular domain.

With the doubtful human sciences, human beings emerge as both subject and object of knowledge. In the context of the disciplines of the human sciences, Foucault investigates the internal relation of power and knowledge: power and knowledge directly imply one another, for there is no power relation without the corresponding constitution of a field of knowledge. The human sciences will be capable of distinguishing between true and false when they will free themselves from their involvement with power (Dreyfus & Rabinow, 1983, p. 116), that is, once it has overcome the problem of objectivity. Yet given that the human sciences are an integral part of the social practices, which they seek to investigate, it is doubtful whether they will ever achieve objectivity and, thus, attain the status of normal science in Kuhn's sense of the term. Thus, relations of power inhere in the human sciences for they cannot meet the objectivity criterion and scientists are as much a product of the cultural practices that they investigate as their subjects. It is these power relations which sustain and regulate the procedures by which statements in the discourses of the human sciences are regulated. In other words, regimes of truth are the discursive productions of the human sciences.

The shift from regimes of truth to games of truth, McKerrow (2001, p. 7) claims, is indicative of the shift in Foucault's thinking concerning the agency of the subject and not of Foucault's notion of truth which remains essentially Nietzschean. For reasons suggested earlier I dispute this interpretation. The Nietzschean perspective on truth is not straightforwardly the concept that governs Foucault's account of truth in the human sciences. McKerrow quotes a late interview with Gauthier (1988, p. 3) where Foucault says:

> I have tried to discover how the human subject entered into games of truth, whether they be games of truths which take on the form of science or which refer to a scientific model, or games of truth like those that can be found in institutions or practices of control.

And Foucault elaborates the concept of game in the following way:

> when I say game I mean an ensemble of rules for the production of truth. .... It is an ensemble of procedures which lead to a certain result, which can be considered in function of its principles and its rules of procedure as valid or not, as winner or loser. (Gauthier, 1988, cited in McKerrow, p. 7)

In fact, Foucault, in a little known paper delivered to a Japanese audience in 1978, takes up the concept of game in relation to analytic philosophy (and probably Wittgenstein's influential notion of 'language-games', although his name is not mentioned) to criticise its employment without an accompanying notion of power. Arnold Davidson (1997a, p. 3) mentions a lecture *La Philosophie analytique de la politique* in which Foucault (1978) makes an explicit reference to Anglo-American analytic philosophy:

> For Anglo-Saxon analytic philosophy it is a question of making a critical analysis of thought on the basis of the way in which one says things. I think one could imagine, in the same way, a philosophy that would have as its task to analyze what happens every day in relations of power. A philosophy, accordingly, that would bear rather on relations of power than on language games, a philosophy that would bear on all these relations that traverse the social body rather than on the effects of language that traverse and underlie thought. (as cited in Davidson, 1997a, p. 3)

In the rest of the quotation, Foucault goes on to make a series of implicit criticisms of analytic philosophy in that it refrains from asking questions concerning power relations and how they operate in language. Language in this conception 'never deceives or reveals' rather simply, as Foucault asserts: 'Language, it is played. The importance, therefore, of the notion of game'. Further on he makes the comparison:

> relations of power, also, they are played; it is these games of power that one must study in terms of tactics and strategy, in terms of order and of chance, in terms of stakes and objective. (cited in Davidson, 1997a, p. 4)

As he tried to indicate, discourse considered as speaking, as the employment of words, could be studied as strategies within genuine historical contexts, focusing upon, for example, the history of judicial practices or:

> even the discourse of truth, as rhetorical procedures, as ways of conquering, of producing events, of producing decisions, of producing battles, of producing victories. In order to rhetoricize philosophy. (as cited in Davidson, 1997a, p. 5)

'Games of truth', as McKerrow (2001) correctly points out, signifies a changed sense of agency on the part of Foucault, who, investigating practices of self, becomes interested in questions of the ethical self-constitution of the subject and self-mastery, especially in his analysis of classical texts. Thus,

> Unlike Habermas who postulates an ideal speech situation wherein games of truth would have the best chance of success, Foucault is a

> realist ... Instead of an absolutely free discourse community, the best one can attain is a com munity in which one commands the requisite rules of procedure, as well as the ethics, the ethos, the practice of self, which would allow these games of power to be played with a minimum of domination. (Gauthier, as cited in McKerrow, 2001, p. 7)

I think this is a valuable comment for not only does it point to the idealism of Habermas' quasi-transcendentalism but also signals the new possibilities inherent in an aesthetics of existence where the self learns the obligations involved in care for the self. This is clearly exemplified in Foucault's analysis of the meanings and practices of *parrhesia*.

Parrhesia, Education and Practices of Truth-Telling

The Meaning and Evolution of Parrhesia

Foucault claims that the word *parrhesia* occurs for the first time in Euripides (c. 484–407 BC) and then is used in the Greek world of letters from the end of the 5th century BC. The word is normally translated into English as 'free speech' and *parrhesiastes*, the person who uses *parrhesia*, is the one who speaks the truth. Indeed, the meaning of the word as it evolves in Greek and Roman culture, develops five major characteristics. First, it is associated with frankness: *parrhesia* refers to a special type of relationship between the speaker and what he says.[7] Unlike rhetoric, which provides the speaker with technical devices to help him persuade an audience, covering up his own beliefs, in *parrhesia*, the speaker makes it manifestly clear what he believes. Second, *parrhesia* is linked with truth. In the Greek, *parrhesia* is a speech activity where there is an exact coincidence between belief and truth. Foucault (1999, p. 3) claims: The "*parrhesiastic* game" presupposes that the *parrhesiastes* is someone who has the moral qualities which are required, first, to know the truth, and secondly, to convey such truth to others.

The moral courage of the *parrhesiastes* is evidence of his sincerity, for there is a clear risk or danger in telling the truth. This is the third characteristic. The *parrhesiastes* is someone who has the courage to tell the truth even though he may be putting his life at risk. *Parrhesia* is also strongly linked to criticism – the fourth characteristic – for the truth that the *parrhesiastes* speaks is capable of hurting the interlocutor. *Parrhesia* is thus a form of criticism, directed either towards oneself or another, where the speaker is always in a less powerful position than the interlocutor. The last characteristic concerns duty, for in *parrhesia* telling the truth is a duty. Foucault (1999, p. 5) summarises his discussion of *parrhesia* as follows:

> *Parrhesia* is a kind of verbal activity where the speaker has a specific relation to truth through frankness, a certain relationship to his own life through danger, a certain relation to himself or other people through criticism ..., and a specific relation to moral law through freedom and duty. More precisely, *parrhesia* is a verbal activity in which a speaker expresses his personal relation ship to truth, and risks his life because he recognizes truth-telling as a duty to improve or help other people (as well as himself). In *parrhesia*, the speaker uses his freedom and chooses frankness instead of persuasion, truth instead of falsehood or silence, the risk of death instead of life and security, criticism instead of flattery, and moral duty instead of self-interest and moral apathy.

Foucault analyses the evolution of the *parrhesiastic* game in ancient classical Greek culture (from the fifth century BC) to the beginnings of Christianity in terms of three aspects: its opposition to rhetoric; its relation to politics as an essential characteristic of Athenian democracy (from the 4th century BC); and its importance in philosophy as an art of life (*techne tou biou*).

The opposition between *parrhesia* and rhetoric is clear in the Socratic-Platonic tradition (in both the *Gorgias* and the *Phaedrus*) where the difference is spelled out in terms of the '*logos* which speaks the truth and the *logos* which is not capable of such truth-telling' (Foucault, 1999, p. 6). In politics, *parrhesia* was not only an ethical characteristic of the good citizen but also a guideline for democracy. The Athenian constitution (*politeia*) guaranteed citizens the equal right of speech (*demokratia isegoria*), equal participation in the exercise of power (*isonomia*) and *parrhesia*, as a prerequisite for public speech both between citizens as individuals and as an assembly. With the rise of the Hellenistic monarchies *parrhesia* becomes centred in the relation between the sovereign and his advisors, whose duty it is to help the king in making decisions but also to prevent him from abusing his power.

As an art of life (*techne tou biou*) *parrhesia* is typical of Socrates, although Plato, while using the word several times, never refers to Socrates in the role of the *parrhesiastes*. Socrates, for instance, appears in the *parrhesiastic* role in the *Apology* and *Alcibides Major* where he demonstrates his care for others in their concern for truth and the perfection of their souls. As Foucault (1999, p. 7) comments: 'Philosophical *parrhesia* is thus associated with the theme of the care of oneself (*epimeleia heautou*)' and he suggests that by the time of the

Epicureans *parrhesia* was primarily regarded as a *techne* of spiritual guidance for "the education of the soul".[8]

The Educational Practices of Socratic Parrhesia

Until now, Foucault's seminars been followed chronologically. Next in order he treats *parrhesia* in six tragedies of Euripides, where he focuses on *Ion* as a play that pursues the problem of *parrhesia*: who has the right, the duty, and the courage to speak the truth? For reasons of space, I shall not review or comment upon his analysis of *parrhesia* in Euripides, or his discussion of *parrhesia* and the crisis of democratic institutions, where Foucault analyses a form of *parrhe-sia*, as free speech, that may become dangerous for democracy itself.[9]

In the fifth and sixth seminars Foucault devotes himself to an analysis of the philosophical form of *parrhesia* as practices used in specific types of human relationships (specified as Socratic, community life, public life, and personal relationships) and, in the final seminar, as the procedures and techniques employed in these relationships.

Socratic *parrhesia* is a new form, different from political *parrhesia* that began to emerge before Socrates. Foucault analyses the dialogue Laches (*On Courage*) for the instance of *parrhesia* that occurs when two elderly men, Lysimachus and Melesias, express a concern about the kind of education they should give their sons. They are worried for, as they admit publicly, while they were both from noble families and their fathers were illustrious, they themselves achieved nothing special in their time. Clearly belonging to a noble family is not sufficient in itself to achieve a prominent city role. They realise that education is required, but what kind?

Foucault explains, at the end of the fifth century BC, educational techniques revolved around rhetoric (learning to speak before an assembly), various sophistic techniques and sometimes also a form of military training. At this time in Athens, when there was a debate about what constituted a good military education,[10] all the political, social and institutional concerns about education are related to the problem of *parrhesia*: in particular, how to recognise a truth-teller, or as Foucault expresses the issue:

> For if you are not well-educated, then how can you decide what constitutes a good education? And if people are to be educated, they must receive the truth from a competent teacher. But how can we distinguish the good, truth-telling teachers from the bad or inessential ones? (Foucault, 1999, p. 35)

Lysimachus and Melesias consult Nicias, an experienced general, and Laches, who cannot agree on what constitutes a good education, and turn to Socrates. Socrates reminds them that education concerns the care of the soul, and Nicias, in a passage that Foucault quotes from the dialogue, explains why he will play the *parrhesiastic* game with Socrates, allowing himself to be 'tested'. In analysing Nicias' speech which depicts Socrates as a *parrhesiastes*, Foucault extracts the following characteristics of Socratic *parrhesia*. First, the game requires close proximity between the *parrhesiastes* and the interlocutor – it takes place in a personal, face to face context; second – where the listener is led by the Socratic *logos* into giving an account (*didonai logon*) of himself and the kind of life he has lived. Foucault is at pains to point out that we should not read this through our Christian cultural lens as giving a confession. Rather, giving an account of one's life or *bios*, is a demonstration of:

> whether you are able to show that there is a relation between rational discourse, the logos, you are able to use, and the way you live. Socrates is inquiring into the way the logos that gives form to a person's life; for he is interested in discovering whether there is a harmonic relation between the two. (Foucault, 2001, p. 98)

Foucault explains that Socrates' role is to determine 'the degree of accord between a person's life and its principle of intelligibility or logos (ibid.), and as a result in such an examination, as Nicias explains,

> one becomes willing to care for the manner in which he lives the rest of his life, wanting now to live in the best possible way; and this willingness takes the form of a zeal to learn and to educate oneself no matter what ones age. (Foucault, 2001, p. 97)

It emerges that why Socrates is considered a good teacher, and why respected older men, citizens of Athens, are willing to submit themselves to Socrates, is the fact there is an ontological harmony between his words (*logoi*) and his deeds (*erga*). The harmony between word and deed in Socrates' life is courageous.[11] Unlike the Sophist, Socrates, the *parrhesiastes*, can 'speak freely because what he says accords exactly with what he what he thinks, and what he thinks accords exactly with what he does'.

Foucault compares three contemporary forms of *parrhesia*: the problematization of *parrhesia* in the form of a game between *logos*, truth and *genos* (birth) in relations between the Gods and mortals (as portrayed in Euripides' *Ion*); the problematization of *parrhesia* involved in a game between *logos*, truth and *nomos* (law) in the realm of politics; and, the problematization of *parrhesia* in the game between *logos*, truth and *bios* (life) in the form of a personal teaching relationship. The problem for Plato and Socrates is how to bring the latter two games into line with one another so that they coincide, i.e., 'How can philosophical truth and moral value relate to the city through the *nomos*?' This is a problem, Foucault tells us, that Plato explores in the *Apology*, the *Crito*, the *Republic* and in the *Laws*. Indeed, the dialogues of *The Last Days of Socrates* demonstrate the courage of the *parrhesiastic* Socrates – someone who is willing to tell the truth, risking his very life with the prospect of facing a death sentence pronounced by the city fathers. As Foucault comments 'even in the city ruled by good laws there is still a need for someone who will use *parrhesia* to tell the citizens what moral conduct they must observe' (Foucault, 2001, p. 106).

This new kind of philosophical *parrhesia*, which arises in Greco-Roman culture, Foucault characterises, first, as 'a practice which shaped the specific relations that individuals have to themselves (ibid). Much of the philosophy that emerged with Socrates and Plato, and shaped the philosophical tradition that is still ours today and which defines the roots of our moral subjectivity, involved the playing of certain games of truth. The philosophical role involved three types of activity: the philosopher-teacher (my construction) assumed an *epistemic* role insofar as he had to teach certain truths about the world; the philosopherteacher assumed a *political* role insofar as he took a stand towards the city, its laws and political institutions; and, the philosopher-teacher assumed a *therapeutic* or *spiritual* (my construction) role in that he took responsibility for and clarified the relationship between truth and ones style of life, or 'truth and an ethics and aesthetics of the self' (Foucault, 2001, p. 107).

Second, this new kind of philosophical *parrhesia* is conceived in a personal teaching relationship aimed at convincing someone he must take care of himself and of others, by *changing his life* – a conversion theme important from the fourth century BC to the beginnings of Christianity – rather than aimed at persuading citizens in the Assembly. Third, these new practices 'imply a complex set of connections between self and truth' (Foucault, 2001, p. 107) endowing an individual with self-knowledge sufficient to be able to pursue and gain access to the truth. Fourth, these new philosophical practices were dependent upon a range of techniques different from those developed earlier and linked to rhetoric and persuasive discourse. What is more these practices are no longer linked to the court but can be used in diverse situations.

Foucault goes on to problematize the new practices as they emerged in community and public and personal relationships.[12] Limitations of space do not permit me to review or examine Foucault's analysis of these practices, if I am to reserve some room for commenting upon Foucault[s examination of the techniques of *parrhesia*, Foucault's concluding remarks, and conclude, myself, by offering some general comments of the importance of Foucault's method and studies for the discipline of education.[13]

I shall deal in summary fashion with what Foucault calls 'techniques of the *parrhesiastic* games', where he focuses upon the techniques employed in truthgames 'which can be found in the philosophical and moral literature of the first two centuries of our era' (Foucault, 2001, p. 142). These techniques indicate a shift from the classical Greek conception of *parrhesia* where the game was 'constituted by the fact that someone was courageous enough to tell the truth to other people to another truth game which now consists in being courageous enough to disclose the truth about oneself' (Foucault, 2001, p. 143). This new kind of truth game of the self requires '*askesis*', which, while the root for 'ascetic', denotes a kind of practical training or exercise directed at the art of living (*techne tou biou*). The Greek conception of *askesis* differs significantly from Christian ascetic practices in that its goal is 'the establishment of a specific relationship to oneself' – a relationship of self possession and self-sovereignty – rather than the Christian renunciation of the self. Whereas Christian asceticism involves detachment from the world, Greco-Roman moral *askesis* is concerned with 'endowing the individual with the preparation and the moral equipment that will permit him to fully confront the world in an ethical and rational manner' (Foucault, 2001, p. 165). That is, the crucial difference consists in the Greek ethical principle of *self-mastery* versus that of Christian *self-renunciation*.[14]

Foucault examines the differences between the practices of these new truth games involving an examination of culture. He refers in turn to Seneca's *De ira* ('On Anger'), Seneca's *De tranquillitat e animi* ('On the Tranquillity of the Mind'), and the *Discourses of Epictetus*, emphasizing that despite the differences these practices share an implied relation between truth and the self very different from what is found in the Christian tradition. These practices he examines exhibit a shift in the relationship between master and disciple as the master no longer discloses the truth about the disciple, but rather the disciple takes on this responsibility as a duty toward himself. It is not enough to say that this personal relation of self-understanding derives from the general principle 'know thyself' (*gnothi seauton*) for the 'relationships which one has to oneself are embedded in very precise techniques which take the form of spiritual exercises – some of them dealing with deeds, others with states of equilibrium of the soul, others with the flow of representations, and so on' (Foucault, 2001, p. 166). Finally, what is at stake in these practices is not the disclosure of a secret but 'the relation of the self to truth or to some rational principles' (Foucault, 2001, p. 169). These exercises constitute what Foucault calls an 'aesthetics of the self'.

In his 'Concluding remarks', Foucault states that 'My intention was not to deal with the problem of truth, but with the problem of truth-teller or truth-telling as an activity'. He expands this idea into the following point:

> What I wanted to analyze was how the truth-tellers role was variously problematized in Greek philosophy. And what I wanted to show you was that of Greek philosophy has raised the question of truth from the point of view of the criteria for true statements and sound reasoning, this same Greek philosophy has also raised the problem of truth from the point of view of truth-telling as an activity. (Foucault, 2001, p. 169)

Truth-telling as a speech activity revolving around four questions – 'who is able to tell the truth, about what, with what consequences, and with what relation to power? – emerged as distinct philosophical problems with Socrates, and were pursued in his confrontations with the Sophists in dialogues concerning politics, rhetorics, and ethics. He adds as a further expansion:

> And I would say that the problematization of truth which characterizes both the end of Presocratic philosophy and the beginning of the kind of philosophy which is still ours today, this problematization of truth has two sides, two major aspects. One side is concerned with insuring that the process of reasoning is correct in determining whether a statement is true (or concern [sic] itself with our ability to gain access to the truth). And the other side is concerned with the question: what is the importance for the individual and for the society of telling the truth, of knowing the truth, of having people who tell the truth, as well as knowing how to recognize them. (Foucault, 2001, p. 170)

One side he characterises as the great philosophical tradition concerned with how to determine the truth-value of a statement, which he describes as the 'analytics of truth'. The other side, 'concerned with the importance of telling the truth, knowing who is able to tell the truth, knowing why we should tell the truth', Foucault explains as the roots of the 'critical' tradition in the Western philosophical tradition and he describes his own purpose in the seminars in precisely those terms 'to construct a genealogy of the critical attitude in the [sic] Western philosophy' (Foucault, 2001, pp. 170–171).[15]

Conclusion: Foucault and the Prospects for *Parrhesiastical* Education

What can we conclude from this brief exposition and analysis? I think we can make some quite significant conclusions. First, in the set of lectures entitled *Discourse and Truth*, delivered at Berkeley a year before his death, we see Foucault at his best, utilising Nietzschean genealogy to problematize the practices of *parrhesia* in classical Greek culture – a set of practices, culturally speaking, that are deep-seated for the West. These practices that link truth-telling, on the one hand, and education, on the other, are not only the roots of our present-day cultural practices and conceptions, but they are still operative in shaping our subjectivities and, therefore, also still relevant in understanding the exercise of power and control in contemporary life.

Second, Foucault's problematization of *parrhesia* and especially his investigation of what he calls Socratic *parrhesia*, provides a genealogical analysis which demonstrates the cultural significance of truth-telling as a set of educational practices, strongly wedded to the Socratic beginning of the Western philosophical tradition, and, therefore, also to the West's cultural self-image or self-understanding. Foucault excavates from a variety of sources in classical literature, with the lightness of the palaeontologist's brush, a series of conceptual, historical and practical relations that link education and philosophy through truth-telling. Perhaps, more importantly, he links this parrhesiastical form of education to democracy, in a way that turns historical ideals into living practices. There is much more that we could develop from this thought: perhaps, the analysis of the ways in which today our schools, bent on teaching students' generic skills as preparation for the knowledge economy, have deviated from our historical models and begun to shed the concern for truth and truth-telling in favour of entrepreneurship (see Peters, 2001b).

Third, the six lectures he gives at Berkeley demonstrate Foucault's direct concern for education and educational practices. In these lectures we see the full intellectual weight of Foucault settled on educational issues rather than having to infer, deduce or apply his genealogical insights or methods to education.

And in relation to this point, fourth, we might begin to understand, in terms of Foucault's analysis of the human sciences – indeed of his epistemological model for becoming a science – that education has a history and that 'the history of non-formal thought had itself a system' (Foucault, 1973, p. x) capable of revealing a '*positive unconscious* of knowledge' (p. xi) but that it is incapable of becoming a science, as recent national research planning in the U.S.A. and U.K. now demand (Peters, 2001b). until it meets the 'objectivity criterion'.

Fifth, I think we see a very different Foucault in these six lectures than we do in, say, his neostructuralist period when he was writing *Archaeology of Knowledge* or *The Order of Things*, especially when it comes to truth-telling. The lectures reveal how Foucault thought that the 'critical' tradition in Western philosophy – the tradition concerned with the importance of telling the truth, rather than truth as the criteria for determining the truth-value of a statement (as we might express it today) – begins precisely at the same time as the 'analytics of truth' with the end of Presocratic philosophy and the institutionalization of philosophy in the Athenian academies. This genealogy of the critical attitude in philosophy is to be traced to the same beginnings that all Western contemporary philosophy is heir to. Foucault's attitude here does not smack of the same antagonism he displayed earlier against analytic philosophy.

Sixth, with his genealogical investigations of the critical attitude in Western philosophy, Foucault delivers us both a fresh reading of the Socratic tradition and the role of education in relation to cultivating practices of truth-telling that subsequently became the basis for the West's cultural and philosophical self-definition. He provides us with the outline of a Nietzschean programme of philosophical research that seeks to question the genealogy of educational ethics. We should remember that Nietzsche, who's *Genealogy of Morals* clearly provides Foucault with a model, also gravitates back to Socrates as an archetype of the philosopher as cultural physician or sets the conditions for culture and the creation of new value. In more concrete terms, in terms of Foucault's Berkeley lectures we might discover anew the continuing relevance of the Socratic tradition. Let me briefly elaborate.

One of the most vexing questions in contemporary philosophy is the question of the relation between the philosopher and his or her work: in more precise terms the possibilities of the genre of philosophical biography. It stands at the door of questions concerning philosophical genres and philosophy as a kind of writing, especially with the emergence of the form of confession as an autobiographical philosophical genre in the work of Augustine and Rousseau, and thus helps to broach a wider set of questions concerning the relation between philosophy and literature that have become a standard reference in the work of thinkers such as diverse as Stanley Cavell and Jacques Derrida. As James Conant (2001, p. 19) comments, in contemporary thought we are offered an apparent deadlock:

> We are offered a forced choice between reductivism and compartmentalism an understanding of an author's work is to be found wholly outside his work (in the external events of his life) or an understanding of

the work is to be sought by attending solely to what lies wholly within the work (and the life is held not to be part of the work).

The case of Socrates, as the fountainhead of Western philosophy, provides an interesting example precisely because he did not *write* anything. As Conant (2001, pp. 19–20) writes: 'Socrates' life is his work and his work is his life ... there is no understanding of his philosophy apart from an understanding of the sort of life he sought to live'. Conant turns to Pierre Hadot, Foucault's colleague at the Collège de France, in order to explain how and why philosophy, during the Hellenistic and Roman era, was 'a way of life', where philosophy was a mode of existing-in-the-world and the emphasis fell on the transformation of the individual's life through *philosophia* as the love of wisdom. On this conception, one which motivated the late Foucault in his studies of the classical texts, 'a philosopher's life is the definitive expression of his philosophy' (Conant, 2001, p. 21) and his writings are merely the means to facilitate work on the self.

Yet this conception of philosophy as an ethical form of life is not restricted to an understanding of Socrates or to truth-telling practices that invest Socratic *parrhesia*. It can be argued that it is central also to understanding some of the inherited forms of modem philosophy and modem philosophers themselves such as Nietzsche and Wittgenstein (see Peters & Marshall, 1999; Peters, 2000, 2001c). It may not be too far-fetched to argue that this problematic could act as a framework for entertaining Foucault's own life and philosophy and the question of ethical self-constitution that concerned him late in his life or that it offers great prospects for a rehabilitation of Socratic *parrhesia* – of parrhesiastical education – in philosophy of education as a possible innovative research programme for a form of applied professional ethics in education.

Acknowledgement

This chapter was previously published as Michael A. Peters, 'Truth-Telling as an Educational Practice of the Self', *Oxford Review of Education*, 29(2), 2002, 207–224 and is reprinted here with permission from Taylor & Francis (https://www.tandfonline.com/loi/core20).

Notes

1 On Nietzsche's influence on Foucault see Shrift (1995). On Heidegger's influence on Foucault see Dreyfus (1998, 1999). Foucault's books are, of course, scattered with

references to both thinkers. In regard to Heidegger, it is an interesting question, given his intellectual debts, why Foucault provided little direct acknowledgement of his work or influence upon him.
2 See Nietzsche's famous and, apparently, only footnote in the entire corpus of his work, which appears after the first essay of the *Genealogy of Morals* (orig. 1887, 1956, p. 188).
3 A shift from ontology to the history of Being is reflected in Heidegger's philosophy.
4 These lectures were edited by Joseph Pearson in 1985, compiled from tape-recordings made in English by Foucault. As Pearson notes Since Foucault did not write, correct, or edit any part of the text, … it lacks his imprimatur and does not represent his own lecture notes. Pearson's version was re-edited in 1999 for the web site www.repb.net (accessed 25 July, 2001), which serves as the text to which I refer. These lectures have subsequently appeared in book form as Fearless Speech (Foucault, 2001b).
5 There are significant differences in the themes Foucault pursues in these two sets of lectures, the way he pursues them and his characterization of the Platonic model. In the Vermont set he characterises the Platonic model as defective in that it is dualistic (teacher/pupil) and directed at knowing oneself rather than care for the self; in the more considered Berkeley lectures he treats the Socratic/Platonic model with greater sympathy, emphasising that the tradition is not only the source of the search for truth (as in the truth value of a statement) but also of a critical philosophy based upon an understanding of the practices of truth telling.
6 I base this account on van Gigch's (1998) thoughtful essay.
7 I use the male pronoun here on purpose as the parrhesiastes must know his own genealogy and status and is usually a male citizen (see Foucault, 1999, p. 5).
8 I am bound to say that Foucault's friend and colleague at the Collège de France, Pierre Hadot, professor emeritus of the History of Hellenistic and Roman Thought, on whom Foucault relies for so much his interpretation of classical texts in his last years, takes Foucault to task for his reading of the care of the self (see Harlot, 1995, 1997; also Davidson, 1997b).
9 Foucault examines an aristocratic lampoon against Athenian democracy attributed to Xenophon, Isocrates' *On the Peace and Areopagiticus*, and Plato's *Republic*.
10 The debate concerns infantry soldiers, who were inferior to their Spartan counter parts.
11 Foucault explains that there were four kinds of harmony, which Plato distinguishes as Lydian (too solemn), Phrygian (too tied to the passions), Ionian (too soft and effeminate), Dorian (courageous).
12 Foucault examines parrhesia in the community life of the Epicureans, the practice of *parrhesia* in public life through the example of the Cynic philosophers (including, critical preaching, scandalous behaviour and provocative dialogue), and the

parrhesiastic game in the framework of personal relationships, from examples taken from Plutarch and Galen.
13 It is important, however, to note that Foucault provides a reading of a fragmentary Greek text by Philodemus (with the help of the Italian scholar, Marcello Gigante) which helps him to make some observations about the practice of *parrhesia* in Epicurean community life, and in particular, the important distinction between two categories of teachers and two types of teaching, which became a permanent feature of western culture (43/66). As he says: With the Epicurean schools, however, there is the pedagogical relation of guidance where the master helps the disciple to discover the truth about himself, but there is now, in addition, a form of authoritarian teaching in a collective relation where someone speaks the truth to a group of others (43/66).
14 Foucault's interest in comparing Greek askesis and Christian ascetic practices is, of course, to a large extent governed and closely related to his reading of Nietzsche, especially the *Genealogy of Morals*. See, in particular, the third essay What do Ascetic Ideals Mean?, where Nietzsche suggests that (Christian) ascetic ideals arose to give meaning to human suffering, under the perspective of guilt – a kind of will to nothingness, injurious to health and life, but, nevertheless a willing. As he says man would sooner have the void for his purpose than be void of purpose (Nietzsche, 1956, p. 299).
15 Foucault ends with a note defending his notion of problematization of practices. It is not a form of historical idealism, not a way of denying the reality of such phenomena (65/66), rather the problematization is an answer to a concrete situation which is real (66/66). It is not a representation or an effect of a situation, but rather a creation that explores the relation between thought and reality to give an answer – the original, specific, and singular, answer of thought – to a certain situation (66/66).

References

Baker, B. (2001). *In perpetual motion: Theories of power, educational history, and the child*. New York, NY: Peter Lang.
Ball, S. (1990). *Foucault and education: Disciplines and knowledge*. London: Routledge.
Conant, J. (2001). Philosophy and biography. In J. C. Klagge (Ed.), *Wittgenstein: Biography and philosophy*. Cambridge: Cambridge University Press.
Davidson, A. (1997a). Structures and strategies of discourse: Remarks towards a history of Foucault's philosophy of language. In A. Davidson (Ed.), *Foucault and his interlocutors*. Chicago, IL: University of Chicago Press.
Davidson, A. (1997b). Introductory remarks to Pierre Hadot. In A. Davidson (Ed.), *Foucault and his interlocutors*. Chicago, IL: University of Chicago Press.

Dreyfus, H. L. (1998). *Being and power: Heidegger and Foucault.* Retrieved from http://socrates.berkeley.edu/%7Ehdreyfus/html/paper_being.html

Dreyfus, H. L. (1999). *Heidegger and Foucault on the subject, agency and practices.* Retrieved from http://socrates.berkeley.edu/%7Ehdreyfus/html/paper_heidandfoucault.html

Dreyfus, H. L., & Rabinow, H. L. (1983). *Michel Foucault: Beyond structuralism and hermeneutics* (2nd ed.). Chicago, IL: University of Chicago.

Foucault, M. (1972). *The archaeology of knowledge.* New York, NY: Pantheon Books.

Foucault, M. (1973). *The birth of the clinic: An archaeology of medical perception* (A. M. Sheridan, Trans.). London: Tavistock.

Foucault, M. (1978). La Philosophie analytique de la politique. In D. Defert, F. Ewart, & J. Lagrange (Eds.), *Dits et ecrits, 1954–1988* (Vol. 3, pp. 540–541). Paris: Grasset.

Foucault, M. (1979). *Discipline and punish: The birth of the prison.* New York, NY: Vintage Books.

Foucault, M. (1980). *Power/knowledge: Selected interviews and other writings 1972–1977* (C. Gordon, Ed.). London: Harvester.

Foucault, M. (1980). *The history of sexuality* (Vol. I). New York, NY: Vintage Books.

Foucault, M. (1985). *The use of pleasure: The history of sexuality* (Vol. II). New York, NY: Vintage Books.

Foucault, M. (1988). *Politics, philosophy, and culture: Interviews and other writings, 1977–1984* (M. Morris & P. Patton, Eds.). New York, NY: Routledge.

Foucault, M. (1988). *Technologies of the self: A seminar with Michel Foucault* (L. H. Martin, H. Gutman, & P. H. Hutton, Eds.). Amherst, MA: University of Massachusetts Press.

Foucault, M. (1990). *The care of the self: The history of sexuality* (Vol. III). New York, NY: Vintage Books.

Foucault, M. (1991). Governmentality. In G. Burchell, C. Gordon, & P. Miller (Eds.), *The Foucault effect: Studies in governmentality, with two lectures by and an interview with Michel Foucault.* London: Harvester Wheatsheaf.

Foucault, M. (1992). *Madness and civilization: A history of insanity in the age of reason* (R. Howard, Trans.). London: Routledge.

Foucault, M. (1997). Michel Foucault: Ethics, subjectivity and truth. In P. Rabinow (Ed.), *The essential works of Michel Foucault 1954–1984* (Vol. 1). London: Allen Lane.

Foucault, M. (1999). *Discourse and truth: The problematization of parrhesia* (Lectures given by Michel Foucault at the University of California at Berkeley, October–November 1983). Retrieved from http://foucault.info/documents/parrhesia/

Foucault, M. (2001a). The subject and power. In J. D. Faubion (Ed.), *The essential works of Michel Foucault 1954–1984* (Vol. 1). London: Allen Lane.

Foucault, M. (2001b). *Fearless speech* (J. Pearson, Ed.). Los Angeles, CA: Semiotext(e).

Gauthier, J. D. (1988). The ethic of the care of the self as a practice of freedom: An interview (G. D. Gauthier, Trans.). In J. Bernauer & D. Rasmussen (Eds.), *The final Foucault.* Cambridge, MA: MIT Press.

Hadot, P. (1995). *Philosophy as a way of life*. Oxford: University of Oxford Press.
Hadot, P. (1997). Forms of life and forms of discourse in ancient philosophy. In A. Davidson (Ed.), *Foucault and his interlocutors*. Chicago, IL: University of Chicago Press.
Marshall, J. D. (1996). *Michel Foucault: Personal autonomy and education*. London: Kluwer Academic.
Martin, R. (1988). Truth, power, self: An interview with Michel Foucault. In L. Martin, H. Gutman, & P. H. Huttons (Eds.), *Technologies of the self*. Amherst, MA: University of Massachusetts Press.
McKerrow, R. (2001). *Foucault and surrealism of the truth*. Retrieved from http://oak.cats.ohiou.edu/-mckerrow/foucault.htm
Nietzsche, F. (1956). *The birth of tragedy and the genealogy of morals* (F. Golffing, Trans.). New York, NY: Doubleday.
Nietzsche, F. (1974). *On truth and lie in an extra-moral sense*. New York, NY: Viking Press.
Olssen, M. (1999). *Michel Foucault: Materialism and education*. Westport, CT: Bergin & Garvey.
Peters, M. (2000). Writing the self: Wittgenstein, confession and pedagogy. *Journal of Philosophy of Education, 34*(2), 353–368.
Peters, M. (2001a). Education, enterprise culture and the entrepreneurial self: A Foucauldian perspective. *Journal of Educational Enquiry, 2*, 1. Retrieved from http://www.education.unisa.edu.auf]EE/
Peters, M. (2001b, September 27–29). *Does Scotland need a national research strategy in education?* Paper presented to SERA Annual Conference, University of Dundee, Dundee.
Peters, M. (2001c). Philosophy as pedagogy: Wittgensteins styles of thinking. *Radical Pedagogy, 4*, 1. Retrieved from http://radicalpedagogy.icaap.org/
Peters, M., & Marshall, J. (1999). *Wittgenstein: Philosophy, postmodernism, pedagogy*. Westport, CT: Bergin & Garvey.
Plato. (1993). *The last days of Socrates: Euthyphro, apology, crito, phaedo* (H. Tredenick & H. Tarrant, Trans.). London: Penguin Books.
Popkewitz, T. S., & Brennan, M. (1998). *Foucault's challenge: Discourse, knowledge, and power in education*. New York, NY: Teachers College Press.
Shrift, A. (1995). *Nietzsches French legacy: A genealogy of poststructuralism*. London & New York, NY: Routledge.
van Gigch, J. P. (1998). The epistemology of the social sciences according to Michel Foucault, 1926–1984 (Design of the modern inquiring system, part 14). *Systems Research and Behavioral Science, 15*(2), 154–159.

CHAPTER 4

Interculturalism, Ethnocentrism and Dialogue

Introduction: Interculturalism and Ethnocentrism

The European Commission's website sets out a 'toolkit for intercultural dialogue' and states:

> We need *intercultural skills* to be able to engage in a meaningful dialogue with others. Among these skills, *communication in foreign languages, social and civic competences,* and *cultural awareness and expression* are essential bridge-builders between people from different cultural, ethnic, religious and linguistic backgrounds. (Original emphasis)[1]

One of these tools and the most recent policy formulation of the desire to address cultural diversity, is the Council of Europe's *White Paper on Intercultural Dialogue: living together as equals in dignity*, which describes dialogue as 'A Key to Europe's Future'. We decided a first move for the new Centre for Global Studies in Education at University of Waikato would be a call for papers for a special issue of *Policy Futures in Education* on the White Paper, which was launched by the Council of Europe Ministers of Foreign Affairs at their 118th Ministerial Session (Strasbourg, 7 May 2008) and provides the following statement:

> Managing Europe's increasing cultural diversity – rooted in the history of our continent and enhanced by globalisation – in a democratic manner has become a priority in recent years. How shall we respond to diversity? What is our vision of the society of the future? Is it a society of segregated communities, marked at best by the coexistence of majorities and minorities with differentiated rights and responsibilities, loosely bound together by mutual ignorance and stereotypes? Or is it a vibrant and open society without discrimination, benefiting us all, marked by the inclusion of all residents in full respect of their human rights?
>
> The Council of Europe believes that respect for, and promotion of, cultural diversity on the basis of the values on which the Organisation is built are essential conditions for the development of societies based on solidarity.
>
> The 'White Paper on Intercultural Dialogu' presented here, emphatically argues in the name of the governments of the 47 member states of

the Council of Europe that our common future depends on our ability to safeguard and develop human rights, as enshrined in the European Convention on Human Rights, democracy and the rule of law and to promote mutual understanding. It reasons that the intercultural approach offers a forward-looking model for managing cultural diversity. It proposes a conception based on individual human dignity (embracing our common humanity and common destiny). If there is a European identity to be realised, it will be based on shared fundamental values, respect for common heritage and cultural diversity as well as respect for the equal dignity of every individual.

Intercultural dialogue has an important role to play in this regard. It allows us to prevent ethnic, religious, linguistic and cultural divides. It enables us to move forward together, to deal with our different identities constructively and democratically on the basis of shared universal values.[2]

'Intercultural dialogue' is a concept and discourse that has emerged as a distinct form of communication practice only since the 1980s. It has been adopted as the basis for interreligious and interfaith initiatives, and has become increasingly associated with a liberal theory of modernity and internationalism that presupposes freedom, democracy, human rights and tolerance. The concept has been adopted by many of the world's major policy organizations such as the United Nations (UN), UNESCO and the Council of Europe as the dominant thread and paradigm for cultural policy, and increasingly the educational basis for the development of intercultural understanding. Intercultural education, communication and understanding have been themes of international cooperation for a long time, but notions of dialogue of civilizations and intercultural dialogue have only recently begun to appear on the political agenda of international institutions.

In one influential formulation, *intercultural education* is viewed as the global forum for the analysis of issues dealing with education in plural societies focusing on the management of cultural diversity and including such issues as multiculturalism, multilingualism, intercultural communication, the maintenance and fostering of human rights, anti-racist education, pluralism within democracies, pluralism in post-communist and in post-colonial countries, conflict resolution and avoidance, international mediation, migration and problems of migrant labor, indigenous cultural and minority rights, refugee education, language policy and, perhaps above all, the question of cultural identity and emerging global forms of identity, especially with youth cultures. Yet the prevalent formulation of interculturalism, while taking a position of openness to the Other and looking for commonalities, ignores a whole range of cultures such as youth cultures, urban cultures, rural cultures, gay cultures, etc., in favor of ethnic-based cultures. The expectation is that an attitude of openness to people of other cultures will lead to dialogue, comparisons and understanding and acceptance between cultural groups, not based simply on awareness of differences, but in finding commonalities.

Yet interculturalism cannot be considered separate from associated discourses of ethnocentrism, which is tangled in a web of meanings of other concepts including cultural relativism and universalism. Strategically, ethically and practically, ethnocentrism (and associated racism) is the major presumption and problematic of interculturalism and intercultural understanding and education. Ethnocentrism was first defined by William G. Sumner in *Folkways: a study of the sociological importance of usages, manners, customs, mores, and morals* as the view "in which one's own group is the center of everything and all others are scaled and rated with reference to it" (Sumner, 1907, p. 13). This hierarchical thinking applies to cultures and nations. Sumner argues that ethnocentric people would judge other groups in relation to their own particular ethnic group or culture, and they would have a feeling of superiority against others. Summer claims that throughout history, almost all cultures have located themselves at the center of the world and civilization:

> The Jews divided all mankind into themselves and Gentiles. They were the 'chosen people'. The Greeks and Romans called all outsiders 'barbarians'. … The Arabs regarded themselves as the noblest nation and all others as more or less barbarous. In 1896, the Chinese Minister of Education and his counsellors edited a manual in which this statement occurs: 'How grand and glorious is the Empire of China, the middle kingdom. She is the largest and richest in the world. The grandest men in the world have all come from the middle empire'. … In Russian books and newspapers the civilizing mission of Russia is talked about, just as, in the books and journals of France, Germany, and the United States, the civilizing mission of those countries is assumed and referred to as well-understood. Each state now regards itself as the leader of civilization, the best, the freest, and the wisest, and all others as inferior. (Sumner, 1907, p. 14)

Ethnocentrism holds that people are born and socialized into a certain world view and almost inevitably perceive the world from their particular positionality, and, over time, come to believe their cultural/national superiority as a given, as normal and natural, often bolstered by religious texts. When they come across other cultures with different values and norms, their ideas are challenged to a greater or lesser extent, especially if the other culture holds very different values and attitudes to their birth culture. They will tend to assess the differences and decide how they rate or accept them in comparison and relation to their own culture – ranging from OK, to OK for them but not for me, or not OK at all. However, since people are accustomed to their birth culture, it can be difficult for them to see the behaviours of people from a different culture from the viewpoint of that culture rather than from their own.

No culture is static, and all cultures change to varying degrees in response to contact with other cultures, especially in the contemporary world with increased mobility, migration and globalization. The question needs to be asked as to if/how different cultures, including Western society/philosophy with its current privileged position, overcome their ethnocentric world view. After Wittgenstein, we understand that language is embedded in a culture, which shapes language, values and behaviour, conditioning people to see things from within a particular cultural frame of reference – "the limits of my language are the limits of my world" (Wittgenstein, 1922, proposition 5.6). The claim of the universality of ethnocentrism acknowledges that we cannot easily shed our cultural assumptions; climb out of our culture and language into some privileged position to view things as they really are. Wittgenstein basically argues that the mind is social or cultural and always already embedded in the external world. We are born into language and culture, and we learn 'language games' practically.

Dialogue

The other key notion in the White Paper is that of dialogue. Dialogue has multiple cultural origins in the great classical literatures of the world, perhaps beginning with classical Indian literature in the form of the dialogue hymns (*samvāda-sūktas*) of the *Rigveda*, which are reputedly the earliest surviving form or genre and a precursor of Sanskrit drama, dating back to roughly the twelfth to tenth centuries BC. In classical Chinese literature, and especially in Ch'an Buddhism, 'dialogue encounter' is used to refer to the questions and responses that take place between Ch'an masters and their students. To this picture we add, of course, the dialogues of Plato and Socrates, and, much later, the scriptural hermeneutics of Abrahamic religions (Old Testament studies in Judaism, Christianity and Islam).

Dialogue takes three main forms: a conversation or other form of discourse between two or more individuals; a literary form, where the presentation resembles a conversation, or a dramatic or literary presentation referring to the verbal parts of the script or text and the verbalizations (dialogue) of the actors or characters; and, in addition, a pedagogical form of question and answer between master and pupil or disciple, as in the classical texts.

Dialogue has been the most venerable pedagogical form for philosophical discourse in the West since the early days of the Academy when Socrates first defined dialectics and the dialogical method of argumentation. Since Socrates, dialogue has taken many different forms including: religious communion (Martin Buber); philosophical hermeneutics (Gadamer); rational deliberation (Habermas); radical pedagogy (Freire); dialogism and dialogical imagination (Bakhtin); dialogue as the awakening of consciousness (Bohm); and dialogue as conversation and the medium of liberal learning (Oakeshott and Rorty), which we briefly elaborate below. Using the philosophy of dialogue to promote intercultural understanding is very recent.

Dialogos: In the Beginning Was the Word

An etymology from the Ancient Greek provides a series of deep metaphors for understanding dialogue as meaning conversation and discourse, and implying some exchange:
- *dialogos* – conversation, discourse
- *dia* – through, inter
- *logos* – speech, oration, discourse
- *dialegomai* – to converse
- *legein* – to speak

Dialogos is a noun derived from the verb *dialegomai*, which means 'to become involved in a conversation with another'. Socrates transformed the erotic relation between himself and the partners in the dialogues to a love for the truth. This is taken to indicate that philosophical knowledge is never possessed by one-person alone and although asymmetric dialogical relations exist between partners, Socrates' famous dictum, 'I know that I do not know anything' (espoused with irony), aimed at equality and used the *maieutic* (midwifery) process to lead to establishing the intersubjective nature of knowledge. Scholars tend to differentiate between Plato and Socrates, indicating the different forms of dialogue:
- *eristic* is the sophistic method of contradiction with the sole purpose of proving the other person wrong, no matter which is the truth;
- *elenchus* is considered the Socratic method of refutation, the method that has as its purpose the purification of unhealthy souls – souls that think they have knowledge while what they have is only an appearance of knowledge;
- *dialectic*, distinct from the Socratic elenchus, refers to the Platonic method of cross-examination, but also is a way of thinking that aims toward discovering truth.

In this context, we must not forget that dialogical logic is a research tradition that can be traced back to Greek antiquity, when logic was first conceived as the systematic study of dialogues in which two parties exchange arguments over a central claim. Thus, *dialogue as argument*, which refers to Plato's dialectics in its modern form, uses concepts of game theory to design dialogue games to provide a semantics for a wide range of logical systems.

One of the important observations to emerge from a study of *dialogus* is that it is a relationship, and Socratic dialogue is not a relationship between a teacher and his disciples but rather a relationship between lovers, which is sublimated to the common love for searching for the truth. Socratic dialogical intercultural philosophy, then, might be described as a methodology of listening, of reading an argument with an emphasis of equality and difference and an openness with regard to possible results. In this context, we might also recognize the extra rational and linguistic means, including emotional and bodily means, which are used to reach common understanding (including the encounter with the face of the Other).

Dialogue as a Process: A Social Relation
Gadamer's notion of dialogue, as a process of understanding each other, makes it

> a characteristic of every true conversation that each opens himself to the other person, truly accepts his point of view as worthy of consideration and gets inside the other to such an extent that he understands not a particular individual, but what he says. The thing that has to be grasped is the objective rightness or otherwise of his opinion, so that they can agree with each other on a subject. (Gadamer, 1989, p. 347)

Thus, dialogue is a *social* relation, an interaction that goes back and forth to ascertain another person's viewpoint without necessarily agreeing with them, and is not so much a specific communicative form of question and answer. Being part of this social relation requires an engagement of participants which entails certain virtues and emotions. Nick Burbules lists six of these as concern, trust, respect, appreciation, affection and hope:
- *Concern*. In being *with* our partners in conversation, to engage them with us, there is more going on than talk about the overt topic. There is a social bond that entails interest in, and a commitment to the other.
- *Trust*. We have to take what others are saying on faith – and there can be some risk in this.

- *Respect.* While there may be large differences between partners in conversation, the process can go on if there is mutual regard. This involves the idea that everyone is equal in some basic way and entails a commitment to being fair-minded, opposing degradation and rejecting exploitation.
- *Appreciation.* Linked to respect, this entails valuing the unique qualities that others bring.
- *Affection.* Conversation involves a feeling with, and for, our partners.
- *Hope.* While not being purely emotional, hope is central. We engage in conversation in the belief that it holds possibility. Often it is not clear what we will gain or learn, but faith in the inherent value of education carries us forward (Burbules, 1993, p. 19; original emphasis).

Crucially, Burbules goes on to argue:

> When we assert a belief that we hold, we also offer an implied promise to provide at least some of the evidence and reasons behind that belief, if asked. We may not be asked; we may not be able to provide those reasons fully; and we may not convince others if we do – but by making the assertion we commit ourselves to that broader obligation. (Burbules, 1993, p. 75)

In important ways, Burbules' analytic approach shares some characteristics with David Bohm's more spiritual view, drawn from Eastern sources in his dialogues with Jidhu Krishnamurti:

> Dialogue ... enables inquiry into, and understanding of, the sorts of processes that fragment and interfere with real communication between individuals, nations and even different parts of the same organization. In our modern culture[,] men and women are able to interact with one another in many ways: they can sing[,] dance or play together with little difficulty but their ability to talk together about subjects that matter deeply to them seems invariabl[y] to lead to dispute, division and often to violence. In our view this condition points to a deep and pervasive defect in the process of human thought. (Bohm et al., 1991)

Mark Smith outlines the ideas of David Bohm and colleagues who, without prescribing how to conduct a dialogue, stipulate three basic conditions for dialogue:

> *Participants must suspend their assumptions* [their thoughts, impulses, judgments to enter the spirit of dialogue, which differs from discussion

> where people usually firmly hold a particular view]. [T]he spirit of dialogue ... is ... the ability to hold many points of view in suspension, along with a primary interest in the creation of common meaning (Bohm & Peat, 1987, p. 247). Suspending an assumption does not mean ignoring it, but rather 'holding it in front of us ready for exploration' ...
> *Participants must view each other as colleagues or peers* ... involved in a mutual quest for understanding and insight. 'A Dialogue is essentially a conversation between equals' (Bohm et al., 1991).
> *In the early stages there needs to be a facilitator who holds the context of dialogue* ... 'point[ing] out ... sticking points for the group[3] to aid the process of collective proprioception, but these interventions should never be manipulative nor obtrusive' (Bohm et al., 1991). [Bohm et al.] continue, 'guidance, when it is felt to be necessary, should take the form of "leading from behind" and preserve the intention of making itself redundant as quickly as possible'. (Smith, 2001)

David Bohm and his colleagues write of dialogue as a means of addressing the significant crises that we face in the world today and he writes of dialogue as a process of awakening and provides insight into the group process. Once people get beyond defending their initial fixed positions, they realize that maintaining the friendship within the group is more important than holding a position. The friendship is not a close, personal one, but more a new mentality that emerges

> based on the development of a common meaning that is constantly transforming in the process of the dialogue. People are no longer primarily in opposition, nor can they be said to be interacting, rather they are participating in this pool of common meaning which is capable of constant development and change. In this development the group has no pre-established purpose, though at each moment a purpose that is free to change may reveal itself. The group thus begins to engage in a new dynamic relationship in which no speaker is excluded, and in which no particular content is excluded. Thus far we have only begun to explore the possibilities of dialogue in the sense indicated here, but going further along these lines would open up the possibility of transforming not only the relationship between people, but even more, the very nature of consciousness in which these relationships arise. (Bohm, 1987, p. 175)

'Dialogue among Civilizations'
In 1998, the UN decided to name 2001 the 'Year of Dialogue among Civilizations' in a clear rejection of the concept of a clash of civilizations which assumes that

intercivilizational understanding is impossible, and a direct response to Samuel P. Huntington's 1996 book, *The Clash of Civilizations and the Remaking of World Order*. Dialogue among civilisations is a theory in international relations that was first introduced by Seyed Mohammad Khatami, the former President of Iran. Prior to the tragedy of 9/11, the UN General Assembly expressed its firm determination to facilitate just such a dialogue, which is aimed at increasing mutual understanding and tolerance among peoples of different cultural backgrounds through an active exchange of ideas, visions and aspirations. Khatami later established the Foundation for Dialogue among Civilizations in Geneva in 2007, introducing dialogue as a new paradigm for international relations and intercultural understanding with the following objectives:

1. to promote and facilitate the peaceful resolution of conflicts and/or disputes;
2. to reconcile tensions between cultures, countries and religions;
3. to promote and facilitate the much needed dialogue between Muslim societies and other societies around the world; and
4. to contribute to academic research and enrich the wider debate around peace in the world.[4]

In the upheavals and wars of the post-9/11 world, dialogue among civilizations would seem to be more important than ever. Yet Khatami's organization seems to have stalled.

UNESCO has taken up part of this challenge, as its website states:

> the promotion of dialogue in the service of peace – in order to build 'peace in the minds of men' – is clearly one of the main themes of UNESCO's mission. Globalization and the emergence of new contemporary challenges and threats to humankind make the need for dialogue among peoples ever more topical. A principal objective of a dialogue is to bridge the gap in knowledge about other civilizations, cultures and societies, to lay the foundations for dialogue based on universally shared values and to undertake concrete activities, inspired and driven by dialogue, especially in the areas of education, cultural diversity and heritage, the sciences and communication and media.[5]

Between 2003 and 2006, UNESCO held a series of conferences, symposia and workshops in New Delhi, Tokyo, Ohrid (Macedonia), Moscow, Libreville (Gabon), Abuja (Nigeria), Paris, Sanaa (Yemen), Issyk Kul (Kyrgyzstan), Barcelona, Bishkek (Kyrgyzstan), Tirana (Albania), Hanoi, Quebec, Rabat (Morocco) and Opatija (Croatia).[6] In 2010, UNESCO stated, with respect to intercultural dialogue:

Equitable exchange and dialogue among civilizations, cultures and peoples, based on mutual understanding and respect and the equal dignity of all cultures is the essential prerequisite for constructing social cohesion, reconciliation among peoples and peace among nations.

This action is part of the global framework of an Alliance of Civilizations launched by the United Nations. More specifically, within the larger framework of intercultural dialogue, which also encompasses interreligious dialogue, special focus is placed on a series of good practices to encourage cultural pluralism at the local, regional and national level as well as regional and sub-regional initiatives aimed at discouraging all expressions of extremism and fanaticism and highlighting values and principles that bring people together.

UNESCO will continue to exercise its watch function by highlighting the role that can be played by culture in conflict or post-conflict situations as a vehicle for reconciliation through cultural heritage and as common spaces for exchange via its Routes of Dialogue programme. (Original emphasis)[7]

Religious Communion: Dialogue and Existence
One of the changes in UNESCO's 2010 statement concerns religion, where the organization

... aims to promote dialogue among different religions, spiritual and humanistic traditions in a world where conflicts are increasingly associated with religious belonging.

It stresses the reciprocal interactions and influences between, on the one hand, religions, spiritual and humanistic traditions, and on the other, the need to promote understanding between them in order to challenge ignorance and prejudices and foster mutual respect.[8]

While forms of religious dialogue can be traced through Søren Kierkegaard to Martin Buber, we restrict ourselves here to the example of Martin Buber's (1970) *I and Thou*, which is based upon the premise of existence as encounter. Inspired by both Feuerbach and Kierkegaard, Buber used word pairs to propose dual modes of being – *Ich–Du* or 'I–Thou' (dialogue) and *Ich–Es* or 'I–It' (monologue) – to categorize the modes of consciousness, interaction and being through which an individual engages both with other individuals and reality. Buber's dialogism makes several assumptions: that human communication entails the interaction of diverse perspectives; that dialogue is embedded in a socio-historical context; that the meaning of a communication can be different to the various participants; that it is important to examine the consequences of a communication; and that each participant in a communication is, to some degree, orienting to the orientation of the other.

Philosophical Hermeneutics

While philosophical hermeneutics can be traced to Husserl's phenomenology and Heidegger's hermeneutics, it was with the great humanist Hans-Georg Gadamer that it was raised to the level of a philosophy in itself. Gadamer was strongly influenced by Plato and takes up the idea of *phronesis* (practical wisdom) from Aristotle. The significant aspect of *phronesis* is a mode of being based on practical insight that cannot be reduced to rules or directly taught. The recognition that all understanding inevitably involves some prejudice gives the hermeneutical problem its real thrust. By the light of this insight it appears that historicism, despite its critique of rationalism and of natural law philosophy, is based on the modern Enlightenment and unknowingly shares its prejudices. "And there is one prejudice of the Enlightenment that is essential to it: the fundamental prejudice of the enlightenment is the prejudice against prejudice itself, which deprives tradition of its power" (Gadamer, 1989, pp. 239–240). In this sense, prejudices are prejudgments – we always begin to understand and interpret from a particular point of view, so understanding always occurs against the background of our prior involvement, so it always occurs on the basis of our *history* – what Gadamer (1989) calls the happening of tradition. There are clear connections here with what we call the *presumption of ethnocentrism* and ethnocentrism as the problematic of intercultural education.

For Gadamer, dialogue is an encounter with the Other in the process of understanding, which can be seen as reaching an agreement, where reaching an agreement means establishing a common framework or horizon and understanding is the fusion of horizons. In *Truth and Method*, Gadamer arrives at 'conversation' as the basic model of understanding:

> A conversation involves an exchange between conversational partners that seeks agreement about some matter at issue; consequently, such an exchange is never completely under the control of either conversational partner, but is rather determined by the matter at issue.
>
> Thus all understanding takes place in language; all understanding is interpretative and involves the active translation between the familiar and the strange. (Gadamer, 1989, p. 269)

Rational Deliberation through Dialogue as Discourse

Jürgen Habermas (1984, 1987), in his major theoretical work *The Theory of Communicative Action*, maintains that conversation is a powerful regulative ideal that can orient our practical and political lives. He calls this the 'ideal speech situation' where each has an effective equality of chances to take part in dialogue and where dialogue is unconstrained and not distorted, and only the sheer force of argumentation alone reigns supreme. Habermas criticizes Gadamer for not addressing the question of power and ideology in dialogue, and he points out that while dialogue does not require egalitarian relationships, it does entail some sort of reciprocity and symmetry. So, Habermas maintains that, in conversation, there is always hope and the claim to reason that underlies it with the prospect of resolving issues rationally through dialogue. He advances a theory of *communicative rationality* and action located in the space of interpersonal conversation, where all speech acts have the goal of mutual understanding as an inbuilt *telos* or purpose. The key to liberation, then, is rather to be found in language and communication between people, and 'communicative action' serves to transmit and renew cultural knowledge in a process of achieving mutual understandings. It then coordinates action towards social integration and solidarity, finally providing the process through which people form their intersubjective identities.

Freirean Dialogue: Radical Pedagogy

Paulo Freire developed his theory of dialogue in Brazil, amid Third World underdevelopment and exploitation, where as an educator he built the tradition of critical pedagogy on the foundation of dialogue. Freire was concerned with *praxis* or 'informed action', where dialogue is not just about deepening understanding but rather is part of making a difference in the world. Dialogue in itself is a cooperative activity that leads to community action and community building. In *Pedagogy of the Oppressed*, Freire (1972, p. 76) states that "dialogue is the encounter between men, mediated by the world, in order to name the world"; dialogue becomes the means to liberate the colonized through the promotion of *cultural action*, which stands in marked contrast to 'anti-dialogics' or the 'banking' concept of education, which use as their basis conquest, manipulation and cultural imperialism as opposed to the 'problem-posing' education he favored. As Freire argues:

> As we attempt to *analyze* dialogue as a human phenomenon, we discover something which is the essence of dialogue itself: *the word*. But the word is more than just an instrument which makes dialogue possible; accordingly, we must seek its constitutive elements. Within the word we find two dimensions, reflection and action, in such radical

interaction that if one is sacrificed – even in part – the other immediately suffers. There is no true word that is not at the same time a praxis. Thus, to speak a true word is to transform the world. (Freire, 1972, p. 87; original emphasis)

The Dialogic Imagination

Mikhail Bakhtin's major work, *The Dialogic Imagination* (1981), develops a literary work on language and the novel that introduces the concepts of 'dialogism', 'heteroglossia' and 'chronotope'. Bakhtin contrasts the dialogic and the 'mono Logic' work of literature. The dialogic work carries on a continual dialogue with other works of literature and other authors. It does not merely answer, correct, silence or extend a previous work, but informs and is continually informed by the previous work. Dialogic literature is in communication with multiple works. For Bakhtin, all language and thought is dialogic, which means that everything anybody ever says always exists in response to things that have been said before and in anticipation of things that will be said in response. We never, in other words, speak in a vacuum. As a result, all language (and the ideas that language contains and communicates) is dynamic, relational and engaged in a process of endless redescriptions of the world (see White & Peters, 2011).

Dialogue as Conversation

In *The Voice of Poetry in the Conversation of Mankind*, Michael Oakeshott develops a view of conversation which

> is non-hierarchical, non-directive, non-assertive. In a conversation, as opposed to disputation, one voice cannot hope to dominate others. There is no fixed agenda. There is no standard external to the conversation itself by which to judge the utterances made. There is no final point or destination or resolution or decision to be reached. (Oakeshott, 1959, p. 10)

Further, he writes:

> In a conversation … there is no truth to be discovered, no proposition to be proved, no conclusion sought. [The participants] are not concerned to inform, to persuade, or to refute one another [rather] thoughts of different species take wing and play round one another, responding to each others movements and provoking one another to fresh exertions. Nobody asks where they have come from or on what authority they are present: nobody cares what will become of them when they have played their part. (Oakeshott, 1959, p. 10)

Later, Dorothy Leland makes a critical comparison with the leading pragmatists:

> a conversation is distinguished from an inquiry, which presupposes a common interest or goal, and from a debate, which presupposes a struggle between interests, a competition to be won ... A conversation, then, is a 'flow of speculation', in which ideas are important not for their truth, their consequences, or their evidential basis, but for their contribution to an 'unrehearsed intellectual adventure'. (Leland, 1988, p. 274)

The Voice of Liberal Learning (Oakeshott, 1989) is a collection of Oakeshott's major writings, edited by Timothy Fuller that emphasizes the distinctive features of his educational philosophy based on the concept of 'conversation'. This collection draws its inspiration from an earlier and smaller work, *The Voice of Poetry in the Conversation of Mankind* (Oakeshott, 1959). Oakeshott began his writing career publishing on the teaching of history and then wrote on Hobbes, contemporary social and political philosophy, universities, and political education. Richard Rorty, the American neo-pragmatist, was fond of quoting the phrase 'the conversation of mankind' and used it as the major motif and theme for his own philosophy. This encourages us to see Rorty's notion of conversation within the liberal tradition of pedagogy and learning, "to [see] conversation as the ultimate context within which knowledge is to be understood'" (Rorty, 1979, p. 389). Following in the footsteps of Oakeshott and Gadamer, Rorty's modern classic, *Philosophy and the Mirror of Nature* (1979), reduces philosophy to the model of conversation,[9] arguing that:

> To see keeping a conversation going as a sufficient aim of philosophy, to see wisdom as consisting in the ability to sustain a conversation, is to see human beings as generators of new descriptions rather than beings one hopes to be able to describe accurately. (Rorty, 1979, p. 378)

Rorty proposes a hybrid notion of conversation based on a combination of Oakeshott and Gadamer as a means of 'saving' philosophy from obscurity and irrelevance in a post-philosophical culture. There is no mistaking his purpose when he writes in the closing sentence of *Philosophy and the Mirror of Nature*: "the only point on which I would insist is that philosophers' moral concern should be with continuing the conversation of the West" (Rorty, 1979, p. 378). Rorty's remark encapsulates the direction he takes as a 'pedagogical philosopher' in carrying out the basic humanist tasks of changing our habits of discourse, deconstructing the ruling metaphors and inventing new vocabularies in order to change, broaden and recreate a sense of ourselves, world history and what matters most to us. In proposing a model of philosophy as conversation, he is in good company, as the hybrid he proposes emerges as a curious blend of two of the greatest contemporary humanists: Oakeshott and Gadamer.

Conclusion

From this brief presentation of Western models of dialogue, we can clearly see different strands of thinking of dialogue in a complex skein, which follow ontological, epistemological, ethical and political lines of inquiry: dialogue as argument; dialogue as an existential encounter with the Other; dialogue as communion; dialogue as hermeneutics (interpretation); dialogue as communication action, as the rational means for redeeming validity claims inherent in ordinary discourse; dialogue as a pedagogical means for cultural action; dialogue as the dialogical imagination; and dialogue as conversation and the seat of liberal learning. Embracing the concept of intertextuality or interdialogue, we might describe the Western philosophy of dialogue as an encounter with itself – the great dialogue of dialogues, each engaging with its predecessors to some extent but all seeking to provide a basis for the ethics of dialogue (some as first philosophy) and for the engagement that has as its object the unrestrained encounter with the Other without coercion or force as a basis for understanding. This leads us to suggest that Western models of dialogue provide a very useful set of models for intercultural understanding, which need to be explored in more detail, especially in relation to the different tasks of intercultural and international understanding, where any rational discussion and resolution of claims in an argumentative sense requires also both the pedagogical and the ethical. As well as encouraging a deeper understanding of the forms of Western dialogue, we would also encourage the genuine first step towards intercultural philosophy, which means the radical openness of this tradition in the encounter with the worlds of other philosophical traditions and the opportunity to subject – in the name of criticism, which is the hallmark of modern Western philosophy – the Western philosophy of dialogue to encounter its Other in a series of active engagements. Only through this process can we hope to attain a truly world concept of dialogue (or dialogues, in the plural) that can do the work that is expected of it.

There clearly is a *strategic, ethical and practical imperative* for attempting to understand other cultures, especially in an age of increasing globalization where communication technologies have enhanced the prospect and the means of intercultural exchange and understanding largely unmediated by states. And we also argue that the emphasis should fall on identifying, analyzing and combating all forms of ethnocentrism as obstacles to intercultural understanding, rather than technical and complex philosophical arguments about the states of various forms of relativism. We argue that this is the *major presumption* of intercultural understanding and education. We do not have time to wait for philosophers to sort out their intellectual positions (if that is ever possible in any final sense), although we acknowledge that intercultural dialogue requires the sophistication of philosophical analysis and that, in particular, philosophy of culture has a great deal of light to shed on the process of intercultural understanding. Thus, we hearken to the prospect of dialogue and the forms of dialogue as a basis for promoting cultural understanding, even if we at the same time are committed to questioning the Western history of the philosophy of dialogue and to interrogating the forms that it has taken to discover whether it is up to the task assumed of it.

Acknowledgement

This chapter was previously published as Tina Besley & Michael A. Peters, 'Interculturalism, Ethnocentrism and Dialogue', *Policy Futures in Education*, 9(1) 2011, 1–12 and is reprinted here with permission from the copyright holder (Michael A. Peters).

Notes

1 See http://ec.europa.eu/culture/our-programmes-and-actions/doc491_en.htm
2 The White Paper and media releases can be found at: http://www.coe.int/t/dg4/intercultural/
3 They recommend groups be between twenty and forty people seated facing one another in a single circle (Bohm et al., 1991).
4 See http://www.dialoguefoundation.org/?Lang=en&Page=33-01
5 See http://www.unesco.org/dialogue/
6 See http://www.unesco.org/dialogue/en/conferences.html
7 See http://portal.unesco.org/culture/en/ev.php
8 URL_ID=35020&URL_DO=DO_TOPIC&URL_SECTION=201.html
9 See http://portal.unesco.org/culture/en/ev.php
10 URL_ID=35270&URL_DO=DO_TOPIC&URL_SECTION=201.html
11 See Peters (2011), on which these comments are based, and Peters and Patel (2010).

References

Bakhtin, M. (1981). *The dialogic imagination: Four essays* (C. Emerson & M. Holquist, Trans.). Austin, TX: University of Texas Press. (Written during the 1930s)
Bohm, D. (1987). *Unfolding meaning: A weekend of dialogue with David Bohm*. London: Ark.
Bohm, D., Factor, D., & Garrett, P. (1991). *Dialogue: A proposal*. Retrieved from http://www.infed.org/archives/e-texts/bohm_dialogue.htm
Bohm, D., & Peat, D. (1987). *Science, order, and creativity*. New York, NY: Bantam Books.
Buber, M. (1970). *I and thou*. New York, NY: Scribners.
Burbules, N. C. (1993). *Dialogue in teaching: Theory and practice*. New York, NY: Teachers College Press.
Freire, P. (1972). *Pedagogy of the oppressed*. Harmondsworth: Penguin.
Gadamer, H.-G. (1960). *Wahrheit und methode: Grundzüge einer philosophischen Hermeneutik* (5th ed.). Tübingen: J.C.B. Mohr.
Gadamer, H.-G. (1989). *Truth and method* (2nd ed.). London: Sheed & Ward.
Habermas, J. (1984). *Reason and the rationalization of society* (T. McCarthy, Trans.). Boston, MA: Beacon Press. (originally published in German in 1981)
Habermas, J. (1987). *Lifeworld and system: A critique of functionalist reason* (T. McCarthy, Trans.). Boston, MA: Beacon Press. (originally published in German in 1981)
Huntington, S. P. (1996). *The clash of civilizations and the remaking of world order*. London: Simon & Schuster.
Leland, D. (1988). Rorty on the moral concern of philosophy: A critique from a feminist point of view. *Praxis International, 8*(3), 273–283.
Oakeshott, M. (1959). *The voice of poetry in the conversation of mankind*. London: Bowes & Bowes.
Oakeshott, M. (1989). *The voice of liberal learning: Michael Oakeshott on education* (T. Fuller, Ed.). New Haven, CT: Yale University Press.
Peters, M. (2011). Rorty and the cultural politics of conversation. In M. Peters (Ed.), *The last book of postmodernism* (pp. 173–192). New York, NY: Peter Lang.
Peters, M., & Patel, R. (2010). Philosophys – pedagogies – dialogue or street talk? *Nordic Studies in Education, 30*(4), 201–213.
Rorty, R. (1979). *Philosophy and the mirror of nature*. Oxford: Blackwell.
Smith, M. K. (2001). Dialogue and conversation. *The Encyclopaedia of Informal Education*. Retrieved from http://www.infed.org/biblio/b-dialog.htm
Sumner, W. G. (1907). *Folkways: A study of the sociological importance of usages, manners, customs, mores, and morals*. Boston, MA: Athenæum Press.
White, J., & Peters, M. (Eds). (2011). *Bakhtinian pedagogy: Opportunities and challenges for research, policy and practice*. New York, NY: Peter Lang.
Wittgenstein, L. (1922). *Tractatus Logico-Philosophicus (TLP)*. London: Routledge.

CHAPTER 5

Understanding the Sources of Anti-Westernism
A Dialogue between Michael A. Peters and Jan Nederveen Pieterse

MP: Anti-Westernism is a widespread phenomenon in the world today. It is complex and takes many different forms including most prevalently anti-Americanism and anti-science. In this context notions of *Orientalism* and *Occidentalism* occur. Curiously, while many in the West do not subscribe to Samuel Huntington's view regarding a 'clash of civilizations', fundamentalist Muslims and Islamists emphasize the Islamic world's clash with Western civilization. Of course, much of this anti-Americanism is based on aggressive American foreign policy in Iraq, Afghanistan and Pakistan. I think it is important to analyze the sources of anti-Westernism especially in the context of what you have called a 'global rebalancing'. Can you say how your recent works bears on this question?

JNP: I'm not sure its widespread; many are just tired of the West. Anti-Americanism was strong in 1980s and 1990s and has been shrinking. Anti-science is increasingly rare too. In emerging societies the key mottos of advancement are science and innovation. This doesn't sound right. Huntington inspired the American neoconservatives in their foreign policies and new wars; and American media without exception interpreted 9/11 through the clash of civilizations lens. It's practically irrelevant. Short version: while the U.S. obsesses over the Middle East, Islam etc., emerging societies from Brazil, South Africa to China are interested in new dynamics and forces and deal with an entirely different global horizon. They're not interested in anti-Westernism; that vastly exaggerates the importance of the West. They're interested in pragmatic cooperation but worry about American policies, the U.S. dollar.

MP: OK let me reformulate the anti-Westernism thesis to get the conversation going. Some recent work like Cemil Aydins (2007) *The Politics of Anti-Westernism in Asia: visions of world order in panIslamic and pan-Asian thought* demonstrates that the Eurocentric global system we see in transition today carries with it a legacy of resistance and change from an earlier era. Aydin looks back at the period between 1880 and 1945 to an era marked by the heights of late European imperialism in order to understand resistance to Western globalism. Others like Melinda Cooper have reflected on the convergence of revolutionary anti-capitalism and moral fundamentalism in the contemporary Islamic revival. Still others suggest that Western scholars have interpreted criticisms of the West by Islamist and Middle Eastern intellectuals as expressions of anti-modernism and anti-globalization aimed at the attempt to fashion an alternative global modernity. Buruma and Margalit (2004) in *Occidentalism: a short history of anti-Westernism* argue that the idea of 'the West' in the minds of its self-proclaimed enemies is still largely unexamined and woefully misunderstood and they tell us that the 'venomous brew' of Occidentalism consists of four main elements: hostility to the city; revulsion for the material life; abhorrence of the Western mind; and hatred of the infidel. There are plenty of sources that document the forms of anti-Westernism in various parts of the world and indeed though wrongly it is a form of anti-Westernism that often informs forms of postcolonialism. This anti-Westernism has in the past taken the form of anti-modernization that is equated with anti-Westernism, the rejection of modernity because its core values and institutions are redeemably Western and tied historically to forms of colonialism. Today it seems that some of the strongest critics of the West are indicating possibilities of multiple or alternative modernities; yet with the rise of the rest and the decline of the West the tenor of these arguments has changed somewhat. I am interested in trying to understand anti-Westernism in its historical forms, its continued prevalence today, and the way in which many on the Left who are themselves Western embrace a form of anti-Westernism and even anti-science.

JNP: From Herodotus to Pliny, the ancient Greeks and Romans invariably found monsters on their far-away shores, which was not a good sign. The Crusades were not a great success either. The Jesuits were kicked out of sixteenth-century Japan because they were 'too Christian'. In the late eighteenth century, the envoy of the British monarch to the Chinese emperor encountered total lack of interest in English goods. But in the course of the nineteenth century relations changed drastically and several nonwestern countries actively sought to adopt European technologies and reforms, such as the Ottoman Tanzimat reforms, Egypt and Persia seeking to industrialize, and Japan sending out missions to the West.

At the turn of the century and into the twentieth century, relations changed again. Decolonization became the dominant strain and the vast bloodletting of the two world wars dramatically undermined Europe's prestige as the harbinger of civilization. When Gandhi was asked what he thought of Western civilization, he replied that it would be a good idea. In the 1970s during the waning years of decolonization, dependency thinking, turning against neocolonialism, became a major motif. This included cultural components such as resistance against Coca-Colonization. In time this spread to McDonaldization, Barbiefication, Disneyfication, all ordinary motifs, also within the West. In Iran after the Islamic revolution westoxification became a theme and there were similar sensibilities among Islamist movements. Yet, of course, some of the same movements accepted American and Western support in the war against the Soviets in Afghanistan.

I note then in anti-Westernism as a theme the following problems. First, presentism – the implicit assumption that only developments since recent decades matter (or at most from the late nineteenth century). Go back in time and many generalizations simply don't hold. Second, bundling – the category of 'the West' glosses over differences between Europe and the United States and over different strands and dimensions of (critique of) Western influence. Third, the risk of stereotyping is not far off. Because the West = modernity and modernity = science, anti-Westernism quickly turns into anti-modernity and anti-science. From there it is a small step to the white man's burden. Fourth, to most literature you cite there is a both a regional, the Middle East, and a time element, the 1980s–1990s. We are then in the neighborhood of the 'clash of civilizations', which is a thoroughly discredited thesis. Fifth, if some so-called anti-Westernism is a response to Western Orientalism and Western double standards in the Middle East and in relation to Israel, some literature you mention may be viewed as pro-Israeli pushback and as part of a game of mirrors. Sixth, these questions have been largely overtaken by the Arab Spring, which is driven by 'post-Islamic' social forces, essentially a new urban educated middle class. Seventh, finally, to the theme of anti-Westernism there is a binary structure, for or against, which is limiting in itself. It ignores intertwining. I have made this a key motif in globalization, arguing that 'globalization is braided' (notably through East-West osmosis, which is the theme of a new chapter in the 2010 edition of the book *Globalization and Culture*).

MP: Yes, I agree that the concept of the West is semantically highly unstable and that it has a long history where it has changed its meaning over time: from Charlemagne, Christendom and the Holy Roman Empire to the constitutional integration and enlargement of the EU. I realize that we are dealing here with representations and semantic categories sometimes promulgated by religious authorities and sometimes developed under the influence of philosophy. So for instance Christendom from the Latin word *Christianus* really meant the Christian body (polity) and suggests a global community of Biblical Christianity which has also geopolitically taken on a kind of cultural hegemony in the West. Early Christendom defined itself against forces in the Greco-Roman world although the post-apostolic era in my view could not be usefully discussed in terms of West and emerging anti-Western sentiments but I do think that when Christendom in the period of the Renaissance came to refer to a theocracy and sociopolitical unity based on Christian values then it also become possible to talk of the West at least in terms of one set of emerging references. It is also possible given this historical entity to talk of anti-Western sentiments which is the basis of some aspects of present accounts on the Left to criticize Judaic-Christian culture by the likes of Žižek, Badiou and others. This tells us that both 'the West' and 'anti-Westernism' are strongly ideological and historical where meanings are fluid and open to change. We might even use Charles Taylor's 'social imaginaries'. I have argued for this kind of approach in a number of publications. I make clear that I do not hold Huntington's 'clash of civilizations' thesis in any shape or form although the term has come to be accepted by fundamentalists just as 'orientalism', as Edward Said (1995) tells us, was adopted by Islamists contrary to his intentions as a form of anti-Westernism.

I would say that the meaning of 'the West' gets another set of references and emerges strongly in relation to a concept of modernity at the hands of German philosophy and historiography in the nineteenth century. Hegel's philosophy of history was instrumental in creating this concept of the West and we have been living in its shadow for some time. I begin an essay on this subject with this thought:

The concept of 'the West' has served important political purposes both historically and in the present foreign policy context. On the one hand it has been a cultural and philosophical unity achieved through an active historical projection back to the origins of Western civilization, at least to the classical Greeks, while on the other, it has been used as a modernist category, politically speaking, to harness the resources of Enlightenment Europe as a basis for giving assurances about the future of liberal democratic societies and the American way of life. The concept was an implicit but key one assumed in an influential analysis of new world order by Samuel Huntington (2001), who in his *The Clash of Civilizations* predicted a non-ideological world determined increasingly by the clash among the major civilizations. In Huntington's analysis 'the Wes't functions as an unquestioned and foundational unity yet the concept and its sense of cultural and historical unity has recently been questioned not only in terms of its historical fabrication but also in terms of its future continuance. Martin Bernal (1991, 2001) in *Black Athena* and a set of responses to his critics, questions the historical foundations of the West demonstrating how the concept is a recent fiction constructed out of the Aryan myth propagated by nineteenth-century historiography. Even more recently, accounts of the so-called 'new world order' have emphasized either the dominance of an American hegemonic Empire (Hardt & Negri, 2001) or an emerging E.U. postmodern state system (Cooper, 2000, 2002). These accounts offer competing and influential conceptions of the new imperialism based on different visions of world government and proto-world institutions. They give very different accounts of questions of international security, world order and the evolving world system of states. (Peters, 2003)

I would follow Bernal's analysis against Huntington, although much more has to be said about forms of Western racism. I do think also that Weber gives another kind of stamp to the notion of the West in the 'Introduction' to *The Protestant Ethic and the Spirit of Capitalism* where he states his belief in the cultural specificity of the West in terms of a process of rationalization and 'disenchantment of the world' that sets the West apart from the East and, indeed, the rest of humanity:

> A product of modern European civilization, studying any problem of universal history, is bound to ask himself to what combination of circumstances the fact should be attributed that in Western civilization, and in Western civilization only, cultural phenomena have appeared which (as we like to think) lie in a line of development having universal significance and value. (Weber, [1920]1992, p. 13)

As you well know he characterizes the West in terms of a process of rationalization, a kind of 'metahistorical teleology'.

My aim in this dialogue with you is not to assert the categories but to investigate their changing forms and also to use the opportunity to explore this theme in relation to your work as a world scholar on globalization – 'the decline of the West and the rise of the rest'.

JNP: The pattern of conversation is that you keep reinvoking the West and while noting the instability of the category, keep going back to it nonetheless. That is understandable because you establish it as the premise of the discussion. So be it, however, I find some references anachronistic.
First, re Christianity and the West: In seventh-century Europe, Christian means urban and is equivalent with modern (*modernus*), in contrast to rural, hence 'pagan' derives from *paysan*. In the Renaissance 'the West' does not figure as a theme or *topos*. In relation to the Americas there is mention of the New Golden Land, i.e. a recovery of the golden land dreamt of in ancient times (Herodotus), as in Hugh Honour's book.

You write, 'when Christendom in the period of the renaissance came to refer to a theocracy and sociopolitical unity based on Christian values then it also become possible to talk of the "West"'. This is a stretch too far. The link between Christianity and the West emerges only AFTER the West is established as a theme and framework, mostly in the twentieth century.

Second, re Hegel and the West: There's no category of the West in Hegel either; his typical categories are history, progress, development, *Zeitgeist*, the role of the state. Europe does come up, in relation to other continents, but not the West.

These links (Christianity, Hegel) seek to give the West a deep historical philosophical grounding, but I think the references are wrong. You note, 'The concept of the West ... has a long history where it has changed its meaning over time: from Charlemagne, Christendom and the Holy Roman Empire to the constitutional integration and enlargement of the E.U'.. None of these, however, are relevant to the West. The West does NOT have a long history. The condition of emergence of this theme is recognition of North America as a significant and equivalent civilizational sphere, which happens only at the end of the nineteenth and mostly from the beginning of the twentieth century. Thus, the West is largely a twentieth-century theme which has two meanings: a civilizational sphere, comprising Europe and North America, and a geopolitical unit that takes on meaning in the context of the Cold War; hence the East-West relationship, with the East bloc and the Western world, the Warsaw Pact and NATO. Later, after Said's Orientalism, the East takes on a different meaning. In this setting terms such as 'Western racism' become appropriate. Retroactively also Christianity is associated with the West, which is later modified to Judeo-Christianity.

I do agree with the link between modernity and the West, notably in Weber. In relation to Europe this takes shape in the nineteenth century, but in relation to the West this takes shape in the twentieth rather than in the nineteenth century. Weber's work on the Protestant ethic refers primarily, of course, to differences *within* Europe, between northwest and Catholic Mediterranean Europe and has been criticized widely (e.g. Bryan Turner). Weber's large-scale comparative history of religions refers to Europe rather than the West. Weber's work has deeply Eurocentric traits.

On the theme of modernity and the West: as first-comer to modernity Europe has monopolized the definition of modernity, but it doesnt own modernity and the new perspective is modernities in the plural (to which I have devoted several articles).

You further note: 'more recently, accounts of the so-called 'new world order' have emphasized either the dominance of an American hegemonic Empire (Hardt & Negri, 2001) or an emerging E.U. postmodern state system' (Cooper, 2000, 2002). These points refer to the U.S. and Europe, not to the West. Both are rather behind the curve and overlook the new emerging configuration with emerging markets as the drivers of the world economy.

Finally you refer to the 'decline of the West and the rise of the res. The rise of the rest (Alice Amsden coined the phrase) is a paraphrase of the rise of the

West. The decline of the West is not a necessary accompaniment to the rise of the rest. Second, decline may be too strong a term. Third, let's be cautious of 'declinism'.

MP: Yes I am trying to establish the concept of the West as the premise and possibility of a certain kind of discourse: I am not trying to establish its truth, I am trying to establish its sources. I am adopting a historicist approach to the discourse of the West and want to show that at different times it is portrayed or characterized differently. I have not given any indication as to whether I agree with these. I agree with these representations only that they exist and change and that the representations have multiple sources: in the concept of Christendom, in nineteenth-century German historiography, in Hegel, in Weber, in Spengler, in Heidegger and many others in the twentieth century, including Stuart Hall and Edward Said. In each case to establish what these thinkers say is a difficult task because there are contradictions in their thought and because interpretations of their 'views' also change. In Hegel's case a particular view of idealism influences how we should view Hegel's metaphysics and its connection with history and the idea of historical development or progress especially teleological views of history. When I say 'the West' has a long history I do not mean in a continuous unchanging sense only that we can see preexisting elements of the discourse that go back to a distinction among Abrahamic religions. Where you say the concept really only takes hold in the twentieth century I am happy to work with that periodizing; and we seem to agree on the link between 'the West' and modernity which is where I want to go because without prejudice I want to investigate the discursive and historical links among a series of family-related concepts that establish valances among 'the West', modernism, and modernization (sometimes also specific forms of the West, like 'Americanism', 'Eurocentrism', maybe 'ethnocentrism') and their binary oppositions: anti-West, anti-modernism, anti-modernization, etc. I am not embracing the binary opposition simply noting that binaries often exist as a means for the production of discourse. I mention 'new world order' at a second time removed from the texts I discuss, i.e. both Cooper and Robert Kagan refer to a split in the West during the period where Rumsfeld refers to 'old Europe'. I am happy to be suspicious of 'declinism' which is a great point but I want to know something about this discourse (elements of its production) especially given that it is a prevalent mood among the discourse-mongers in the U.S. at the moment.

Let me ask you to elaborate further on the discourse of decline and perhaps its sister concept, that of crisis. I am trying to find a more direct way back to your work.

JNP: About the West and modernity let me note it is an overworked theme. It goes back to the Enlightenment, is thematized in Marx (modern capitalism, etc.) and looms large in sociology, particularly in Weber (modern bureaucracy, the modern state), and in the distinction between Gemeinschaft and Gesellschaft, which is taken up in American structural functionalism. All of this is well known. A further development of course is the postmodern turn. Secondly, modernization looms large in modern development studies. I've written about this extensively and can't repeat it here (notably in *Development Theory: deconstructions/reconstructions*, Sage 2010, 2nd edition). What these discourses share is Eurocentrism.

'Decline' in my view is too simplistic. Amid the ongoing process of global rebalancing some strata and classes win even as particular Western countries lose in a general sense. The U.S. and U.K. will go some notches down, but not Wall Street and the London City. What decline means here is greater social inequality! The pattern of private wealth and public squalor, Galbraith's point, will become more sharply profiled. Northwest Europe and Japan are in a different situation. Mediterranean Europe is different again.

MP: This is helpful because it seems to me in these overworked discourses in sociology one also gets a notion of anti-modernity, where antimodernism forms a strata and *leitmotif* that takes decline as its core and emerges with the realization that technological development and 'progress' has its dark side that has destructive consequences for nature, culture and religion. These anti-modernisms within modernity emerge in the nineteenth century with Thoreau, Ruskin, and William Morris and in the twentieth century with T.S. Eliot, Rainer Maria Rilke, and W.B. Yeats who seem to articulate a voice of *cultural* decline as a direct result of industrial modernity. Wittgenstein, in some ways like Nietzsche and Heidegger, sees himself and his work as trying to avoid the nihilism that industrialscientific society represented. In this context of anti-modernism the term 'postmodernism' at the hands of Lyotard becomes more easily understood. There are of course forms of anti-modernism that critique the cultural wasteland (Eliot) and other forms that champion the notions of arts and crafts (Ruskin, Morris) against the 'alienated labor' of the capitalist factory. Some beginning from radical features of ecology or environmentalism or Christian theology head in different directions. Ecological anti-modernism seems to view modern technoscience as a species of symbolic capitalism that always survives on exporting its environmental costs and disputes the concept of science. There are also violent forms of anti-modernism. Is it true to say that all these versions also share Eurocentrism as a fundamental premise? What is Eurocentrism if not a form of anti-modernism? Can you also say something more about decline within the processes of global rebalancing?

JNP: The category anti-modernism doesn't work for me. We should distinguish between an internal critique (accept the overall premises) and an external one (overall rejection). Most instances you cite seem to me internal critiques of modernity and are in that sense negotiations of modernity, not rejections. Industrialization causing dislocation is a familiar trope from the Luddites to Dickens, Two Cities, and Cardinal Newman. The first origin of development thinking is here: development is needed to mend the dislocations that industrialization brings. Technology bringing alienation is familiar from Marx onward, yet Marx was also an arch-modernist (Berman).

Some forms of modernism (Huysmans, trends in avant-garde art) reject modernity. Indeed, we should distinguish between modernity (a condition) and modernism (art, style), just as we distinguish between postmodernity (condition) and postmodernism (philosophy, art, style).

Some of the themes of modernism resonate with the tropes of decadence, decay that reflect the crisis of aristocracy – for the rise of the modern was also the decline and fall of the *ancien régime* of nobles, monarchy and the church, a decline that lasted well over a century, with dramatic cultural ramifications, as in Shelley, Frankenstein, Count Dracula and images of the' dark castle'.

So to 'the modern' there are several variations: early modernity, high modernity, late modernity, critical modernity (Frankfurt school, critical theory), modernism (art and philosophy of 'willing the modern'), postmodernism, postmodernity. The latest turn that I find interesting and productive is modernities-in-the-plural, a theme more radical in my view than postmodernism. I don't agree that anti-modernity is Eurocentric; on the contrary, most variants of modernity are Eurocentric.

Global rebalancing brings decline in some places (especially U.S., U.K. and the PIGS: Portugal, Ireland, Greece, Spain); mostly moderate adjustments in others (northwest Europe, Scandinavia and Japan), and opportunities or boom in emerging markets.

MP: I agree that we can make a distinction between 'internal' and 'external' critique and it seems to me that a number of strands in modern Western philosophy, those represented separately by Nietzsche, Heidegger and Wittgenstein are forms that reject underlying premises and therefore provide example of external critiques. It is interesting because we can see some interesting results when we trace the contemporary lines of these investigations in the work of post-Nietzscheans, post-Heideggerians, and post-Wittgensteinians. I think we can find some forms of external critique in radical ecologism that begins from the premise that industrialism is functionally opposed to the preservation of nature and that surfaces in various Earth Summits from the early 1990s and in rejections of 'sustainable development'. There are extreme examples in Theodore Kaczynski's *Industrial Society and its Future* and in the Earth Liberation Front. Speaking of religious-based forms we might recognize both Islamic fundamentalism of the kind embraced by Sayyid Qutb and Catholic anti-modernism of Pope Pius X. The Oath against the Errors of Modernism was issued on 1910 and continued to be taken until 1967. The 'sin' of modernism had been defined in the encyclicals *Pascendi Dominici gregis* of 1907 and *Lamentabilli Sane*.

I very much like your comments and your work on multiple or new modernities that transcend and in some cases seek to advance theory with the explicit aim of unseating Eurocentrism. These are so to speak forms of world-making that are taking place in the global south that go against the classical theories of modernization and the convergence of industrial society to explain the history of modernity as a multiplicity of cultural programs. The notion was useful when it emerged in the early 2000s to break the easy association between modernization and Westernization. Yet I still have some problems with the concept, even if we admit capitalisms in the plural, of the extent to which modernities can be different. Of interest here is the uncoupling of democracy with capitalist-driven development in China. It would be good to hear your thoughts on these questions.

JNP: Yes probably Nietzsche's critique is an external one. Given his classical philology background the decline of aristocracy is an important undercurrent in his work. Heidegger strikes me rather as an internal critique. In his case, southern German Catholicism (Lebenswelt) is a subtext, as in phenomenology generally. As to Wittgenstein, the various Viennese schools, from psychoanalysis and linguistics to economics, are surely internal critiques of modernity.

Some strands of radical ecology, such as deep ecology, resemble of course Luddism. There are interesting parallels between Roman Catholic and Islamic takes on modernity; both defend a medieval political economy and social cohesion against modern trends. Yet the Catholic Church came around in the early twentieth century, took up modernism and then participated actively also in electoral politics; there are counter-instances to the ones you cite. The influence of the Center Party in Germany is a case in point, as are Catholic trade unions, newspapers and broadcasting in many European countries. Likewise, most forms of Islamic fundamentalism are of course thoroughly modern in outlook, so represent internal critiques. Islamic Jacobins is the appropriate terminology.

On the uncoupling of democracy and capitalist-driven development in China, a few notes. First, in development studies there is a decade's long debate on what comes first, development or democracy. The usual answer is development first; development is a precondition for democracy, not the other way round. When a middle class develops and pays taxes it becomes concerned about the quality of government and accountability. So China's approach simply matches that of most developing countries. Second, at some stage this will become a growing constraint. In China there are discussions about how far in the dynastic cycle the CCP government is and a growing number argue it is past midway. Third, most important is the CCP s ability to deliver development and to include the majority in growing prosperity; the 12th five-year plan of March 2011 is a major step. At this stage this is more important to China than democracy Western style. Fourth, internal dynamics matter most. Just as China develops capitalism with Chinese characteristics, in time it will develop democracy with Chinese characteristics. This is the gist of the modernities perspective.

MP: Nietzsche, Heidegger and Wittgenstein are what I would describe as anti-philosophers who have at least this in common, that they are battling against the tradition of Western metaphysics, trying to get rid of metaphysical conceptions altogether and replace it with something different like 'historicism' and 'thinking' (Heidegger) or 'radical contingency' (Rorty). Thus Nietzsche and Heidegger talk of the 'end of metaphysics' and each tries to define what should follow philosophy in the West as the spirit and unity of Western culture. For Heidegger it is a form of post-philosophical thinking which he explores in the essay 'The End of Philosophy and the Task of Thinking' (1969) that involves and is based upon a rethinking of Western metaphysics and its development in Western technology: 'We are thinking of the possibility that the world civilization that is just now beginning might one day overcome the technologicalscientific-industrial character as the sole criterion of man's world sojourn'. What is interesting in his analysis for me is that he raises the possibility of something different: 'Perhaps there is a thinking which is more sober-minded than the incessant frenzy of rationalization and the intoxicating quality of cybernetics'. Heidegger points to a form of education. Wittgenstein also struggles against metaphysics – not so much Plato's dualism as Descartes' – and tries to rid us of 'pictures that held us captive'. Actually I must say the internal/external critique does not fit easily with these thinkers in my view.

Is this now the end of the Western, Christian, liberal worldview such that it becomes just one among a number of others? What are the consequences?

JNP: This response changes the terrain of discussion from modernity (internal/external critique) to philosophy: that all three object to the tradition of Western metaphysics is true but refer to a different subject matter. So I have no response here (but I'm thinking of Antonio Damasio's book, *Descartes Error*). This, then, is a different 'West' than the West discussed above; this West is, again, equated with Christian views – which I think is misplaced and anachronistic (although the Pope would probably agree); and with liberal views – which has some validity, but only if we also take on board the dark side of liberalism (as in colonialism and J.S. Mill; note the critical analyses of Parekh and Mehta).

Is this worldview becoming one among others? Of course it is. Surely the fading of Western/American hegemony implies the fading of Western/American ideological hegemony and its assorted claims. What has been strangely missing in this discussion so far is who is asking the question? What positionality is involved here (as they ask in standpoint theory)? If this is considered from the point of view of 'formerly colonized peoples', of those who have been on the receiving end of Western double standards and complicity with autocracies (Middle East), of the Washington consensus, IMF conditionalities and structural adjustment (developing countries), of Western humanitarian intervention (conflict zones, now zones of uranium munitions pollution), of CIA interventions, whether or not under the guise of 'human rights' and the National Endowment of Democracy, of vanity wars of American hegemony, the answer probably is good riddance. What are the consequences? Well, it includes a pretty cleanup.

MP: OK I am used to thinking about modernity in these philosophical terms, even though the West here overlaps and takes on different hues with other definitions. The positionality angle is important because it implies a consistently historicist and situated condition yet I have to note that the viewpoints of 'formerly colonized peoples' are radically diverse – clearly some involve anti-Western sentiments while others willingly remain within the liberal fold and old networks despite the formal post-colonial political phase and move to independence. I certainly do not want to defend any version of Western-U.S. hegemony or the historical plight of colonies yet I do want to understand analytically the sources of anti-Westernism, especially among the left in the West who are among those historically sensitive to double standards and the effects of power. Can I tempt you to make one further statement about the 'cleanup'?

JNP: At the end you ask the same question you started with, which leads me to wonder what has been the point of this exercise? Did we have a discussion or what? You ask me questions but you barely react to my responses. I simply dont know whether you agree or not. At times you change the subject (as in the shift from modernity to philosophy), leaving the conversation unfinished. You agree with positionality – but you note diversity. But positionality implies diversity – why else would people's standpoints matter? You keep coming back to the sources of anti-Westernism, even though I have refuted the category of anti-Westernism.

You ask me to elaborate on the cleanup: I think it should include the cleanup of Western paranoia, which is arrogance in disguise. After all we have contributed the world's leading values, the values of liberal democracy, but what we get in return is ingratitude. Decoded: the barbarians are at the gate! The whole premise smacks of a profound lack of reflexivity.

MP: The point of the interview is really to gauge your thoughts. I'm happy to respond to any questions and to elaborate responses to aspects we have discussed. Let's extend this interview into a conversation and pursue this further. I guess I have a different reading of modernity because I see it as a philosophical issue. Indeed, the philosophers I study – Nietzsche, Heidegger and Wittgenstein ('prophets of postmodernity') – and the Continental tradition I see in relation to modernity. At the level of theory here, the respect for disciplinary boundaries means little to me. I agree that positionality implies diversity and this is consistent with my historicist orientation (in fact I wrote a paper on positioning theory once!).

My position of anti-Westernism is to try to understand it as a category – how it has behaved, what kind of discourse it is, why it emerges in different forms at different times, how significant it is in the contemporary world. This was ostensibly the topic for discussion. I'm not sure what it means to say 'I have refuted the category of anti-Westernism'. You have proposed some arguments against it as a category, right but it exists as a discourse in a complicated relationship with anti-modernism, anti-modernization, anti-colonialism, anti-globalization, anti-Europeanism (or Eurocentrism), anti-Americanism, and anti-Western science. I am not saying that all of these are the same but that they belong to a set of discourses that exist. I want to understand the materiality of these discourses without wagging my finger. In other words, I do not want to take a moral attitude toward them but rather treat them as object of analysis.

Let me explain my position that this interview has enabled me to clarify in my own head. On the question of anti-Westernism I am a realist, materialist and a historicist. I am a realist in that I believe that West/anti-West is an effective historical category that while dynamic and taking different forms nevertheless correlates with a series of other dualisms and oppositions that together make up a mosaic of discourses that represent real political forces and have real political consequences. I am a materialist and realist in the sense that I believe that this opposition is accessible scientifically through the study of the mosaic of discourses that comprise it and that these discourses refer to extra-discursive features (practices and institutions). This mosaic of discourses includes specific forms of anti-Westernism – e.g. anti-Americanism and anti-Europeanism – that can be studied through understanding forms of ethnocentrism (Americentrism, Eurocentrism). It includes aspects associated with the history of the West – precisely modernism, modernity, modernization – so that in the discourse appears anti-modernism, anti-modernization, anti-modernity – especially as these are seen to represent Western, secular and rationalist values. It is evident also that specific historical periods and forms of development occasion a negative assessment – anti-colonization, anti-capitalism, anti-globalization. There are other expressions of oppositional attitudes to Western rationalism and science – anti-rationalism, anti-science, anti-technology. There are other forms that developed around liberalism and liberal modernity, specifically anti-liberal movements, forms of anti-secularism, movements associated with the critique of liberalism giving expression to forms of post-liberalism. One current of anti-Westernism and anti-liberalism has its source in the West as a critique of Western metaphysics most influentially advanced though in different ways by Nietzsche, Heidegger and Wittgenstein. Each in turn struggling with European nihilism wants to provide a way forward and this is why I call them 'prophets of postmodernity'. There are other sources of antiWesternism that originate in the Western academy as a critique of the West's Enlightenment legacy and much of what is called post-structuralism falls into this category – the postmodern critique of Enlightenment values of scientism, instrumental rationality and 'progress'. Much of post-colonial criticism insofar as it also originates with Foucault's assessment of Western modernity is also motivated by similar moves. There are still also neoconservative critiques of contemporary liberalism going back to Leo Strauss that also might be argued to belong to this source. Other currents typically originate outside the West specifically as religious and sometimes fundamentalist oppositions to Western values and these should be seen as country specific – Russia, the radical Islamic and Muslim jihadist elements, Asian countries, and so on – particularly when considered say in relation to anti-Americanism.

We should not dismiss Occidentalism simply as a feeble counterpart to Orientalism, especially if, as Ziauddin Sardar (2004) argues, 'Anti-American and anti-Western sentiments are not going to evaporate. Occidentalism seems poised to become the dominant discourse of the future. This means that attempts to theorise, understand and do something about it will become more common – and more necessary'. He makes the point that the history of orientalism dates back a thousand years. How old is occidentalism? What is the relationship between these two structures of perceiving the Other? I think this is a useful observation. Reviewing Ian Buruma and Avishai Margalits (2004) *Occidentalism: a short history of anti-Westernism*, he writes: "It turns out that what these city-hating, anti-materialist, antirational occidentalists dislike most is 'the selfish greed of capitalism, the moral emptiness of liberalism, the shallowness of American culture'". He makes the argument that Occidentalism cannot be equated with Orientalism: "Orientalism is a discourse – a coherent structure of knowledge through which the West has understood and represented the 'Orient', and through which the West produces self-confirming accounts of the non-west. Occidentalism is nothing more than a collection of a few pet hates, most of which, as the authors themselves admit, are entirely justified, given the excesses of the West". I am not sure that I agree with him here. He goes on to develop a series of contrasts: "orientalism is a discourse of power, with the strength of a dominant, globalised civilization behind it. Occidentalism is the recourse of the powerless"; "Orientalism has a long history, dating back to the inception of Islam itself. Occidentalism … is a relatively recent phenomenon in the non-west, emerging only after the Second World War; orientalism is deeply embodied in Western knowledge and disciplinary structure; it shaped disciplines such as anthropology and development studies, international relations and area studies, history and geography. There is not a single discipline in the world in which occidentalism plays an integral part".

I like the last comment you make and agree that there are profound forms of Western paranoia that are founded mostly on ignorance and a lack of reflexivity. This is a kind of cultural sickness that is an extension of ethnocentrism which needs therapy and education. I am interested in your views on how we might treat the symptoms?

JNP: Re modernity then we follow different readings: sociologicalhistorical perspectives and your philosophical angle (antimetaphysical). We can just leave the matter here, or else follow a sociology of knowledge approach and delve into the sociology of anti-metaphysical views (i.e. the end or waning of the ancient regime in Europe). I think that makes sense and thus, sociological and philosophical approaches overlap.

As to 'anti-Westernism', your position is 'to try to understand it as a category' while I seek to refute it as a category. I think it had some relevance in the second half of the twentieth century (decolonization, dependency theory, the Iranian revolution) but has waned in importance and has no relevance *per se*.

I have noted presentism, bundling, stereotyping, binarism, and redoing 'clash of civilizations' discourse, whose relevance has been overtaken by the Arab Spring.

Still in your view 'it exists as a discourse in a complicated relationship with anti-modernism, anti-modernization, anti-colonialism, anti-globalization, anti-Europeanism (or Eurocentrism), anti-Americanism, and anti-Western science ... I want to understand the materiality of these discourses without wagging my finger'. Michael, let me note that in doing so you are not just *observing* but are also *constructing* it as a category. Any analysis assumes and posits the 'existence' of its object of knowledge.

Breaking 'anti-Westernism' down in specific forms ('anti-Americanism' and 'anti-Europeanism') is a step forward. The relations with the other discourses are contingent and occasional. You quite rightly refer to similar strands *within* Western thinking (such as neoconservative critiques of contemporary liberalism going back to Leo Strauss), which confirms the instability of the discourses.

As to Western paranoia I think the key point is that Western power is waning and some Westerners look at rising powers as rivals, so their world horizon is one of 'present and imminent danger'. The 'rise of the rest' doesn't necessarily undermine the West but does affect its power monopoly and claims of civilizational leadership. Europeans tend to view this differently than Americans. Europeans have already long experienced decline of their power; for Americans this is a new experience. So yes it is 'founded mostly on ignorance and a lack of reflexivity' but it is a particular kind of unworldly ignorance. Does it need 'therapy and education'? That may be a bit like saying that those who fly the Confederate flag in the southern United States need therapy and education. It's not entirely untrue but it's not the first thing that comes to mind. And it comes after a hundred years or so of education already.

Further I generally agree with Zia's points on Occidentalism. Cheers!

MP: Well Jan, we have come a long way and many of the difficulties we encountered along the way – examples perhaps of 'talking past each other' are not just the result of disciplinary education but also of historical interpretation – got resolved once we grappled with the meaning of concepts and their place in current theory. I guess that fundamentally we do have a difference of opinion: unlike you, I do think that the category of 'the West' and even the trope of the 'decline of the West' (along with discourses that talk about the decline of Western metaphysics ... my passionate interest) will be around for a lot longer. More so indeed, I think that it is too early to talk of the 'end of the West'. I am grateful to you for such a spirited exchange that I enjoyed very much and also learned something from.

Acknowledgement

This chapter was previously published as Jan Nederveen Pieterse & Michael A Peters, 'Understanding the Sources of Anti-Westernism', *Policy Futures in Education*, 10(1), 2012, 59–69 and is reprinted here with permission from the copyright holder (Michael A. Peters).

References

Aydin, C. (2007). *The politics of anti-westernism in Asia: visions of world order in pan-Islamic and pan-Asian thought.* New York, NY: Columbia University Press.
Bernal, M. (1991). *Black Athena: The Afroasiatic roots of classical civilization.* London: Vintage Books. (Orig. 1987)
Bernal, M. (2001). *Black Athena writes back: Martin Bernal responds to his critics.* Durham & London: Duke University Press.
Buruma, I., & Margalit, A. (2004). *Occidentalism: A short history of anti-Westernism.* New York, NY: Atlantic Books.
Cooper, R. (2000). *The postmodern state and the world order.* London: Demos, The Foreign Policy Centre. (Orig. 1996)
Cooper, R. (2002). The postmodern state. In M. Leonard (Ed.), *Re-ordering the world: The long-term implications of September 11th.* London: Foreign Policy Centre. Retrieved from http://www.observer.co.uk/Print/0,3858,4388912,00.html
Damasio, A. (1994). *Descartes' error: Emotion, reason, and the human brain.* New York, NY: Putnam Publishing.
Hardt, M., & Negri, A. (2001). *Empire.* Cambridge, MA: Harvard University Press.
Huntington, S. P. (2001). *The clash of civilizations and the remaking of world order.* New York, NY: Simon & Schuster.
Kagan, R. (2003). *Of passion and power: American and Europe in the new world order.* New York, NY: Alfred A. Knopf.
Kaczynski, T. (2008). *The unabomber manifesto: Industrial society and its future.* Wing-Span Classics.
Peters, M. (2003). Deconstructing 'the west'? Competing visions of new world order. *Globalization,* 3(2). Retrieved from http://globalization.icaap.org/content/v3.2/01_peters.html
Pieterse, J. N. (2010). *Globalization and culture: Global Mélange* (2nd ed.). Lanham, MD: Rowman & Littlefield Publishers.
Pieterse, J. N. (2010). *Development theory: Deconstructions/reconstructions* (2nd ed.). Thousand Oaks, CA: Sage Publications.

Pope Pius, X. (1907). *Lamentabilli Sane: Syllabus condemning the errors of the modernists.* Retrieved from http://www.papalencyclicals.net/pius10/p10lamen.htm

Pope Pius, X. (1907). *Pascendi dominici gregis: Encyclical of Pope Pius X on the doctrines of the modernists.* Retrieved from http://w2.vatican.va/content/pius-x/en/encyclicals/documents/hf_p-x_enc_19070908_pascendi-dominici-gregis.html

Said, E. (1995). *Orientalism.* London: Penguin.

Weber, M. ([1920]1992). *The protestant ethic and the spirit of capitalism.* London & Boston: Unwin Hyman.

CHAPTER 6

Islam and the End of European Multiculturalism?
From Multiculturalism to Civic Integration

Introduction

This chapter provides an analysis of the new conservative attitude that has begun to question the ideology of multiculturalism in Europe and the consequent policy shift that emphasises by contract a discourse of civic integration. Multiculturalism has been the dominant paradigm for the West since the 1960s, influencing a range of policies from international development and immigration to democracy promotion and education. Over the decade or so since 9/11 and against the background of the Iraq War, terrorist attacks in New York, Washington, Madrid and London, and a number of other critical incidents, Europe has officially turned away from the doctrine of state multiculturalism. In 2010 Angela Merkel was the first to declare that multiculturalism in Germany had 'failed utterly' and indicated that it was an illusion to think that Germans and 'gastarbeiters' or guest workers could live happily together.[1] Merkes stance was repeated by Nicolas Sarkozy in 2011 when he commented that "We have been too concerned about the identity of the person who was arriving and not enough about the identity of the country that was receiving him".[2] Merkel's and Sarkozy's comments were quickly supported by former Prime Ministers for Australia and Spain, John Howard and José Maria Aznar. Nigel Freitas (2011) in *The Spectator* puts it provocatively, summing up the new conservative attitude:

> Germany's Merkel, Frances Sarkozy, Britain's Cameron, Spain's former Prime Minister José Maria Aznar: all have repudiated multiculturalism. At last, Europe is recognising what John Howard and Peter Costello realised some time ago: integration works. Rather than follow the European experience, we have an opportunity in Australia to learn from their mistakes. Our goal should not be 'multiculturalism' but assimilated 'multiracialism' – people of different races living side by side, but bound by Western culture. To achieve this, we need a fundamental reset of our immigration policy, predicated on a number of new assumptions.[3]

Freitas' comment registers a 'get-tough' Australian immigration policy directed against asylum seekers from Afghanistan, Iran, Sri Lanka and other countries of the Middle East who pay huge sums to people smugglers who set sail in small and unsafe boats from Indonesia. As Janet Phillips and Harriet Spinks (2013) indicate, the 'boat people' has become an emotive and divisive political issue central to the 2013 election (where Tony Abbott's party took the Treasury benches). The numbers of such immigrants to Australia has increased rapidly to over 17,000 in 2012.[4]

On 5 February 2011, then British Prime Minister David Cameron echoed the criticisms of state multiculturalism, arguing:

> Under the doctrine of state multiculturalism, we have encouraged different cultures to live separate lives, apart from each other and the mainstream. We have failed to provide a vision of society to which they feel they want to belong. We have even tolerated these segregated communities behaving in ways that run counter to our values.[5]

Cameron's talk was aimed at Islamic extremism in the United Kingdom and the process of radicalization of Muslim youth. He was careful not to lump all Muslims together and he focused on the need for identity processes that embodied core liberal values of host societies: "we need a lot less of the passive tolerance of recent years and a much more active, muscular liberalism". Partly as a response, in Britain and elsewhere in Europe, there has emerged a call for 'civic integration' and for a 'community cohesion agenda' comprised of tougher immigration and deportation laws, various citizenship tests, compulsory citizenship education, and new employment policies giving preference to British workers.

The combined impact of the Iraq War, the Abu-Ghraib and Guantánamo Bay abuses and the war on terror has been highly damaging to Muslim minorities, leading to claims of social exclusion, discrimination and abrogation of identity rights. At the same time, political Islam is in a state of radical transformation, with the events of the Arab Spring and a spate of revolutionary protests in Tunisia, Egypt, Libya and Yemen that have forced traditional rulers from power and with other protests throughout the Arab world.

From Multiculturalism to the Crisis of Civic Integration

The problems associated with immigration and separate development in multicultural enclaves is not restricted to Mediterranean or central European-countries. In May 2013 Stockholm was rocked by a week of disorder, with up to 200 cars set ablaze, fires in schools, police stations and restaurants, and about a dozen police officers injured. These protests involved an estimated

300 young people, of whom 30 were arrested. Sweden has taken in more than 11,000 refugees from Syria since 2012; more per head than any other European country. It has absorbed more than 100,000 Iraqis and 40,000 Somalis over the past two decades. About 1.8 million of its 9.5 million people are firstor second-generation immigrants. This has led to the phenomenon of 'White flight'. The fact is that inequality has also grown faster in Sweden over the past decade than in any other developed country, according to the Organization for Economic Cooperation and Development (OECD), which puts the blame partly on tax cuts paid for by reductions in welfare spending.[6]

On 22 May 2013 a British soldier, Lee Rigby, was hacked to death by two men in what has been described as an Islamic terrorist attack apparently in revenge for the killing of Muslims by the British armed forces.[7] The perpetrators of this horrific attempted decapitation were Michael Olumide Adebolajo and Michael Oluwatobi Adebowale, both British men of Nigerian descent who were raised as Christians and converted to Islam while studying at the University of Greenwich. Adebolajo apparently had links to Islamic extremist groups.[8]

The trial took place in November 2013 and both men, who pleaded not guilty, were found guilty of murder. They are currently awaiting sentencing. There have been strong anti-Muslim protests and rising sentiments across Britain, with attacks on mosques, verbal and physical attacks on Muslim women and the tearing off of their burqas, and other reported Islamophobic incidents, often provoked and organized by the English Defence League which is also responsible for distributing racist literature.[9]

Cecilia Malmström, E.U. Commissioner for Home Affairs, on 27 May 2013 warned of the rise of right-wing extremism in Europe, commenting:

> We have seen the development of Islamophobic, anti-Semitic and white supremacist ideology in far right groups which are also anti-democratic, intolerant and conducive to violence. We know how these extreme organizations feed off one another and try to create enmity, suspicion and hatred between communities.[10]

In a comprehensive review of multiculturalism Elsa Koleth (2010) documents the crisis of integration that accompanied European post-war immigration, particularly of those of Muslim background, and fears of the growth of Islamic extremism along with acts of terrorism that has seen the rise of far-right nationalist politics and a questioning of multicultural policies:

> In an international security environment that was concerned with the rise of Islamic extremism and the threat of terrorism, events such as the

London bombings of 2005 and the Madrid train bombings of 2004 were – in the context of broader issues about the parameters of diversity, and the place of religion in secular liberal democracies – seen as 'evidence of the incompatibility of Muslim values with modern European societies'. However, concerns about the place of Muslim communities in Europe and the U.K. are not limited to relatively recent fears about the growth of extremism, but are also related to more far-reaching and deep-seated issues of socioeconomic and ethnic marginalization facing Muslim minorities as well as other immigrant communities.

Koleth (2010) documents racial tensions in the cities of Bradford, Burnley and Oldham in northern England during May and July 2001 and she argues:

> The riots, followed by the terrorist attacks of September 2001 in the U.S., the Madrid bombings of 2004 and culminating with the London bombings of July 2005, drove sustained criticism of multiculturalism and led to a shift in Britains policy approach from multiculturalism to integration, with a focus on 'community cohesion' at a local level.[11]

She writes further:

> The Home Office acknowledged that 'links between social deprivation and extremism is [sic] not simple cause and effect', but there was a need to address the underlying 'discrimination, disadvantage and exclusion suffered by Muslim communities (as by other minorities)'.

She goes on to document race riots in the outer suburbs (*les banlieues*) of Paris and other large cities in France in November 2005 followed by further riots in late 2007 by young North Africans protesting against police profiling and economic discrimination. Even in the Netherlands – 'the European bastion of toleration and multiculturalism through the second half of the twentieth century' – there was a perception that integration policies for minorities had failed, that multiculturalism was a threat to social cohesion and the Muslim minority in particular posed a problem for Dutch society.

After years of agitation on issues to do with immigration the Dutch elections of June 2010 saw far-right nationalist politician Geert Wilders and his Freedom Party (PVV) unexpectedly finishing with the third highest number of seats. Wilders, who pledged to 'end the Islamization of the Netherlands', including by ending immigration from Muslim countries, and banning mosques and the Koran, was tried for inciting racial hatred against Muslims in 2011 but was acquitted of all charges.

Dora Kostakopoulou (2010) suggests that increasingly the discourse of civic integration has prevailed as a means for coping with the failures of multiculturalism:

> In official discourses at the national and, increasingly at European levels, civic integration is presented as the required antidote to the alleged failures of multiculturalism and the alleged creation of parallel worlds within societies owing to increasing ethnic and cultural heterogeneity.

Thus, many European countries began to rethink the links between integration and immigration and citizenship and started to impose mandatory civic integration programmes and citizenship tests as part of citizenship education and training.

Sergio Carrera (2006) argues that the trend towards mandatory integration in the European Union (E.U.) masks a form of mandatory assimilation or acculturation. He suggests these are political tools for institutional control where integration has become a 'juridical, policy-oriented and institutional tool of control' through which nation-states determine the parameters for inclusion and exclusion:

> The social conflicts from which some E.U. member states are currently suffering represent a direct expression of opposition to a conservative notion of 'we' and a homogenous and anchored 'national identity'. They are also an intense reaction towards restrictive immigration, citizenship and integration policies and discourses.

David Cameron's 2011 Speech at the Munich Security Conference

In this context, it is worth taking a closer look at David Cameron's speech on 5 February 2011 where he set out his views on radicalization and Islamic extremism. He began by addressing the theme of security with a focus on terrorism and British commitments to NATO. He went on to make the distinction between the existence of a political ideology, 'Islamist extremism', which he distinguished from the religion, Islam, and then focused on the threat of Islamist extremism within the United Kingdom, suggesting that state multiculturalism had failed.

Cameron turned to radicalization and the process by which 'preachers of hate can sow misinformation about the plight of Muslims' and leaders promote separatism by encouraging Muslims to define themselves solely in terms of their religion. The answer Cameron sketched involved, first, confronting and undermining the political ideology by banning hate preachers and scrutinizing Islamic organizations that apply for public funds to determine whether they embrace universal human rights and whether they encourage integration or separatism. Second, he emphasized how the government must stop extremist organizations from radicalizing U.K. citizens at publicly funded institutions like universities and prisons. In addition to attacking and exposing the ideological bases and justifications for extremism, Cameron suggested, we must build stronger societies and stronger identities at home:

> A passively tolerant society says to its citizens, as long as you obey the law we will just leave you alone. It stands neutral between different values. But I believe a genuinely liberal country does much more; it believes in certain values and actively promotes them. Freedom of speech, freedom of worship, democracy, the rule of law, equal rights regardless of race, sex or sexuality. It says to its citizens, this is what defines us as a society: to belong here is to believe in these things. Now, each of us in our own countries, I believe, must be unambiguous and hard-nosed about this defence of our liberty.

Cameron also mentions a number of 'practical things' such as 'making sure that immigrants speak the language of their new home and ensuring that people are educated in the elements of a common culture and curriculum'.[12]

Stating that British Muslims should adhere to the main values of liberty and equality, he announced the end of the 'passive tolerance' in the context of the divided communities, emphasizing that the members belonging to all religions should integrate themselves in the larger society and accept its fundamental values. Cameron maintained that to be a British citizen means to believe in the liberty of speech and in religious freedom, and in democracy and equal rights, irrespective of race, sex or sexual orientation, and he declared that immigrants should learn English and that all schools should teach their children elements connected with a common curriculum and culture. Each individual, from ministers to electors, should have an active confrontation with those sharing extremist opinions and he warned that all organizations and groups who do not promote British values would no longer receive funds from the state budget and would no longer be allowed to cooperate with the state. Cameron promised to elaborate a new plan meant to confront and 'triumph' over the extremist ideologies that incite some to involve themselves in terrorist actions: 'In the name of a multicultural state we have encouraged various cultures to develop independently, apart from one another and apart from the main culture'.[13]

In this speech and subsequently, Cameron positioned himself as an ally of the German chancellor Angela, Merkel and the French president Nicolas Sarkozy, both of whom had strongly criticized multiculturalism. In response to his speech he was criticized for giving a domestic speech about Muslims in

Britain at an international security conference and framing it as essentially a question of national security and counterterrorism.

Cameron was forced to confront the question of Islamist extremism and radicalization again with the killing of Drummer Lee Rigby, mentioning that the government's Prevent strategy and new Cabinet-level group, Tackling Extremism and Radicalization Task Force (TERFOR), set up in response to this brutal murder, had excluded hate preachers and had closed down websites in order to try to prevent people vulnerable to radicalization, especially potential recruits in jails, schools, colleges and mosques, from being targeted by radical preachers.

There was plenty of global debate on his multiculturalism speech. When David Cameron stated that he wanted to see the end of state multiculturalism' his comments created a media firestorm in the United Kingdom. Surprisingly, perhaps, others picked up on his lead in other parts of the world.

While Marine Le Pen, leader of France's far right, aligned herself with Cameron's comments, the speech was condemned by Iranian newspapers that suggested he had been hiding his anti-Islam face.[14] Angela Merkel made some sobering remarks about Muslim guest workers and the separatism that accompanied their settlement. Thilo Sarrazin, a prominent German banker, and also a long-time member of the Social Democratic Party (SPD), published a controversial new book titled *Germany Does Away with Itself*. The book broke Germany's long-standing taboo on discussing the impact of Muslim immigration by highlighting painful truths about the current state of affairs.[15] He argued that Germany's *gastarbeiters* or guest workers are dumbing down the nation, using the phrase a 'genetic minus' to describe migrants from the Middle East.

There is no doubt that there has been a rise of anti-immigration parties and a general move to the Right, with increased numbers of European voters willing to shift in favour of parties manipulating xenophobic sentiments, a political trend that spells big trouble ahead for European multiculturalism. The rise of anti-immigration parties across Europe reflects a growing concern that multiculturalism is destroying the core values of traditional European society.[16]

The Wilson Center sponsored an event (24 May 2012) with the title, 'The End of Multiculturalism in Europe? Migrants, Refugees and their Integration',[17] providing the commentary:

> Europe relies on immigrants to sustain economic growth due to the continent's shrinking and aging population. Yet migrants are increasingly seen as importing risk: they are seen as competing for jobs with the growing number of unemployed; they are seen as a drain on state budgets which are in many places operating under austerity; they are seen as possible

collaborators of global terrorist groups; or as refugees, they are reminders of instability in the neighborhood.

Cristian Jura (2012) suggests that the E.U. lacks a clear perspective on multiculturalism:

> The European political project cannot ignore this plurality of cultures in which each national culture expresses and imposes itself differently. The problem of building a new political area means, among other things, the establishment of a new pattern of society – a pluralist pattern which aspires – through the contribution of the various national/minority cultures – to create a common European culture …
>
> One of the ideas related to a united Europe expressly refers to exceeding the models of the states considered to be particularistic and to using means of linking different juridical, cultural and political areas together; at the same time the proposal refers to maintaining the national sovereignty of each state and to elaborating a constitution able to recognize them all.
>
> Mainstreaming culture in all relevant policies within the E.U. is based on The Lisbon Treaty (Article 167, paragraph 4; the ex-E.U. Treaty, Article 151) which requires the Union to take into account culture in all its actions so as to foster intercultural respect, and promote diversity. (p. 107)

Education and the Rise of Terrorism Studies

Education plays an important role in challenging, combating and understanding terrorism in its different forms, whether as counterterrorism or as a form of human rights education. Just as education has played a significant role in the process of nation-building, so education also plays a strong role in the process of empire-building, globalization, and resistance to global forces. It also plays an important role in terrorism and anti-terrorism, especially where it is linked to emergent statehood (Peters, 2005).

Benjamin Barber (2003) writes in *Jihad vs. McWorld: terrorisms challenge to democracy*:

> [t]he most egregious globalization has been the exploitation and abuse of children in war, pornography, poverty, and sex tourism. Children have been soldiers and victims in the raging ethnic and religious wars; children are the majority of the global cohort that suffers poverty, disease and

starvation. Children are our terrorists-to-be because they are so obviously not our citizens to come. (p. xxvii)

Terrorism is a difficult concept to define, partly because there is disagreement over the status of self-determination and national liberation movements. Nelson Mandela was once classified as a terrorist when he worked for the ANC (African National Congress). For the U.S. State Department the term 'terrorism' means premeditated, politically motivated violence perpetrated against non-combatant targets by subnational groups or clandestine agents, usually intended to influence an audience. The term 'international terrorism' means terrorism involving citizens or the territory of more than one country and the term terrorist group means any group practising, or that has significant subgroups that practise, international terrorism. For the United Nations, by contrast, terrorism is, in most cases, essentially a political act. It is meant to inflict dramatic and deadly injury on civilians and to create an atmosphere of fear, generally for a political or ideological (whether secular or religious) purpose. Terrorism is a criminal act, but it is more than mere criminality. To overcome the problem of terrorism it is necessary to understand its political nature as well as its basic criminality and psychology. The United Nations General Assembly has been negotiating a Comprehensive Convention on International Terrorism, although it has been deadlocked for reasons mentioned above. The definition of the crime of terrorism which has been on the negotiating table of the Comprehensive Convention since 2002 reads as follows:

1. Any person commits an offence within the meaning of this Convention if that person, by any means, unlawfully and intentionally, causes:
Death or serious bodily injury to any person; or
Serious damage to public or private property, including a place of public use, a State or government facility, a public transportation system, an infrastructure facility or the environment; or
Damage to property, places, facilities, or systems referred to in paragraph 1(b) of this article, resulting or likely to result in major economic loss when the purpose of the conduct, by its nature or context, is to intimidate a population, or to compel a Government or an international organization to do or abstain from doing any act. (Ad Hoc Committee established by Resolution 51/210 of 17 December 1996 on Terrorism)

The Report of the Policy Working Group on the United Nations and Terrorism[18] provides a set of 31 recommendations under the headings dissuasion (international legal instruments and non-legal norm-setting), denial (counterterrorism committee, disarmament and preventive measures) and cooperation (non-United Nations [UN] multinational initiatives and coordination of UN system). The UN stresses a universalism based on human rights ideology framed within the international rule of law which places it in some tension with U.S. solutions that tend to be less constrained by the international rule of law and more Americentric. Recommendations 10 and 11 directly address education in relation to terrorism:

> Elements of the United Nations system which address the issue of education should meet to determine how best to mount a coherent worldwide programme to assist countries in which educational systems need support or that are under the control of groups advocating terror.
>
> Continue emphasizing the importance to the fight against terrorism of existing United Nations work in the area of human rights, democratic capacity-building, and social and economic justice.

Education as counterterrorism has emerged as one response. For instance, the Counterterrorism Education Learning Lab (CELL)[19] is a U.S.-based group headquartered in Denver with a mission to prevent terrorism through 'education, empowerment and engagement'. The basis of education is an exhibit described as:

> a dynamic, interactive experience that is continually updated to reflect today's reality of the threat of terrorism. All of the content included in the state-of-the-art exhibit was developed by world-renowned counterterrorism experts and was designed by Academy and Emmy Award-winning artists. Located across from the Denver Art Museum, the exhibit is self-guided and empowers visitors to educate themselves about the threat of terrorism and how they can play a role in enhancing public safety.

The Centre for Terrorism and Counterterrorism (CTC) was established at Leiden University[20] with the following brief:

> Terrorism continues to rank highly on the political agenda. To meet the demands, from national and international policy makers to local security officials, the Centre for Terrorism and Counterterrorism (CTC) at Leiden University – Campus The Hague seeks to provide a uniquely integrated, interdisciplinary approach to the phenomenon of terrorism. Initiated by the National Coordinator for Counterterrorism (NCTb) and Leiden University, the centre contributes to various essential components of terrorism research, education, and consulting.

The website sports the following goals:

> CTC has been created to:
>
> – achieve national and international recognition as a centre of excellence within the academic (counter) terrorism community;
> – contribute to the effectiveness of policy and the quality of intelligence analyses;
> – stimulate national and international collaboration among researchers;
> – contribute to the social and political debate on terrorism, counterterrorism, (de)radicalization and disengagement;
> – develop a successful Masters' program, supervise PhD-theses, and develop a curriculum for internships;
> – serve as a public resource for the understanding of terrorism and counterterrorism.

Starting in 2009, the CTC offered 'practitioners a one-year course in Terrorism and Counterterrorism. In the The CTC [sic] participates in several academic courses. The CTC also offers practitioners several modules and a one-year course in Terrorism, Radicalization, Security and Law'.

Louise Richardson (2008), Executive Dean of the Radcliffe Institute for Advanced Study, Harvard University, in 'Restoration, Education, and Coordination: three principles to guide U.S. counterterrorism efforts over the next five years',[21] indicates the nature of the problem, the degree of perplexity for the American public and the role that education should play in cultivating a resilient public:

> Many Americans responded to the attacks by asking: Why? Why us? Why do they hate us? This is a very important question, but rather than engage in a reasoned analysis, our leaders responded in effect: because we are good and they are bad. If we want to have an effective counterterrorism policy over the next five years, we must engage seriously with this question. The United States needs to understand what it means to be the most powerful country in the history of the planet and how that affects perceptions around the world. We must not only educate our children in the languages and cultures of other societies, but also educate our citizens as to what it means to be on the receiving end of U.S. policies in countries where our good intentions are not self-evident.

Her conclusions are also revealing and useful to refer to in their fullness:

> Over the next five years we should acknowledge the failures of the past seven years. We should publicly repudiate the departures from American

principles evident in our counterterrorism policy. We should abandon the language of the 'war on terror'. Instead, we should make a concerted effort to restore our prestige in the world, demonstrate our commitment to multilateralism, and reframe the war against terrorism as a transnational campaign against isolated extremists. We should try to persuade the American people that we can be most effective against terrorism when we abide by our principles, keep the threat in perspective, and play to our strengths. We should educate our children in the languages and cultures of others. We should educate our public about how to evaluate risk and how terrorists try to manipulate us. We should educate ourselves about the nature of our adversary and we should educate the rest of the world about America's virtues. Finally, we should coordinate the actions of our intelligence and security forces, ensuring that their short-term successes are advancing our long-term goals. This means that we should exploit our technological strength to reduce our adversaries' reliance on new technologies. We should also articulate a set of goals for our policies, principles to guide us in pursuing them, and means to evaluate the success of our actions in achieving them.

The rise of Terrorism Studies within universities is also another feature of the role that education is now mandated to play. Here is one example from the University of St Andrews that offers an Advanced Certificate in Terrorism Studies[22]:

> If it's part of your responsibility to protect people, infrastructure, organizations or investments, understanding the threat is key – whether this is to governments and homeland security, transport networks, investments, private organizations or to the public. Understanding this threat involves knowing who is involved, how and why they act and their capacity to inflict harm.

The programme offers the following modules (abridged from the website):
- Key Issues in International Terrorism – It explores the concept of terrorism, the types of terrorism and prominent terrorist groups.
- Terrorist Ideologies, Aims, Beliefs and Motivations – Understanding the terrorist mindset is critical to countering terrorism effectively.
- Terrorist Modus Operandi – This module explores how the ideologies of various terrorist groups can have an impact on group structure, tactics, strategies and target selection.
- International Policing Policy – By exploring initiatives in various countries such as the United States, the United Kingdom, Australia and across

Europe, this module examines in detail the role of police and other agencies involved in the efforts to prevent terrorism and manage terrorist attack incidents.
- Aviation Terrorism & Security – Beginning with a brief historical survey of aviation terrorism from Dawsons Field to Lockerbie, 9/11 and beyond, this module examines aviation terrorism from both theoretical and tactical perspectives.
- Maritime Terrorism & Security – This module provides participants with a solid foundation in the complex and often obscure world of maritime security.
- Critical Infrastructure Protection – What is infrastructure and what makes it critical? Why is it imperative to protect it and what would happen if we chose not to protect it?
- Cyberterrorism – This module examines the concept of cyberterrorism and provides an introduction to the ways in which terrorists use the Internet and the politics of cybersecurity.
- Radicalization and De-Radicalization – Why people turn to terrorism, how they become involved, and then eventually participate in terrorist activity is a complex area in the study of terrorism (http://www.terrorismstudies.com/page/Content).

Another aspect of education's role is the emphasis on peacebuilding. Here is an example of a UNICEF (2011) report[23] that looks at experiences of education in relation to peacebuilding in Lebanon, Nepal and Sierra Leone, beginning with this summary:

> Education is deeply implicated in processes of socialization and identity formation, is vital for economic growth and individual and national advancement, and can act as an important vehicle for social cohesion and reconciliation. On the other hand, education can also undermine all these processes and therefore we need to ensure that it is delivered effectively and equitably and is a driver of peace rather than war. Crucially, education is not a marginal player in peacebuilding, but a core component of building sustainable peace. Peacebuilding is essentially about supporting the transformative process any post-conflict society needs to go through and these change processes unfold over generations.

Education has a role to play in a variety of activities, not just peacebuilding or counterterrorism or human rights education but also critically around all the aspects of civics, multiculturalism and citizenship education.

Reactions to Islamic Extremism: Hate Preachers and 'Poisonous Narratives'

The total number of Muslims in Europe in 2010 was about 44 million (6%) with some 19 million living in the E.U. (3.8%).[24] In the United Kingdom the total Muslim population had reached 2.7 million in 2011, some 4.8% of the total population. It is estimated that there are fewer than 50,000 Muslims living in Scotland, less than 1% of the population (about 30,000 live in Glasgow, mostly of South Asian [Pakistani] descent).

In a split society education has a difficult role to play, especially where divisions are both religious and ideological. For instance, the Scottish Defence League (SDL), a far-right organization, says it aims to stop the 'Islamification' of Britain. The SDL has taken to the streets of Edinburgh to stage protests outside the Scottish Parliament, following the Woolwich attack on Lee Rigby. The SDL is mobilizing due to high demand and boasts of up to 4000 members.[25] The Muslim Council of Scotland condemned the Woolwich Attack:

> This is a truly barbaric act that has no basis in Islam and we condemn this unreservedly. Our thoughts are with the victim and his family. We understand the victim is a serving member of the Armed Forces. Muslims have long served in this countrys Armed Forces, proudly and with honour. This attack on a member of the Armed Forces is dishonourable, and no cause justifies this murder.[26]

Clearly there are political problems that surround immigration on a continent that is experiencing long-term aging of the population and shrinkage of the potential workforce, and a kind of terrorist risk from young Muslims who become radicalized.

In response to the Woolwich attack Cameron launched the Tackling Extremism and Radicalization Task Force (TERFOR):

> When young men born and bred in this country are radicalised and turned into killers, we have to ask some tough questions about what is happening in our country. It is as if that for some young people there is a conveyor belt to radicalization that has poisoned their minds with sick and perverted ideas. We need to dismantle this process at every stage – in schools, colleges, universities, on the internet, in our prisons, wherever it is taking place.
>
> We are looking at the range of powers and current methods of dealing with extremism at its root, as opposed to just tackling criminal violent extremism.

And we will look at ways of disrupting individuals who may be influential in fostering extremism. We cannot allow a situation to continue where extremist clerics go around this country inciting young people to commit terrorist acts This new group will study the issue in great depth before acting. There is no question of restricting freedom of speech – this is about preventing people spreading the message of extremism and radicalization in a totally irresponsible and reckless way.[27]

The First Report of the Working Group on Radicalization and Extremism that Lead to Terrorism emphasized engaging and working with civil society, focusing on:
– prison programmes;
– education;
– promoting an alliance of civilizations and intercultural dialogue;
– tackling economic and social inequalities;
– global programmes to counter radicalization;
– the Internet;
– legislation reforms;
– rehabilitation programmes;
– developing and disseminating information; and
– training and qualifying agencies involved in implementing counter-radicalization policies.

'Radicalization' as 'Education'

Radicalization is an important concept, especially for U.K.-born Muslim youth who are 'turned" by radical imams, who through skilful rhetoric and manipulation are able to get mostly young men to turn against their country on the basis of faith. Much more is required to understand this concept which stands in a family relationship to the concept of 'education'. Alex P. Schmid (2013) in an International Centre for Counter-Terrorism Research Paper provides a useful introduction to the concept and process, remarking that:

> The terms 'radicalisation', 'de-radicalisation' and counter-radicalisation are used widely, but the search for what exactly 'radicalisation' is, what causes it and how to 'de-radicalise' those who are considered radicals, violent extremists or terrorists has so far been a frustrating experience. The popularity of the concept of 'radicalisation' stands in no direct relationship to its actual explanatory power regarding the root causes of

terrorism. In Europe, it was brought into the academic discussion after the bomb attacks in Madrid (2004) and London (2005) by policymakers who coined the term 'violent radicalisation'. It has become a political shibboleth despite its lack of precision.

He also points out that in 'polarised political situations not only non-state actors but also state actors can radicalise ... [the use of] torture techniques and extrajudicial renditions ... [has been a] departure from democratic rule of law procedures and international human rights standards'. Yet when it comes to answers he admits it is 'difficult to identify what works and what does not work in general, or what is even counter-productive'. Local context matters very much and academics and policy makers alike are increasingly recognising this fact.

Educational theory can contribute to this understanding. One example is the application of learning theory to transformative radicalization. Wilner and Dubouloz (2011) provide the following abstract of their attempt to use learning theory to understand Islamic radicalization:

> While a consensus has emerged concerning the role radicalization plays in persuading Westerners to participate in terrorism, little research investigates the cognitive processes inherent to radicalization processes. Transformative learning theory, developed from the sciences in education and rehabilitation, offers an interdisciplinary lens with which to study the processes of personal change associated with radicalization. Transformative radicalization explains how triggering factors lead to critical reflection of meaning perspectives and personal belief systems that guide and alter behavior. Using an autobiographical account of the radicalization process, this study offers a plausibility probe of an inherently interdisciplinary and novel theoretical framework. (p. 418)

The hypothesis of 'radicalization as education; education as radicalization' might also draw attention to the way in which existing institutions and ideologies are Islamophobic and record a set of deep fears about Islam as the fastest growing religion in the world, and often depicted as posing a threat to the West. We need to understand the historical and cultural dimensions of the role that Islamophobia plays in Western culture going back to the Crusades. At the same time it is necessary to embrace a robust analysis that recognizes power and influence exhibited in funded activity. In *The Looming Tower: AlQaeda and the road to 9/11*, Lawrence Wright states that while representing only 1.5% of the world's Muslims, Saudis fund and essentially control around 90% of the

Islamic institutions from the U.S. to Kazakhstan and Xinjiang and from Norway to Australia.

The literalism of extremist Islam that insists on oversimplified and rigid, sectarian Wahhabi-Salafist interpretations of religious texts tends to prevent the important internal debate about Islam and modernity, and also actively oppose Western forms of schooling associated with modernization.

One promising research approach to the study of extremist Islam and to questions of multiculturalism is based on the approach of narrative inquiry (Peters & Besley, 2012; Besley & Peters, 2012), including the resources of narrative pedagogy.

The 'Crisis of Integration'

By the beginning of the twenty-first century many European states appeared to be undergoing a so-called 'crisis of integration' as governments became concerned about the socio-cultural integration of immigrants, particularly those of Muslim background. In official discourses at the national and, increasingly at European levels, civic integration is presented as the required antidote to the alleged failures of multiculturalism and the alleged creation of parallel worlds within societies owing to increasing ethnic and cultural heterogeneity. However, critics have questioned whether restrictive and more onerous sanctions-based legal and policy measures are in fact counterproductive for achieving integration and social cohesion, as they can further compound the marginalization of immigrant communities and have a deleterious impact on their sense of belonging. Sergio Carrera argues, "[m]any E.U. states need to go through a painful process of readjusting their own conceptualization of their perceived national identities and values from one that emphasises a mythical national unity to one that is heterogeneous, diverse and multicultural" (Carrera, 2006, p. 19).

The turn against 'multiculturalism' and new political calls for integration try to develop a sense of common citizenship based on shared values and policies designed to strengthen civic/national identity and social cohesion. European states have increasingly focused on immigration limits, citizenship tests, new school programmes and citizenship ceremonies for new citizens. Clearly the issues faced by multicultural societies transcend national borders and raise broader political questions about how liberal democracies are to effectively respond to the challenges of diversity. In these respects we would ask the following questions as part of an ongoing research agenda in education:
– What is the reality of multiculturalism on the street as opposed to multicultural policies at state and institutional levels?

– What is the link between multiculturalism and terrorism in public discourse and in institutional practices?
– What is the status of multiculturalism as a state educational doctrine?
– What is involved in the shift from multiculturalism to an integrationist ethos in education?
– Is the new integrationist ethos compatible with the E.U. emphasis on diversity and interculturalism enshrined in the constitution?
– Can social cohesion and national identity coexist with valuing cultural diversity in the public sphere?
– What is the role of education in these issues and processes and in counter-terrorism, peacebuilding and narrative analysis and pedagogy?

Acknowledgement

This chapter was previously published as Michael A. Peters & Tina Besley, 'Islam and the End of European Multiculturalism? From Multiculturalism to Civic Integration', *Policy Futures in Education*, 12(1), 2014, 1–15 and is reprinted here with permission from the copyright holder (Michael A. Peters).

Notes

1 See, for example, http://www.theguardian.com/world/2010/oct/17/angela-merkelgermany-multiculturalism-failures
2 See http://www.telegraph.co.uk/news/worldnews/europe/france/8317497/NicolasSarkozy-declares-multiculturalism-had-failed.html; and http://www.france24.com/ en/20110210-multiculturalism-failed-immigration-sarkozy-live-broadcast-tfifrance-public-questions
3 See http://www.spectator.co.uk/australia/6811278/the-multicultural-whiteout/
4 See http://apo.org.au/research/boat-arrivals-australia-1976-updated-january-2012. For updates and other stories by Janet Phillips for Australian Policy Online see http://apo.org.au/author/janet-phillips
5 See https://www.gov.uk/government/speeches/pms-speech-at-munich-securityconference
6 See http://www.gatestoneinstitute.org/3729/sweden-multiculturalism
7 See http://en.wikipedia.org/wiki/Death_of_Lee_Rigby#Suspects
8 Some 51 international terrorist organizations are proscribed under the Terrorism Act 2000; see https://www.gov.uk/government/uploads/system/uploads/attachment_data/file/232176/List_of Proscribed_organisations.pdf
9 See http://en.wikipedia.org/wiki/English_Defence_League

10 See http://europa.eu/rapid/press-release_SPEECH-13-464_en.htm, but also see http://blogs.lse.ac.uk/europpblog/2013/08/22/contrary-to-popular-opinioneurope-has-not-seen-a-rise-in-far-right-support-since-the-start-of-the-crisis/
11 Multiculturalism: a review of Australian policy statements and recent debates in Australia and overseas. http://www.aph.gov.au/About_Parliament/ Parliamentary_ Departments/Parliamentary_Library/pubs/rp/rp1011/11rp06#_Toc275248146
12 The issue of the Burqa was prominent on the media agenda in France where fewer than than 2000 women wear it. Some commentators suggest that various forms of hijab should be seen in the context of women's rights and inconsistencies, especially in European countries that have legalised prostitution.
13 See the speech at http://www.youtube.com/watch?v=VsGQvOq8cEs
14 http://www.bbc.co.uk/news/uk-politics-12415597
15 http://townhall.com/columnists/patbuchanan/2011/02/15/will_multiculturalism_end_europe/pa ge/full
16 http://www.gatestoneinstitute.org/1612/european-multiculturalism-end
17 http://www.wilsoncenter.org/event/the-end-multiculturalism-europe-migrantsrefugees-and-their-integration, see also http://www.france24.com/en/20101030europe-multiculturalism-integration-germany-merkel-multikulti
18 http://www.globalsecurity.org/security/library/report/2002/un-wrkng-grpterrorism.htm
19 http://www.thecell.org/
20 http://campusdenhaag.leiden.edu/organisation/ctc/about-ctc.html
21 http://www.acslaw.org/files/Restoration-Education-Coordination.pdf
22 http://www.terrorismstudies.com/
23 http://www.unicef.org/spanish/evaldatabase/index_61271.html
24 http://www.pewforum.org/files/2011/01/FutureGlobalMuslimPopulation-WebPDFFeb10.pdf
25 http://www.powerbase.info/index.php/Scottish_Defence_League
26 http://www.mcscotland.org/
27 http://rt.com/news/terfor-tackle-extremism-cameron-830/

References

Barber, B. R. (2003). *Jihad vs. McWorld: Terrorisms challenge to democracy*. London: Corgi.
Besley, T., & Peters, M. (Eds.). (2012). *Interculturalism, education and dialogue*. New York, NY: Peter Lang.
Carrera, S. (2006). A comparison of integration programmes in the E.U.: Trends and weaknesses. *Liberty & Security Challenge Papers*. Retrieved July 26, 2010, from http://www.libertysecurity.org/article851.html

Jura, C. (2012). Multiculturalism: A confusing European approach. *Journal of Politics and Law, 5*(2), 107–115. Retrieved from http://dx.doi.org/10.5539/jpl.v5n2p107

Koleth, E. (2010). *Multiculturalism: A review of Australian policy statements and recent debates in Australia and overseas* (Research Paper No. 6, 2010–2011). Retrieved from http://www.aph.gov.au/About_Parliament/Parliamentary_Departments/Parliamentary_Library/pubs/rp/rp1011/11rp06#_Toc275248146

Kostakopoulou, D. (2010). Introduction. In R. van Oers, E. Ersboll, & D. Kostakopoulou (Eds.), *A re-definition of belonging? Language and integration tests in Europe*. Leiden: Martinus Nijhoff.

Peters, M. A. (2005). *Education, globalization, and the state in the age of terrorism*. Boulder, CO: Paradigm Publishers.

Peters, M. A., & Besley, T. (2012). The narrative turn and the poetics of resistance: Towards a new language for critical educational studies. *Policy Futures in Education, 10*(1), 117–127. Retrieved from http://dx.doi.org/10.2304/pfie.2012.10.1.117

Schmid, A. P. (2013). *Radicalization, de-radicalization, counter-radicalization: A conceptual discussion and literature review*. Retrieved from http://www.icct.nl/download/file/ICCT-Schmid-Radicalisation-De-Radicalisation-Counter-Radicalisation-March-2013.pdf

Wilner, A., & Dubouloz, C.-J. (2011). Transformative radicalization: Applying learning theory to Islamist radicalization. *Studies in Conflict and Terrorism, 34*(5), 418–438. Retrieved from http://dx.doi.org/10.1080/1057610X.2011.561472

Wright, L. (2006). *The looming tower: Al-Qaeda and the road to 9/11*. New York, NY: Alfred A. Knopf.

Relevant Websites

- Treaty of Lisbon: http://europa.eu/lisbon_treaty/glance/index_en.htm
- UNESCO Convention on the Protection and the Promotion of the Diversity of Cultural Expression: http://portal.unesco.org/en/ev.phpURL_ID=31038&URL_DO=DO_TOPIC&URL_SECTIO N=201.html
- 2008 European Year of Intercultural Dialogue: http://www.interculturaldialogue2008.eu/
- GD Education and Culture: http://ec.europa.eu/dgs/education_culture/index_en.htm
- Declaration on multiculturalism of Angela Merkel: http://www.bbc.co.uk/news/world-europe-11559451
- Declaration on multiculturalism of David Cameron: http://www.bbc.co.uk/news/uk-politics-12371994 Declaration on multiculturalism of Nicolas Sarkozy:

- http://www.france24.com/en/20110210-multiculturalism-failed-immigrationsarkozy-live-broadcast-tf1-france-public-questions

Other sites

http://ec.europa.eu/dgs/education_culture/
http://en.wikipedia.org/
http://europa.eu/
http://portal.unesco.org/
http://www.bbc.co.uk/
http://www.britannica.com/
http://www.culturalpolicies.net
http://www.france24.com/
http://www.interculturaldialogue2008.eu/
(Compiled from Cristian Jura, 2012)

CHAPTER 7

'Western Education Is Sinful'
Boko Haram and the Abduction of Chibok Schoolgirls

Western education is a sin! What does that mean to you? It's the definition of 'Boko Haram', the Islamist group of which I, Abul Qaga, am the spokesman. The group, founded in 2002 by Muhammad Yusuf in Maiduguri, capital of Borno State in north-eastern Nigeria, has been making a name for itself in Africa and throughout the world. Its original name in Arabic is Jamaatu Ahlis Sunna Liddaawati Wal-Jihad.
THE CONGREGATION OF THE PEOPLE OF TRADITION FOR PROSELYTISM AND JIHAD

∙∙∙

We do not beat around the bush. Our goal? The application of Sharia law throughout Nigeria. How do we go about it? Through kidnappings, bombings and suicide attacks aimed at the United Nations, churches and symbols of the federal government such as police stations.
HTTPS://EN.RSF.ORG/PREDATOR-THE-ISLAMIST-GROUP-BOKO-HARAM,44536.HTML

∙∙

Introduction

This chapter describes and analyses the abduction of Chibok schoolgirls by the West African Radical Islamic terrorist group. It details the aasualt on these girls as part of an ideological and terroristic attack on Western education with a clear agenda designed to introduce Sharia law in Nigeria and displace Western colonisers.

A number of new sources including Aljazeera, the BBC and the *Guardian* reported that 276 girl students were kidnapped from the Chibok Government Girls Secondary School, Borno state, on April 14, by the Islamist group popularly called Boko Haram. The leader, Abubakar Shekau, also known as Darul Tawheed (specialist in Taweed, the 'abode of monotheism'), who claimed responsibility for the abduction, is recorded as saying that he will sell them in the marketplace.[1] The abductions caused an international outcry: United

Nations Special Envoy for Global Education Gordon Brown condemned the actions of the group, and President Obama with the agreement of Nigerian leaders deployed US personnel to help find them. Since the abduction another eight girls aged 12 to 15 have been taken. While some 53 girls managed to escape, conflicting reports suggest nearly three hundred girls were taken as hostages and are thought to have been smuggled over the border into Chad and the Cameroon. The abductions have also caused mass protests within Nigeria. Nigeria's First Lady, Patience Jonathan, ordered the two protest leaders, Saratu Angus Ndirpaya and Naomi Mutah Nyadar, to be arrested, accusing them of fabricating the incident, giving the Nigerian government a bad name and of belonging to Boko Haram.

Abubakar Shekau became leader after Muhammad Yūsuf was captured and executed by Nigerian police in 2009. Under his leadership the group has become more radical, engaging in a range of terrorist acts that have left hundreds killed in multiple bomb attacks.[2]

Boko Haram in Hausa (the tribal language of northern Nigeria) in popular parlance means 'Western education is sinful'. Ḥarām is an Arabic term. In Islamic jurisprudence the term Ḥarām is used to refer to any act that is forbidden by Allah. As Paul Newman (2013) indicates, *boko* is an indigenous Hausa word originally connoting sham, fraud, deceit, or lack of authenticity. He continues:

> When the British colonial government imposed secular schools in northern Nigeria at the beginning of the 20th century, *boko* was applied in a pejorative sense to this new system. By semantic extension, *boko* came to acquire its current meaning of Hausa written in Roman script and Western education in general. (p. 2)

In 'The Boko Harām Group in Nigeria: its beginnings, principles and actions in Nigeria', Ahmad Murtadā (2012)[3] from the Islamic Studies Department, Bayero University, Kano, Northern Nigeria, provides the following description of the name of the group:

> The name Boko Harām is a Hausa name which only the Hausa peoples understood and is a compound name comprised of Hausa and Arabic. The Hausa applied the term Boko to Western forms of education so when the term 'Harām' is appended to it the intent is: the Western education system is haram. Yet it is perhaps more adequate to explain the term not in its literal linguistic sense but in its more technical sense as meaning traversing the Western education system of education is haram. (p. 4)

The group's intention is to prohibit all forms of Western education, as Muhammad Yūsuf explained in a lecture: 'education within schools which have been established by missionaries which includes the education curriculum from elementary education to secondary schooling and institutes to national service to employment' (Murtadā, 2012, p. 4).

Ahmad Murtadā explains that before 2002 the group did not have an ideological agenda, and he describes the formation of 'Jamāt Ahl us-Sunnah lid-Dawah wal-Jihād' (The Group of the People of Sunnah for Preaching and Struggle) and the armed confrontations that took place after 2002. Muhammad Yūsuf travelled the north-east (and later north-west) of Nigeria giving lectures and 'calling the youth to preparation for jihad'. He details the Massacre of Shabān in July 2009 and the killing of Muhammad Yūsuf shortly thereafter. The group issued a statement indicating that they were to begin a series of bombings 'to make Nigeria ungovernable'. There were reportedly some 115 attacks during 2011 in which 550 people lost their lives. In 2012 warnings were issued to all Christian Nigerians living in the North demanding they leave the region, and further bombings and killings followed.

In terms of principles Muhammad Yūsuf stated, 'the western education system conflicts with Islamic education'. In terms of the group's credo they hold that 'democracy totally conflicts with Islām' (Murtadā, 2012, p. 16), quoting the hadeeth of Abū Saīd al-Khudrī. Ahmad Murtadā refers to Muhammad Yūsufs *Hadhihi Aqeedatuna* (pp. 82–99) to ascertain the prohibition against Western education.[4]

> They prohibit studying in the educational system from primary through to university level for a number of reasons: (a) missionaries and colonialists established these schools as a means to serve their missionary interests among Muslims in Nigeria. They argue that the Islamic system of education was widespread in our country before the missionaries arrived and it was still fully functioning until the colonialists took over the entire country. Thus, their system took over all aspects of life, important the educational system, which results in a Muslim bit by bit becoming a disbeliever; (b) mixing between the genders [Ikhtilāt] and Tabarruj [uncovering and wearing impermissible revealing attire], while Allāh says: And abide in your houses and do not display yourselves as [was] the display of the former times of ignorance {al-Ahzāb (33): 33}; (c) the study of subjects, ideas and theories which conflict with the religion such as Darwin's theory of evolution which conflicts with Allāh's saying: Say, [O Muúammad], "Travel through the land and observe how He began creation. Then Allāh will produce the

final creation. Indeed Allāh, over all things, is competent". {ar-Rūm (29): 20} (pp. 17–18)

The Boko Haram educational programme involves sermons, lessons, and lectures from books including: tafseer of the *Qurān*; *Saheeh ul-Bukhārī*; *Riyadh us-Sāliheen*; *Bulūgh ul-Marām*; *ar-Risālah* by Imām Ibn Abī Zayd; *Usūl uth-Thalāthah* and *Kitāb ut-Tawheed* by Muhammad ibn Abdul Wahhāb; *Ahkām ul-Janāiz*; *Kitāb us-Salāh* by Shaykh al-Albānī; *al-Walā wal-Baraā* by Shaykh Fawzān and other works (p. 21).[5] These are texts and sources from scholars from the past that are used to justify the fatāwā and rebellion against leaders. It is important to note that the translator added several appendices including Appendix 5: Boko Haram Are Not Salafi.[6]

Zenn and Pearson (2014) document the gender-based violence (GBV) and the targeting of women as a significant development in Boko Harams tactics in 2013. They report that more than 3500 people have been killed since 2010 in attacks modelled on al-Qaeda with whom Shekau has developed links, not only Ayman al-Zawahri and the late Abu Musaab al-Zarqawi, but also Al-Qaeda in the Islamic Maghreb (AQIM) and Al-Shabaab. They indicate that GBV 'transcends region, religion and ethnicity, with physical and sexual abuse affecting as many as 35.1% of Igbo women and 34.3% of Hausa-Fulani women', commenting that 'Nigerian cultural traditions have included female genital mutilation, forced marriage and widowhood practices, including hair-shaving and restriction to the home' (Ifemeje, 2012, p. 138).

In addition, Nigerian law is discriminatory against women, including lack of legal recognition for rape within marriage. Zenn and Pearson (2014) also note the targeting and abuse of Christian women, documenting how the victimization of women has become an explicit part of Boko Haram's ideology. It is clear that the attacks on girls, and on girls' education especially, in the North-East has become a deadly focus of recent tactics, as a refinement of ideology and tactics.

It is useful to follow the work of Roman Loimeier (2012), who analyses Boko Haram from a historical perspective, "viewing the movement as a result of social, political and generational dynamics within the larger field of northern Nigerian radical Islam" (p. 137) to maintain that if "basic frame conditions such as social injustice, corruption and economic mismanagement do not change" (p. 137) the Boko Haram movement will continue to recruit and flourish. Loimeier (2012) views the theological dimension of the movement as the first to advocate jihad (armed struggle) in the region. He also explains how the British colonial schools challenged the hegemonic position of Islamic education and how reformers (Ahmadu Bello, Aminu Kano, Abubakar

Gumi) sought to 'Islamize modernity'. These efforts have been rejected by fundamentalists (e.g. Maitatsine) as radically anti-modern, as un-Islamic or another form of Westernization. Loimeier (2012) provides some background on the development of the Yan Izala movement, established in 1978, which rejects everything un-Islamic to offer a vision of Islam no longer tied to forms of established religious authority. Abubakar Gumi translated into Hausa his programmatic text, *al-aqida al-sahiha bi-muwafaqat al-sharia* (The Right Faith According to the Prescriptions of the Sharia, first published in Arabic in 1972) in 1978 and Loimeier records the movement's first crisis due to the rise of Pentecostal Christianity in the 1980s whose members won seats in local government. He also records the regional divisions of Yan Izala and disputes over leadership. Loimeier (2012) provides a useful analysis of the struggle for Islamic education as a central debate:

> The struggle for modern Islamic education had been one of the major programmatic features of the Yan Izalas development and had led not only to the establishment of numerous Yan Izala schools in northern Nigeria but also to the emergence of a second generation of Yan Izala followers who had gone through this new system of education, only to discover that modern Islamic education 'Yan Izala-style' did not necessarily provide jobs. In particular, the stress on sound training in Arabic in Yan Izala schools as well as Yan Izala-sponsored university education in Saudi Arabia did not provide enough career options in Nigeria. (p. 145)

He documents the way that second-generation dissidents became militant supporters of legal and political sharia and he suggests that an increasing fragmentation of ultra-radical religious groups after 2000 indicates the importance of understanding the theological disputes that ensued. Where Jaafar Mahmud Adam, for instance, did not make Western education a sin, "Muhammad Yusuf rejected the modern Islamic schools of the Yan Izala and related groups as well as Nigerias secular system of education and summarized this specific position as boko haram (Hausa: 'Western education is forbidden')" (p. 149). It is also important to acknowledge the sources alluded to in these bitter theological debates:

> Central to Muhammad Yusufs argumentation was a text written by a Saudi Arabian Wahhabi-oriented scholar, Abubakar b. 'Abdallah Abu Zayd (d. 2008), titled *al-madaris al-'alamiyya al-ajnabiyya al-isti'mariyya:*

ta'rikhuha wa-makhatiruha (*The Secular, Foreign and Colonialist Schools: Their History and Dangers*). This text specifically served as the theological basis for his rejection of a natural science-based (Western and secular) view of the world. (p. 149)

The dispute turned to open conflict in 2003 and escalated again in 2009 (as described above) with clashes between Boko Haram and Nigerian security forces. With increasing radicalization and even more violent tactics Boko Haram claims to be the supreme authority on the definitions of both 'Sunna' and 'Islam' (p. 152).

Loimeier (2012) demonstrates that 'Muslims in Nigeria do not form a homogeneous' group and are divided into bitterly disputed splinter factions of which some oppose the Nigerian State and 'others are deeply involved in governmental dynamics and politics of positioning' (p. 152). He suggests that the Boko Haram movement will be defeated in part because it has strong opposition and enemies *within* the Nigerian Muslim community and he concludes by making the following claim:

> Yet, as long as the basic social and economic context does not decisively change – specifically, Nigeria's on-going inability to achieve sustained economic growth as well as some degree of social justice – militant movements such as Boko Haram will rise again.

There is no sound justification for the abduction of girls or the gender violence of Boko Haram. At the same time, Western educators far removed from the scene need to understand the ideological closure and bitter theological disputes at the heart of 'Western education is sinful', as well as the economic, social and cultural conditions of Borno and the north-east of Nigeria and the wider tribal and religious splits within the country. Education is at the heart of modernization (and modernity): is there an Islamic modernization that allows for Western-style education that enhances this process while making room for traditional Islamic religious education in Nigeria.

Acknowledgement

This chapter was previously published as Michael A. Peters, 'Western Education is Sinful: Boko Haram and the Abduction of Chibok Schoolgirls', *Policy Futures in Education*, 12(2), 2014, 1–5 and is reprinted here with permission from the copyright holder (Michael A. Peters).

Notes

1. See, for example, http://www.aljazeera.com/news/africa/2014/05/boko-haramclaims-nigeria-abductions-201455134957975542.html and Who are Nigeria's Boko Haram Islamists? by Farouk Chothia, http://www.bbc.com/news/worldafrica-13809501
2. See this profile at: http://www.bbc.com/news/world-africa-18020349
3. The English translation carries the following acknowledgement: Dr Ahmad Murtada, Jamaat Boko Harām: Nashatuhā, Mabadiuhā wa Amāluhā fi Naygeeriyah [The Boko Harām Group in Nigeria: its beginnings, principles and actions in Nigeria], 13 November 2012. Refer to the Arabic language Islamic and African studies journal *al-Qiraāt, Rabī al-Ākhir-Jumādā al-Ākhira* 1433AH/April –June 2012 CE vol., no. 12, pp. 12–25. From the blog of our Shaykh, Dr Khālid al-Anbarī (hafidhahullāh). It can be referred to here: http://dralanbary1.blogspot.co.uk/2013/02/blog-post_21.html?m=1 Summarised translation by AbdulHaq ibn Kofi ibn Kwesi al-Ashantī.
4. Hadeeth or hadith is translated as 'tradition' in relation to the deeds and sayings of the Prophet Muhammad but does not qualify as primary source material.
5. See also pp. 21–22 for the movement's academic sources.
6. See http://muslimmatters.org/wp-content/uploads/On-Salafi-Islam_Dr.-Yasir-Qadhi.pdf

References

Ifemeje, S. C. (2012). Gender-based domestic violence in Nigeria: A socio-legal perspective. *Indian Journal of Gender Studies, 19*(1), 137–148.

Loimeier, R. (2012). Boko haram: The development of a militant religious movement in Nigeria. *Africa Spectrum, 47*(2–3), 137–155.

Newman, P. (2013). *The etymology of Hausa boko*. Retrieved from http://www.megatchad.net/publications/Newman-2013-Etymology-of-Hausa-boko.pdf

Zenn, J., & Pearson, E. (2014). Women, gender and the evolving tactics of Boko Haram. *Journal of Terrorism Research, 5*(1), 46–57. Retrieved from http://ojs.st-andrews.ac.uk/index.php/jtr/article/view/828/707

CHAPTER 8

Global Citizenship Education
Politics, Problems and Prospects

Introduction

This chapter speaks to the recent development of the concept of global citizenship and what kind of political community it promotes. The chapter responds to the question of how far globalization and citizenship revolves around the free movement of peoples.

In *Global Citizenship Education* (Peters et al., 2008) we noted that the modern concept of citizenship – a recent concept historically – implies the existence of a civil or political community, a set of rights and obligations ascribed to citizens by virtue of their membership in that community, and an ethic of participation and solidarity needed to sustain it. Most traditional accounts of citizenship begin with the assertion of basic civil, political and social rights of individuals and note the way in which the modern concept as inherently egalitarian, took on a universal appeal with the development of the liberal tradition which is often understood as synonymous with modernity. Yet the concept has appealed to both conservatives and radical democrats: the former emphasize individual freedom at the expense of equality and see state intervention as an intolerable and unwarranted violated of the freedom of the individual while the latter stress the democratic potential of citizenship. Increasingly, on the Left the concept has been seen as a means to control the injustices of capitalism. For the Left, the most pressing question has been the status of citizenship in the modern state and what kind of political community best promotes it.

In relation to these issues there are a set of pressing philosophical and conceptual problems at the heart of the philosophy, theory, and pedagogy of global citizenship education that require investigation. We do not have the time to dwell on them here but can at least mention them. Global citizenship education (GCE) requires an understanding of citizenship and human rights as 'international norms that help to protect all people everywhere from severe political, legal, and social abuses' (Nickle, 2006). GCE therefore requires an understanding of the philosophy of human rights [that] addresses questions about the existence, content, nature, universality, justification, and legal status of human rights (Nickle, 2006) together with the history of struggle and international human rights law and organizations. What are rights? What are human rights? How do we distinguish between different kinds of rights – civil and political rights, social rights, minority and group rights, environment rights? These philosophical questions are important and students at all levels need to be taught the main approaches and theories of rights. They also need to understand the historical specificity of the struggle for rights as well as the global significance of the Black struggle for equality and civil rights in the U.S., the importance of the struggle for indigenous rights, women's rights, cultural rights and children's rights – what Norberto Bobbio (1989), the late Italian professor of jurisprudence called *The Age of Rights*. We might also inquire with Jacques Rancière (2004) 'Who Is the Subject of the Rights of Man?'[1]

In addition, Global Citizenship Education (GCE) might also begin to foreground the development of international organization associated with the development of human rights including the UN and its agencies and the International Court of Criminal Justice, a European initiative established in 2002 that does not yet carry the signatures of U.S. and China.[2]

At the beginning of the twenty-first century, the world experiences processes of both integration and disintegration. The expansion of world markets as a form of economic globalization can be understood as a process of integration composed of international flows of capital, goods, information, and people. The same process is both a form of economic integration and a polarization of wealth that exacerbates existing tendencies toward greater global inequalities between rich and poor countries and regions. It also accentuates the need for reviewing the templates of the global system of governance that emerged with the Bretton Woods agreement, which founded many of the world institutions that comprised the architecture of the postwar world system. Now, more than at any time in the past, with the end of the Cold War, the collapse of the Soviet system, the consolidation of the E.U., the entry of China in the WTO, and the growth of India, we are witnessing an accelerated set of changes – economic, cultural, technological and political – that impinge on one another in novel ways and create new possibilities and dangers both for the democratic state and the notions of citizenship and national identity that underpin it.

In the U.S. under the neoconservatives, and the U.K. under the so-called Third Way, a mantle inherited by Prime Minister Gordon Brown, there has been a shift from the concept of rights to responsibilities and a move away from state intervention towards the market and the construction of 'consumer-citizens' who are increasingly forced to invest in themselves at critical points in their life-cycle (education, work, retirement) or go into debt. At the same time, there has been a shift to the third sector with community and church involvement in the definition of social welfare policy and an emphasis on giving, gifting and voluntary work often thinly disguising a moral re-regulation of social life, especially of single women and their children. Increasingly, with the development of information and communications technologies, there has been a rise in state surveillance and, especially after 9/11, an erosion of liberal rights and a shift from active political citizenship to passive political literacy; concomitantly, the same technologies have supported new public spaces and civil networks that are interest-based and transcend the geography of face-to-face communities and even larger collectivities like states. We have come to think that the new movement referred to as Open Education Resources (OER), what we prefer to call simply Open Education has the potential to encourage and shape global civil society – what we call *The Virtues of Openness* (Peters & Roberts, 2010).[3]

At one point, we had conceived a book project with the title *Old America, New Europe*, inverting Rumsfield's notorious comment, because what we perceived was an old style *defensive modernity* developing strongly under the U.S. neoconservatives – with the largest reorganization of several government departments as Homeland Security that focused on surveillance, constant war alert, strengthening borders etc. Even the preemptive first strike doctrine was *in defense* of American *values* and American *identity*, if the neoconservative play on Leo Strauss is to be believed – both the 'war on terror' abroad and the 'war on culture' at home. We think these two are systematically linked and show, for instance, the transparent and openly ideological nature of Lynne Cheney's attack on history standards and on, postmodernism or Foucault as the source of the value crisis that confronts America. Remember that Strauss, at one time a student of Heidegger who he regarded very highly, viewed the crisis of modernity (after Nietzsche) as predominantly a crisis of values. The three waves of modernity symbolized in Hobbes, Rousseau and Nietzsche had led, respectively, to liberalism, socialism and fascism. Only liberalism could be rescued from the relativism and historicism of modern philosophy by a return to classical political philosophy (basically in the form of Plato) and the eternal values inherent in what he calls the 'theological-philosophical problem' that begins with Athens *and* Jerusalem, reason *and* faith (York & Peters, 2010).

We have since become more skeptical about the promise of Europe and the kind of claims made by Habermas and Derrida in 2003 especially a mere sixty years after Auschwitz and the recent ethnic cleansing in Kosovo involving war crimes committed by Serbian forces, including summary execution, burning of homes, and forcible displacement of Kosovar Albanians.[4]

Perhaps, more than ever before the question of globalization and citizenship revolves around the free movement of peoples. By this we mean not only the modern diaspora, or the planned colonial migrations, or the more recent global mobility of highly skilled labour that is rewarded by citizenship. But more importantly, we mean refugees of all kinds and asylum-seekers and all that that entails – enforced border crossings, ethnic cleansing policies, the huge illegal movement of so-called 'aliens' or the 'undocumented', detention camps the likes of Woomera in Australia and even Guantanomo Bay, where the concept of rights is fragile or has entirely disappeared. Derrida (2001) argues for a form of cosmopolitanism that entails the right to asylum while Dummett (2001) focuses on refugee and immigration policy, increasingly a defining policy issue for the U.S., France, and the U.K.

We are interested in how central the camp rather the prison is to contemporary society remembering Giorgi Agamben's (1998) reworking Foucault's biopolitics based on the model of the prison in *Discipline and Punish*.[5] Not only Abu Ghraib prison in Iraq (the Baghdad Correctional Facility) or Guantanamo Bay detention camp but also immigration detention camps like Woomera in Australia and across the western world and a variety of concentration, detention and refugee camps in Serbia, Asia and Africa. We note that in 2006 one of Halliburtons subsidiaries was awarded a $385 million dollar contract by Homeland Security to construct detention and processing facilities in the event of a national emergency.[6]

The terms 'globalization' and 'citizenship' are not normally juxtaposed in social and political analysis. They tend to appear as contradictory or, at least, conflicting: the former points to a set of economic and cultural processes of unequal and uneven world integration, based on the unregulated flows of capital and underwritten by developments in new information and communications technologies, while the latter serves mainly as a metaphor for political community or solidarity. To what extent does globalization (as financialization) threaten the sovereignty of the nation-state and with it the notion of citizenship that developed during the modern era? To what extent can citizenship be severed from questions of national identity? Within the context of globalization how can we maintain or develop a sense of community and local identity to establish or defend the hard-won entitlements of social citizenship? What possibilities are there for developing genuine transnational alliances and defining entirely new sets of rights within supranational political arenas? To what extent can the movement of individuals and peoples come to be regarded as genuinely free within states, regions, and continents; and how might states that encourage the free-floating globally integrated enterprise also extend universal and lawful protections to migrants, refugees and those seeking asylum? These are critical questions that ought to inform a democratic response to citizenship and to the question of global citizenship education.

Acknowledgement

This chapter was previously published as Michael A. Peters, 'Global Citizenship Education: Politics, Problems and Prospects', *Citizenship, Social and Economics Education*, 9(1), 2010, 43–47 and is reprinted here with permission from the copyright holder (Michael A. Peters).

Notes

1   In this context it is worth repeating the first three paragraphs of Rancière's essay:
    As we know, the question raised by my title took on a new cogency during the last ten years of the twentieth century. The Rights of Man or Human Rights had just been rejuvenated in the seventies and eighties by the dissident movements in the Soviet Union and Eastern Europe – a rejuvenation that was all the more significant as the 'formalism' of those rights had been one of the first targets of the young Marx, so that the collapse of the Soviet Empire could appear as their revenge. After this collapse, they would appear as the charter of the irresistible movement leading to a peaceful posthistorical world where global democracy would match the global market of liberal economy.
    As is well known, things did not exactly go that way. In the following years, the new landscape of humanity, freed from utopian totalitarianism, became the stage of new outbursts of ethnic conflicts and slaughters, religious fundamentalisms, or racial and xenophobic movements. The territory of posthistorical and peaceful humanity proved to be the territory of new figures of the Inhuman. And the Rights of Man turned out to be the rights of the rightless, of the populations hunted out of their homes and land and threatened [End Page 297] by ethnic slaughter. They appeared more and more as the rights of the victims, the rights of those who were unable to enact any rights or even any claim in their name, so that eventually their rights had to be upheld by others, at the cost of shattering the edifice of International Rights, in the name of a new right to "humanitarian interference" – which ultimately boiled down to the right to invasion.
    A new suspicion thus arose: What lies behind this strange shift from Man to Humanity and from Humanity to the Humanitarian? The actual subject of these Rights of Man became Human Rights. Is there not a bias in the statement of such rights? It was obviously impossible to revive the Marxist critique. But another form of suspicion could be revived: the suspicion that the "man" of the Rights of Man was a mere abstraction because the only real rights were the rights of citizens, the rights attached to a national community as such.

2 The Rome statue at established the court is to be found at http://www.un.org/law/icc/index.html. The ICC is to be distinguished from the International Court of Justice (ICJ) establish at the Hague, see it website at http://www.icj-cij.org/homepage/index.php?lang=en

3 For an introduction to the issues see the paper and video 'Openness and Open Education in the Global Digital Economy: An Emerging Paradigm of Social Production', paper to be presented at Economic and Social Research Council (ERSC, U.K.) Seminar Series on Education and the Knowledge Economy, University of Bath, March 6–7th, 2008, at http://www.bath.ac.uk/education/seminars/esrc_seminars/listenagain/?p=5

4 See M. A. Peters, "Ghosts in the Promise of Enlightenment Europe: Habermas, Derrida and Education", lecture sponsored by the Center for European Studies, Global Studies, and Department of Curriculum and Instruction at the University of Wisconsin-Madison, Monday April 14th, 2008.

5 The camp, according to Agamben, is the space that opens up when the state of exception turns into a normality. The state of exception signifies a temporary (zeitliche) abrogation (Aufhebung) of the rule of law, and the camp gives a spatial expression to this state of exception, even if this expression remains outside of the normal order.

6 Rachel L. Swarns of the NY Times (Feb 3, 2006) reports The Army Corps of Engineers has awarded a contract worth up to $385 million for building temporary immigration detention centers to Kellogg Brown & Root, the Halliburton subsidiary that has been criticized for overcharging the Pentagon for its work in Iraq. K B R would build the centers for the Homeland Security Department for an unexpected influx of immigrants, to house people in the event of a natural disaster or for new programs that require additional detention space, company executives said. K B R , which announced the contract last month, had a similar contract with immigration agencies from 2000 to last year at http://www.nytimes.com/2006/02/04/national/04halliburton.html

References

Agamben, G. (1998). *Homo sacer: Sovereign power and bare life* (D. Heller-Roazen, Trans.). Stanford, CA: Stanford University Press.
Bobbio, N. (1996). *The age of rights*. London: Polity Press.
Derrida, J. (2001). *On cosmopolitanism and forgiveness*. London: Routledge.
Dummett, M. (2001). *On immigration and refugees*. New York, NY: Routledge.
Nickle, J. (2006). Human rights. *Stanford Encyclopedia of Philosophy*. Retrieved from http://plato.stanford.edu/entries/rights-human/

Peters, M. A. (2008). Citizenship in the age of globalization. *Global-e: A Global Studies Journal, 1*(3). Retrieved from http://www.global-ejournal.org/index.php/global-e/article/view/20/62

Peters, M. A., Blee, H., & Britton, A. (Eds.). (2008). *Global citizenship education: Philosophy, theory and pedagogy*. Rotterdam, The Netherlands: Sense Publishers.

Ranciere, J. (2004). Who is the subject of the rights of man? *South Atlantic Quarterly, 103*(2–3), 297–310.

CHAPTER 9

The Refugee Crisis and the Right to Political Asylum

Introduction

This chapter examines the concept and history of political asylum as it developed in liberal societies in Europe, grounded in the emergence of human rights in the eighteenth century. Against this historical review the chapter then analyses the way the conflict in Syria led to the largest contemporary migration to Europe.

The right to asylum is a historic right stretching back to Ancient Egyptian, Hebrew civilizations, and the Greek city states that afforded protection against extradition and an inviolable place of refuge to criminals, and debtors from other countries. By the early Christian era, sanctuary was given to those fleeing from religious persecution with refuge in a consecrated place, generally a church. The right of sanctuary was recognized under the Code of Theodosius (399), and later by Roman law under the Justinian Code. Papal sanction came with Leo I in 441. King Æthelbert of Kent enacted laws regulating sanctuary in about 600 AD in laws that governed licenses of church sanctuaries where the asylum seeker had to surrender himself and confess his sins, and be supervised by the abbot or church father.

The political right to asylum, the granting of refuge to an alien in a sovereign state, evolved from the religious notion of sanctuary. France was the first to recognize the right to asylum in its 1793 constitution. In the section *Of The Relations of the French Republic towards Foreign Nations*, the following articles appear:

> 118. The French nation is the friend and natural ally of free nations.
>
> 119. It does not interfere with the affairs of government of other nations. It suffers no interference of other nations with its own.
>
> 120. It serves as a place of refuge for all who, on account of liberty, are banished from their native country.

These it refuses to deliver up to tyrants.

> 121. It concludes no peace with an enemy that holds possession of its territory.[2]

Its expression in the twentieth century was developed by the United Nations in the 1951 Convention Relating to the Status of Refugees, and the 1967 Protocol Relating to the Status of Refugees.[3] The Introductory Note by the Office of the United Nations High Commissioner for Refugees (UNHCR) provides the historical summary of the evolution and scope of the law:

> Grounded in Article 14 of the Universal Declaration of Human Rights 1948, which recognizes the right of persons to seek asylum from persecution in other countries, the United Nations Convention relating to the Status of Refugees, adopted in 1951, is the centrepiece of international refugee protection today. The Convention entered into force on 22 April 1954, and it has been subject to only one amendment in the form of a 1967 Protocol, which removed the geographic and temporal limits of the 1951 Convention. The 1951 Convention, as a post-Second World War instrument, was originally limited in scope to persons fleeing events occurring before 1 January 1951 and within Europe. The 1967 Protocol removed these limitations and thus gave the Convention universal coverage. It has since been supplemented by refugee and subsidiary protection regimes in several regions, as well as via the progressive development of international human rights law.

According to the definition embraced in Article 1, as the Note suggests:

> A refugee ... is someone who is unable or unwilling to return to their country of origin owing to a well-founded fear of being persecuted for reasons of race, religion, nationality, membership of a particular social group, or political opinion. (p. 3)

As a rights-based instrument, the convention is underwritten by three main fundamental principles: non-discrimination, non-penalization, and *non-refoulement* (non-expulsion). The convention currently enjoys the supports of some 147 countries around the world.

The original signing of the Convention was attended by some 26 states. Although World War II had ended hundreds of thousands of refugees still wandered Europe or were still confined to refugee camps. Marilyn Achhiron (2001) remarked:

> On the 50th anniversary of its adoption, the Convention is coming apart at the seams, according to some of the same capitals which had breathed life into the protection regime a half century ago. Crises such as Kosovo

have multiplied, spilling millions of people into headlong flight in search of a safe haven. Intercontinental travel has become easy and a burgeoning business in human trafficking has swelled the number of illegal immigrants. States say their asylum systems are being overwhelmed with this tangled mass of refugees and economic migrants and are urging a legal retrenchment. The Convention, they say, is outdated, unworkable. (p. 6)[4]

Refugee law, as a branch of international law, has developed enormously since the 1938 League of Nations, and come to embrace a set of international and regional legal instruments, including the Bangkok Principles on Status and Treatment of Refugees (1966), OAU Convention Governing the Specific Aspects of Refugee Problems in Africa (1969), Cartagena Declaration on Refugees (1984), the Council of Europe's Situation of de facto Refugees (1976), and the European Council's Directive (2004) on third country nationals and stateless persons as refugees. Refugee law is anchored in an understanding of the history of population movements, the emerging framework of refugee protection, the UNHCR and other international actors, and the political context of statelessness and displacement.[5]

Roger Zetter (2015) in his article, 'Protection in Crisis: Forced Migration and Protection in a Global Era' writes of more than 51 million people worldwide who are forcibly is placed as refugees, asylum seekers or internal displaced persons.[6] He goes on to write:

> The contemporary drivers of displacement are complex and multilayered, making protection based on a strict definition of persecution increasingly problematic and challenging to implement. Many forced migrants now fall outside the recognized refugee and asylum apparatus. Much displacement today is driven by a combination of intrastate conflict, poor governance and political instability, environmental change, and resource scarcity. These conditions, while falling outside traditionally defined persecution, leave individuals highly vulnerable to danger and uncertain of the future, compelling them to leave their homes in search of greater security. In addition, the blurring of lines between voluntary and forced migration, as seen in mixed migration flows, together with the expansion of irregular migration, further complicates today's global displacement picture.[7]

What is known as the European immigration crisis erupted in the mid-2000s, and culminated in 2015 with the worst crisis in immigration, and massive increase of displaced persons seeking asylum in Europe since the end of World War II. The sheer numbers of refugees and migrants flowing across borders involving the Mediterranean to Greece (in particular, to the island of Lebos) in hazardous conditions risking their lives in small overcrowded boats provided by people smugglers who charge 1200 euros per person. Numerous migration corridors from war-torn states like Syrian, Afghanistan, Eritea, and other Middle East and North African states, as well as the Western Balkans take refugees overland through Turkey, Macedonia, Serbia, and Hungary to preferred destinations in Germany, Britain, or France. The numbers are staggering: Frontex 2015 Annual Risk Analysis estimates some 283,000 illegal border crossings in 2014 alone, with some 114,000 refusals of entry.[8] The executive summary records the major features of the geopolitical context:

> As regards the wider geopolitical context, two issues clearly stand out: the conflict in Syria and the continued volatility in North African countries, notably Libya, from where migrants often depart in their attempt to cross the Mediterranean Sea. The large number of displaced Syrians in the Middle East and North Africa suggests that Syria will likely remain the top country of origin for irregular migrants and asylum seekers in the EU for some time to come. In Libya, migrants are in an extremely vulnerable situation, especially those in areas affected by the fighting. Migrants in Libya also face arbitrary detention and very poor conditions of detention, marked by overcrowding, poor sanitation and exploitation. (p. 6)

According to Eurostat statistics, some 626,000 asylum applications were received by E.U. member states in 2014, highest number of asylum applicants within the E.U. since the peak in 1992.[9] The major increase has come from Syrian refugees that increased to over 122,000 in 2014, roughly 20% of the E.U. total, with a huge increase in 2015 although reliable estimates are hard to come by. The New York Times (2105) reports 7.6 million displaced persons within Syrian with some 1.9 million refugees in Turkey, 1.1 million in Lebanon, 629,000 in Jordan, 250,000 in Iraq, and 132,000 in Egypt – roughly 12 million Syrians have been displaced, four million abroad, since 2011 which is over half the Syrian population.[10] World refugee hotspots, according to Patrick Boehler and Sergio Pec͵anha (26 August 2015) include the Balkans, the Middle East, Eastern Europe (Ukraine), and the Mediterranean coast. But the problem is not confined to Europe.

South-East Asia is another hotspot, with thousands of Bangladeshis and Rohingya, an ethnic minority from Myanmar, fleeing by sea from poverty and persecution to Indonesia and Malaysia in the first instance, and risking their lives at sea to make it to Australia.[11] Australia's ex-Prime Minister Tony Abbott had consistently ruled out resettling any of the thousands of refugees stranded at sea amid the South-East Asia asylum seeker crisis arguing that irregular migration should be stemmed at the source.[12] Mexico – U.S. migration is a major issue in the forthcoming U.S. elections with nearly 12 million Mexicans resident in the U.S. up from just over 2 million in 1980.[13] It is one of the defining issues between Republicans and Democrats, and is an issue that has become highly politicized, although there is some evidence that migration patterns have recently changed reversing previous trends.[14]

It is not surprising given this historic upsurge that immigration issues have suddenly gained a great deal of news coverage, and has become one of the dominant issues on political agendas of governments in most countries of the global North, especially the member states of the E.U.. European Commission President Jean-Claude Juncker on 9 September announced a binding quota system distributing an additional 120,000 asylum seekers among E.U. nations. While Germany expects to receive 800,000 asylum seekers this year, other E.U. countries like Hungary have opposed the quota system, and closed its borders.[15]

Estimates are changing almost daily of numbers of refugees making their way over-land to Germany with figures of between 800,000 to 1 million being made in news reports.

The influx of Syrian refugees has divided member states with those like Germany temporarily abandoning border controls and E.U. protocols to accept asylum seekers, and others like Hungary closing and policing their borders.[16] This leads to the emergence of very different philosophies of immigration within the E.U. with very different positions taken on the moral status of refugees, their rights to asylum and the obligations of host countries – issues that standardly raise questions of closed or open borders and of the open society per se (see Wellman, 2010).[17] The refugee crisis has also exacerbated the internal politics of E.U. member states and consolidated the rise of the radical right across Europe based on an anti-immigration platform with immigration emerging as one of the defining issues of the next round of elections.[18]

As Ambrosini and Van Der Leun (2015) write in their introduction to a special issue on civil society and migration policies that while public discourse has mobilized outspoken moral positions, state migration policies have become increasingly restrictive aiming to control unwanted migration to protect labor markets, to fence off state-funded social provisions, and expelling undocumented and unwanted persons (p. 103). They write:

> Despite globalization and the development of an international human rights regime, legal residence and citizenship are still to a large extent dependent on the nation-state. State authorities therefore play a significant role in granting or refusing certain social rights (Bloch & Chimienti, 2012). This power of the nation-state may have diminished in other spheres but

only to a lesser extent in the definition and implementation of citizenship (Mora & Handmaker, 2014). Over the years, many states and federal governments have developed fine-grained policies to select immigrants to regulate who can reside in the territory and who is eligible for certain social rights (Engbersen & Broeders, 2009; Torpey, 2000). The concept of 'mobility regimes' (Faist, 2013) highlights the social and political stratification of people moving beyond national borders. (p. 106)

The truism that planet Earth is one interconnected functioning whole – a self-regulating complex system – has various environmental, cybernetic, and political readings. Earth system science provides some evidence for the regulation of the biosphere to support the conditions for life. The 'global brain' is another such metaphor for an interconnected ICT network connecting human collective or distributive intelligence as a kind of planetary nervous system that emerges as self-organized dynamic semiotic networks in which everything speaks. The political reading adds another dimension that we might call cosmopolitanism with its philosophical roots in Ancient Greece and its juridical notion of a single community based on a shared morality and cosmopolitan law or right anchored in an extended hospitality.

One part of this shared understanding among these different systems is the notion of equilibrium and equalization that operates on the principle that changes in one part of the system causing related changes in other parts. This rudimentary notion of equilibrium or homeostasis is a way of charting the dynamic nature of systems that evolve in unpredictable ways. Liberal internationalism provides an account of an evolving globalization that is based on universal values of *free movement* – the free movement of capital, of trade, and of people where asylum is granted to refugees fleeing persecution. Asylum is seen as a fundamental right philosophically linked to the notion of free movement and also to notions of security and justice pointing to the control of external borders. While in the past, freedom of movement and residence for persons in the E.U. has been the cornerstone of Union citizenship established by the Treaty of Maastricht in 1992, its practical implementation in E.U. law is now at a critical pressure point and there are cracks in the policy and in its implementation that threaten the right to asylum.

The 'European migrant crisis', more aptly named 'refugee crisis', is one of historic proportions and with over million migrants represents the largest movements of people since the establishment of the E.U. and one that will no doubt change European society in the future. Angela Merkel's welcome to Syrian refugees and her refusal to contemplate an upper limit increasingly has come under criticism from within Germany and from Germany's neighborhood states with the danger of splitting the coalition over her plans to build 'transit camps'. Meanwhile, the E.U. has backed an action plan by Turkey to stem the influx promising to re-energize talks on joining the E.U. Many of the E.U. member states have started to raise the issue of increased welfare costs by incoming refugees, especially in areas of education, health, and housing even though these are only a fraction of the cost borne by Syria's neighboring states of Jordan and Lebanon that have taken most of the 4 million plus refugees. A recent Save The Children report (2015) estimates almost 3 million Syrian children are out of school, commenting:

> Education can have a transformative effect on the futures of Syria's children, on economic growth and on stability in Syria and the wider region. Going to school equips children with the skills they need for life and it protects them: when they are in school they are less vulnerable to recruitment into armed groups, early marriage and child labour. Without substantial investment in, and support for, education, the prospects of a generation of Syrian children, and Syria's chance at a prosperous and peaceful future, are bleak. (n.p.)

In Lebanon, the number of Syrian school-aged children is reported to be greater than the number of Lebanese children enrolled in the public system. Even with the 'double system' – two shifts of schooling in one day – most Syrian children are missing out on schooling or have dropped out even in the refugee–host countries and now constitute the 'lost generation'.

Acknowledgement

This chapter was previously published as Michael A. Peters & Tina Besley, 'The Refugee Crisis and the Right to Political Asylum', *Educational Philosophy and Theory*, 47(13–14), 2015, 1367–1374 and is reprinted here with permission from the copyright holder (Michael A. Peters).

Notes

1 See http://www.newadvent.org/cathen/13430a.htm
2 See http://oll.libertyfund.org/pages/1793-french-republic-constitution-of-1793
3 See http://www.unhcr.org/pages/49da0e466.html
4 See http://www.unhcr.org/3b5e90ea0.html

5 See for instance some the current research papers from the Refugee Studies Center at Oxford University at http://www.rsc.ox.ac.uk/publications

6 According to the UNHCR, the number of displaced people worldwide reached 59.6 million at the end of 2014, of which some 14.4 million were refugees. See http://www.nytimes.com/interactive/2015/06/09/world/migrants-global-refugee-crisis-mediterranean-ukraine-syria-ro hingya-malaysia-iraq.html?_r=0

7 See http://www.rsc.ox.ac.uk/publications

8 Frontex is the European Agency for the Management of Operational Cooperation at the External Borders of the Member States of the European Union. See its annual report at http://frontex.europa.eu/assets/Publications/Risk_Analysis/Annual_Risk_Analysis_2015.pdf# page=59

9 See http://ec.europa.eu/eurostat/statistics-explained/index.php/Asylum_statistics. This report also recorded the four major legal instruments that the E.U. has developed since 1999 to work toward creating a common legal framework including: the Qualification Directive 2011/95/E.U. on standards for the qualification of non-E.U. nationals and stateless persons; the Procedures Directive 2013/32/E.U. on common procedures for granting and withdrawing international protection; the Conditions Directive 2013/33/E.U. laying down standards for the reception of applicants for international protection; the Dublin Regulation (E.U.) 604/2013 establishing the criteria and mechanisms for determining Member State responsibility for examining an application for international protection lodged in one of the Member States by a third-country national (national of a non-member country) or stateless person.

10 See Patrick Boehler and Sergio Peçanha (26 August 2015), 'The Global Refugee Crisis, Region by Region", http://www.nytimes.com/interactive/2015/06/09/world/migrants-global-refugee-crisis-mediterranean-ukraine-syria-rohingya-malaysia-iraq.html?_r=0

11 The UNHRC report: 'Since 2014, approximately 94,000 refugees and migrants are estimated to have departed by sea from Bangladesh or Myanmar, including 31,000 departures in the first half of 2015'. See also, the timeline of events detailing those abandoned at sea http://www.unhcr.org/554c6a746.html

12 See Taylor's (2015) account at http://thediplomat.com/2015/07/australia-and-the-southeast-asia-refugee-crisis/

13 See http://www.migrationpolicy.org/article/mexican-immigrants-united-states

14 See http://www.pewhispanic.org/2012/04/23/net-migration-from-mexico-falls-to-zero-and-perhaps-less/

15 Victor Orban, Hungary's PM has erected a fence along it Serbian border, employed the army to police it and gone on record to say Hungary's Christian heritage is at risk'. See Chris Morris' blog http://www.bbc.com/news/blogs-eu-34,144,554

16 See http://www.unhcr.org/cgi-bin/texis/vtx/refdaily?pass=52fc6fbd5&date=2015-07–15&cat= Europe; see also the so-called Schengen Area, that is 26 countries of

the E.U. that have abolished passport and internal border controls for international travel purposes.
17 See also Philosophies of Migration' at https://www.opendemocracy.net/5050/jennifer-allsopp/philosophies-of-migration
18 See Guibernau's (2010) paper at http://www.policy-network.net/publications_list.aspx?Page=12. See also 'Islam and the End of European Multiculturalism', Michael Peters and Tina Besley (2014), Special Issue in *Policy Futures in Education*, Editorial at http://pfe. sagepub.com/content/12/1/1.full.pdf+html, and Besley and Peters (2012).

References

Achhiron, M. (2001). A 'timeless' treaty under attack. *Refugees, 2*, 6–8. Retrieved from http://www.unhcr.org/3b5e90ea0.html

Ambrosini, M., & Van Der Leun, J. (2015). Introduction to the special issue: Implementing human rights: Civil society and migration policies. *Journal of Immigrant & Refugee Studies, 13*, 103–115.

Besley, T., & Peters, M. (2012). *Interculturalism, education and dialogue*. New York, NY: Peter Lang.

Bloch, A., & Chimienti, M. (2012). *Irregular migrants: Policy, politics, motives and everyday lives*. London: Routledge.

Engbersen, G., & Broeders, D. (2009). The state versus the alien: Immigration control and strategies of irregular migrants. *West European Politics, 32*, 867–885.

Faist, T. (2013). The mobility turn: A new paradigm for the social sciences? *Ethnic and Racial Studies, 36*, 1637–1646.

Guiberau, M. (2010). *Migration and the rise of the radical right*. Retrieved from http://www.policy-network.net/publications_list.aspx?Page=9

Mora, C., & Handmaker, J. (2014). Migrants citizenship and rights: Limits and potential for NGOs advocacy in Chile. In T. D. Truong, D. Gasper, D. J. Handmaker, & S. I. Bergh (Eds.), *Migration, gender and social justice: Perspectives on human insecurity* (pp. 281–290). New York, NY: Springer.

Peters, M., & Besley, T. (2014). Islam and the end of European multiculturalism [Special Issue]. *Policy Futures in Education, 12*(1). Retrieved from http://pfe.sagepub.com/content/12/1/1.full.pdf+html

Save the Children. (2015). *The cost of war: Calculating the impact of the collapse of Syria's education system on Syria's future*. Retrieved from http://www.savethechildren.org.uk/sites/default/files/images/The_Cost_of_War.pdf

Torpey, J. (2000). States and the regulation of migration in the twentieth-century North Atlantic world. In P. Andreas & T. Snyder (Eds.), *The wall around the west: State borders and immigration controls in North America and Europe* (pp. 31–54). Lanham, MD: Rowman & Littlefield.

Wellman, C. H. (2010). Immigration. In E. N. Zalta (Ed.), *The Stanford encyclopedia of philosophy*. Retrieved from http://plato.stanford.edu/archives/sum2015/entries/immigration/

Zetter, R. (2015). *Protection in crisis: Forced migration and protection in a global era*. Washington, DC: Migration Policy Institute. Retrieved from http://www.migrationpolicy.org

CHAPTER 10

The Refugee Crisis in Europe
Words without Borders

Introduction

This chapter speaks to the refugee crisis in Europe on the basis of personal observation by the authors, who travelled around Europe visiting Vienna, Budapest, and various cities in France and Sweden in late 2015. It uses some poetry to convey aspects of the crisis, including belonging, homelessness, and the experience of being a refugee. It reviews and comments on the rise of the Right and the closing of borders as the number of refugees in Europe spills over the one million mark, making it the largest migration since World War II. It is estimated that roughly half the refugees are Syrians who are displaced and have been living in camps in Turkey, Lebanon, and Jordon. We pose the question: What are the responsibilities of the West to education and health beyond borders?

> "Managing international migration is not a matter of controlling borders; it is a question of transnational peace". Bardakci, S. (2015, August 26). Ibrahim Sirkeci interview: 'Bu göçün artıları olabilir', Al Jazeera Turkish. Available at: http://www.aljazeera.com.tr/haber/bu-gocunartilari-olabilir (Bardakci, cited in Yazgan et al., 2015)

'Refugee Blues', by W.H. Auden

Say this city has ten million souls,
Some are living in mansions, some are living in holes:
Yet there's no place for us, my dear, yet there's no place for us.

Once we had a country and we thought it fair,
Look in the atlas and you'll find it there:
We cannot go there now, my dear, we cannot go there now.

W.H. Auden's poem 'Refugee Blues' is a poem written about the experience of being a German Jew during the Holocaust. Utilizing the blues genre and making a series of variations on the theme Auden broadens his 'argument' to Jews and

© PETER LANG, 2017 | DOI:10.1163/9789004380776_010

refugees everywhere.[1] In his 1949 essay 'Cultural Criticism and Society' Adorno famously suggest that in the final stage of the dialect of culture and barbarism 'To write poetry after Auschwitz is barbaric' by which Adorno meant to draw attention to the fact that the same culture that produced Auschwitz now produces poetry to memorialize the Holocaust renders cultural criticism unthinkable. Today as Europe faces the Syrian refugee crisis, the largest mass migration since the end of World War II, it seems pertinent to raise this issue again; and yet poetry speaks to us in a way that news reports cannot.

Traveling from Vienna to Budapest in mid-September 2015, we were caught up in the refugee crisis. The trains were cancelled for a day and we had to find alternative transport by bus. The buses weren't running on time, either. When we finally boarded the bus and started on the journey, we came to realise that traffic from Budapest to Vienna had been stopped, and there was a buildup of cars and trucks many kilometres long. Many refugees streamed along the side of the road with few possessions (only what they could carry) and no provisions. There were many thousands. We had never seen such a stream of humanity straggling along a highway that stretched such a huge distance, kilometre after kilometre. These people walk, walk, walk. They carry their children. They assist their old people.

From 'A Mother in a Refugee Camp', by Chinua Achebe

The air was heavy with odors of diarrhea,
Of unwashed children with washed-out ribs
And dried-up bottoms waddling in labored steps
Behind blown-empty bellies. Other mothers there
Had long ceased to care, but not this one:
She held a ghost-smile between her teeth,
And in her eyes the memory
Of a mothers pride ...

We stayed in Budapest for about 10 days. Hungary is a country that has decided to close its borders, sealing off its southern border with Croatia and diverting refugees to Slovenia. Hungary has built a large steel fence almost the entire length of the border "to secure its borders to protect what it calls the prosperity, security and 'Christian values' of Europe". Viktor Orbán, the Prime Minister, is fiercely antiimmigration. When we were there he had closed down Hungary's border with Serbia, forcing thousands of refugees to find alternative routes. Estimates indicate that, at that time, some 5,000-plus migrants per day were trying to find a route through Hungary to preferred destinations in Germany and Austria. The Hungarian police have used water canons, batons, and tear gas on migrants and made it clear that they do not want Muslims in their country. Some estimates suggest that between 800,000 and one million migrants will reach Europe this year. The situation is dangerous and frightening, especially for small refugee children.

One of the consequences of this ongoing migration into Europe is the rise of anti-immigration political parties throughout Europe – the Danish People's Party, the Swedish Democrats, and parties in Finland and Norway, not to mention France's National Front, the Dutch Party of Freedom, Italy's Lega Nord, Greece's Golden Dawn, and the Austrian Freedom Party. The backlash against immigration has begun in earnest, with arguments about national identity, Christian values, and national unity against multiculturalism and specifically against Muslim immigrants.

From 'Home', by Warsan Shire

You have to understand that no one puts their children in a boat unless the water is safer than the land ... no one chooses refugee camps or strip searches where your body is left aching or prison, because prison is safer than a city of fire and one prison guard in the night is better than a truckload of men who look like your father.

The number of forcibly displaced people worldwide is some 59.5 million. According to the UN Refugee Agency (UNHCR), there were '*19.5 million refugees* worldwide at the end of 2014, 14.4 million under the mandate of UNHCR, around 2.9 million more than in 2013'.[2] This is the highest level of displacement of people in the history of the world. UNHCR reports that at least 1.66 million people submitted applications for asylum in 2014, the highest level ever recorded.

The Syrian crisis is an unprecedented historical example of the refugee problem, with more than 4 million leaving the country since the civil war began in 2011 – most fleeing to Turkey, Lebanon, and Jordan. The war followed the Arab Spring uprisings in Tunisia, Egypt, Libya, and Iraq, with Syrians taking to the streets to oppose Bashar El-Assad's administration. Within Syria there are an estimated 7.5 million displaced persons. The Syrian crisis represents one of the largest forced migrations since World War II.[3] What began as a trickle became a torrent this year as Syrian asylum seekers fled to Europe, with roughly half the estimated 800,000 migrants being Syrian refugees. But most are too poor to flee, especially considering the costs of people smuggling.[4] The Syrian exodus has been brought about by a loss of hope concerning the civil war (now in its fifth year with no hope of resolution). In this period the cost of living has soared, and poverty has deepened; there are limited opportunities for work; aid shortfalls have increasingly made life in the camps more difficult; education for children is almost non-existent or has only recently begun to be institutionalised.[5] There is talk of the 'lost generation'. David Miliband reports that more Syrian refugees currently live in Istanbul (some 366,000), and he attributes the roots of the crisis to 'the tumultuous convulsions inside significant parts of the Islamic world'.[6]

From 'When I am Overcome by Weakness', by Najat Abdul Samad (Translated by Ghada Alatrash)

When I am overcome with weakness, I bandage my heart with a woman's patience in adversity. I bandage it with the upright posture of a Syrian woman who is not bent by bereavement, poverty, or displacement as she rises from the banquets of death and carries on shepherding life's rituals. She prepares for a creeping, ravenous winter and gathers the heavy firewood branches, stick by stick from the frigid wilderness. She does not cut a tree, does not steal, does not surrender her soul to weariness, does not ask anyone's charity, does not fold with the load, and does not yield midway.

Pinar Yazgan, Deniz Eroglu Utku, and Ibrahim Sirkeci (2015), in their article "Syrian Crisis and Migration" (*Migration Letters*, 12[3], 181–192), embrace a conflict culture of migration model:

> all human mobility is due to some kind of a conflict. Conflict is defined in a very broad sense which includes latent tensions and disagreements on the one end and goes to armed and violent clashes (e.g. wars) on the other. This is to say, migration is initiated by discomforts, difficulties, restrictions, clashes, and finally violence and wars at the country of origin. People only decide to move when they see that given conflict as a threat, an environment of insecurity, which is unmanageable. This also allows us to factor in potential conflicts that arise as people move from one place to another, including the transit areas. Thus migration changes in response to these new challenges en route and in destinations. This is the dynamic nature of human mobility, which can be helpful to under-

stand why suddenly so many Syrians are also desperate to leave Turkey, a country that welcomed them in millions in the first place. (p. 182)

The authors cast aspersions on the distinction between 'refugee' and 'economic migrant', arguing that

> the root causes in Syria are unlikely to disappear soon. Long before the current violence, this was a country of multifaceted problems: unemployment, income inequality, suppression of minorities, suppression of opposition are just a few issues to name. If one wants economic drivers for migration, the average GDP per capita in Syria has been about a third of – or less – than in Turkey, and about a tenth of the averages in most European countries. This means even without the current violence, there were adequate reasons for many Syrians to leave. The violence is perhaps providing an opportunity framework to facilitate the process. We should also not forget that the conflict migration is not a Syrian problem, it is a widespread issue and the responses to this must be transnational and comprehensive in nature. (p. 183)

From 'I am a Refugee', by Mohamed Raouf Bachir[7] (Translated by Thomas Aplin)

I knocked on Arab doors
The sheikhs, the emirs and the kings
All chased me away;
I came to you.
Will you accept me among you
As a refugee?

My daughters in exile disowned me
In my eighties.
They fought against me;
I have no one left but you.
Will you accept me among you
As a refugee?

My family, my daughters, my kin,
All of them sold me out;
They pilfered my life and forgot me;

> They uprooted me and left me to wither at the embassy gates.
> Foreigner, will you accept me
> As a refugee?
>
> Wretched are the joy
> And servility of thanking ones masters,
> And the fools of my nation,
> And my daughters,
> And the criminals who drove me away,
> And burned down my home.
> I have fled their tyranny
> To become a refugee among you.

What are the Western world's, and particularly Europe's, responsibilities to refugees and migrants? The truism that the planet Earth is one interconnected functioning whole – a self-regulating complex system – has various environmental, cybernetic, and political readings. Earth system science provides some evidence for the regulation of the biosphere to support the conditions for life. The 'global brain' is another such metaphor for an interconnected ICT network linking human collective or distributive intelligence as a kind of planetary nervous system that emerges as self-organized dynamic semiotic networks in which everything speaks. The political reading adds another dimension that we might call 'cosmopolitanism', with its philosophical roots in Ancient Greece and its juridical notion of a single community based on a shared morality and cosmopolitan law or right anchored in an extended hospitality.

One part of this shared understanding among these different systems is the notion of equilibrium and equalization that operates on the principle that changes in one part of the system are caused by related changes in other parts. This rudimentary notion of equilibrium or homeostasis is a way of charting the dynamic nature of systems that evolve in unpredictable ways. *Liberal internationalism* provides an account of an evolving globalization that is based on universal values of *free movement* – the free movement of capital, of trade, and of people, where asylum is granted to refugees fleeing persecution. The free movement of people has an economic interpretation based on the analysis of labor requirements, in addition to the political rights of people. Asylum is seen as a fundamental right that is philosophically linked to the notion of free movement and also to notions of security and justice pointing to the control of external borders. While in the past freedom of movement and residence for persons in the E.U. has been the cornerstone of E.U. citizenship, which was established by the Treaty of Maastricht in 1992, its practical implementation in

E.U. law is now at a critical point, and there are cracks in the policy and in its implementation that threaten the right to asylum.

Cosmopolitanism and the philosophy of migration are based on freedom of movement, seen by the E.U. as encouraging tolerance and understanding among people of different cultures, helping to break down harmful stereotypes and prejudices, and building solidarity between people and governments of different countries. The European Union embodies the ethic of an open society, including values of equality, respect for human rights, democracy, and the rule of law. Member states have recognized that they are interdependent and use the E.U. to cooperate to achieve a greater, collective good. But what does it mean outside the E.U., and what does the right to political asylum entail? In these circumstances we also have to ask: What are the responsibilities of the West to education and health beyond borders? Ethics and universal values do not stop at national borders – they are part of the motivation for strengthening global civil society and in this instance for educating the lost generation of Syrian children.

Acknowledgement

This chapter was previously published as Michael A. Peters and Tina Besley, 'The Refugee Crisis in Europe: Words without Borders', in Peter McLaren & Suzi Soohoo (Eds.) 2017, *Radical Imagine-Nation*, 2017, pp. 191–198, Peter Lang, New York, and is reprinted here with permission from Peter Lang.

Notes

1 Hear Auden's poem set to original blues music by Ted Slowik at https://www.youtube.com/watch?v=krubUqbYslc
2 See http://www.unhcr.org.uk/about-us/key-facts-and-figures.html
3 See "Refuge: 18 Stories from the Syrian Exodus," at http://www.washingtonpost.com/sf/syrian-refugees/story/refuge/
4 See https://www.washingtonpost.com/world/most-syrian-refugees-are-just-too-poorto-flee-to-europe/2015/09/30/06cb785a-673a-11e5-9ef3-fde182507eac_story.html
5 See http://www.unhcr.org/560523f26.html
6 See http://www.theguardian.com/world/2015/oct/27/istanbul-has-more-syrian-refugees-than-all-of-europe-says-david-miliband
7 http://www.wordswithoutborders.org/article/i-am-a-refugee

CHAPTER 11

From State Responsibility for Education and Welfare to Self-Responsibilisation in the Market

Introduction

This chapter profiles the term 'responsibilization' as a term adopted from Foucault to describe the shift from the state to the individual as a consequence of privatization of social welfare. Now market-like arrangements emphasize customer-related forms of assessment and the state encourages a new moral economy that focuses on individual responsibility. Often the term 'responsibilization' is associated with Foucault's analysis of neoliberal governmentality, though not exclusively. Foucault provides a nunaced reading that comes from naturalizing and historicizing Kant and thereby also emphasizing some continuity between liberalism with its accent on individual autonomy and neoliberalism that also emphasizes individuality and rationality from within a perspective that focuses on self-interest where greater good is a result of the 'invisible hand'. Sometimes the term has been used by others embracing Ulrich Beck's concept of the 'risk society' and an analysis of the neoliberal State that has been privatizing and individualizing social provision through the use of market-like arrangements through contracting-out, public-private partnerships, user-pays, and other parallel mechanisms for the privatization of the social welfare state.

We demonstrate the analytical power of the concept of 'responsibilization' to analyse the shift from State responsibility under the old Keynesian welfare state to a responsibilization of teachers, students, and associated forms of discourse, accountability and assessment regimes. Currently market-like arrangements and a market rationality have been employed to responsibilize the individual and to naturalise regimes of self-care in neoliberal environments.

On one hand the focus of the twin themes of responsibility and responsibilisation seeks to disrupt the universalization of responsibilization as a practice and universal characterization of education. There is still room for further theoretical work here beyond its simple application especially in relation to the construction of student identities (Keddie, 2016). On the other hand we caution against conflating responsibility with responsibilization. These are different concepts that originate in different 'moral' traditions. While responsibilization is more of a neoliberal technology of the self that forces an individualism on society and exports responsibility from state to individual, it has not been taken up by all players in education, particularly young people and teachers. They teach us that responsibility remains central to interpersonal relations – how could we possibly escape it? – and that the matter of *who* is responsible cannot be excised from history or social context.

There is some consensus on the way market-like structures and social provision delivered through the market leads to individualization and privatization of both welfare and the self. Ronen Shamir (2008, p. I) comments on the nature of market-embedded rationality:

> Generally recognized and referred to in terms of privatization, deregulation, structural adjustment and corporatization, the economization of the political transforms the very instruments of public authority, replacing laws with guidelines, relying on selfand reflexive-regulation and treating normative prescriptions in general as commodities that are to be produced, distributed and consumed by a host of agencies, enterprises and non-profit organizations.

As he goes on to explain, commercial enterprises progressively take on tasks that 'were once considered to reside within the civic domain of moral entrepreneurship and the political domain of the caring welfare state, dispensing social goods other than profits to constituencies other than their shareholders' (Shamir, 2008). In this regard we can cite the case of Serco, an international service company that operates in public service markets around the world with 100,000 employees in over thirty countries, a company that is active in both Australia and New Zealand especially in running private prisons at a profit.[1]

Shamir (2008) discusses the moralization of markets that also 'entails the economization of morality; a process which is compatible with the general neo-liberal drive to ground social relations in the economic rationality of markets' (p. 3). Responsibilization is one of the major strategies and practices of a neoliberal moralization of markets that shifts responsibility from the State (the so-called welfare State) to the citizen – the user of social services, the citizen-consumer, the client such as students, pensioners, beneficaries – and to professionals who are 'responsible' for providing the service.

In the new market environment the figure of the entrepreneur becomes paramount in understanding the rise of a new individualism that strips away all collective value and responsibilizes the individual to take care of themselves through enhanced choice-making in the market place. In these new arrangements the State forces responsibility, a responsibilization, back on the individual, on families and on professionals, as it steps back from active social provision to devise juridical frameworks that set up the rules governing social distribution, and set criteria for their continual monitoring and performativity.

The concept of 'responsibilization' that originally emerged out of the context of the so-called 'Governmentality Studies' is now widely used in various social sciences to describe a governing technology particularly attuned to the challenge of neoliberalism and focused on the central question of how to govern free individuals that relies heavily on individual choice, freedom and responsibility.

In the Sage *Dictionary of Policing*, Pat O'Malley, one of the leading Australian neo-Foucaudian theorists, defines responsibilization as:

> ... a term developed in the governmentality literature to refer to the process whereby subjects are rendered individually responsible for a task which previously would have been the duty of another – usually a state agency – or would not have been recognized as a responsibility at all. The process is strongly associated with neoliberal political discourses, where it takes on the implication that the subject being responsibilized has avoided this duty or the responsibility has been taken away from them in the welfare-state era and managed by an expert or government agency. (p. 276)

He explains that the term surfaces first in the 1990s governmentality literature to describe the neoliberal assumption that the old welfare state has robbed citizens of their independence and made them dependent on the state. The neoliberal strategy was used to reverse this process, to make subjects responsible for themselves and to take responsibility for governing themselves and their lives. This reversal of responsibility is often dressed up in the catch words 'no rights without obligations'. He details the application of the responsibilization strategy in the field of criminal justice by making subjects more cautious of becoming victims, instituting government-community programs like neighbourhood watch, turning the public into crime reporters, vigilantes and surveillance operators, and holding offenders themselves as responsible for their actions through tougher penalties but also community consultations with their victims.

O'Malley reviews the critique of the neoliberal strategy as 'victim blaming' as the State devolves its responsibilities. He also points out that responsibilization does find willing supporters from both Left and Right which criticize the state and look for greater citizen involvement, control and responsibility.

Neoliberal governmentality is a pragmatic evolving form of post-welfare state politics in which the state systematically downscales its responsibilities outsourcing 'well-being' and social security to its citizen-subjects in the market, emphasizing the concept of 'choice'. The subject, according to neoliberalism, is theorised as a rational autonomous individual in all its behaviour – *Homo economicus* ('economic man') that is expected to 'look after herself' modelled on assumptions of individuality, rationality and self-interest. These highly abstract assumptions of *Homo economicus* reveal the limitations of a kind of economic rationality that does not take into account gender, collective dimensions or cultural variation in everyday economic management and decision-making of households and groups.

Somewhat curiously in some ways this argument gels with arguments mounted in the 1960s and 1970s that were a critique of state power as exercised through big centralised institutions. Arguments concerning deinstitutionalization alongside arguments for community devolution and control were being proposed by Ivan Illich, Michel Foucault and David Cooper in fields of mental health, medicine, and education ('deschooling'). Under neoliberalism State power and authority is rejigged in terms of the marketplace where the citizen subject is provided a kind of freedom through making consumer choices in the marketplace for all aspects of social welfare and provision.

The central aim of neoliberal governmentality ('the conduct of conduct') is the manufacture of social conditions that encourage and necessitate the production of *Homo economicus*, as a historically specific form of subjectivity constituted as a free and autonomous individual of self-interest and based on the following three assumption: the classical liberal assumptions of individuality and rationality, and the assumption of self-interest developed through the work of Adam Smith. The neoliberal subject is thus an individual who is transparent to itself and morally responsible for navigating the social realm using rational choice and cost-benefit calculations – a new kind of prudentialism or actuarial rationality – grounded on market-based principles to the exclusion of all other ethical values and social interests.

Homo economicus is no longer a partner in exchange but as Foucault writes 'Homo economicus is an entrepreneur, an entrepreneur of himself' (Foucault, 2008, p. 226). Trent Hamann (2009) argues:

> the central aim of neoliberal governmentality is the strategic production of social conditions conducive to the constitution of Homo economicus, a specific form of subjectivity with historical roots in traditional liberalism. However, whereas liberalism posits 'economic man' as a 'man of exchange', neoliberalism strives to ensure that individuals are compelled to assume market-based values in all of their judgments and practices in order to amass sufficient quantities of 'human capital' and thereby

become 'entrepreneurs of themselves'. Neoliberal Homo economicus is a free and autonomous "atom" of self-interest who is fully responsible for navigating the social realm using rational choice and cost-benefit calculation to the express exclusion of all other values and interests.

The construction of *Homo economicus* leads to a double strategy of the economization of state and civil society institutions and the moralization of the market where the primary shift in responsibility is away from the State – a State-shedding of responsibility while retaining the power to strike norms of assessment and control – toward the private sector in all areas of social provision including pensions, welfare, health and education. Responsibilization thus functions as a technique for the self-management and self-regulation of social risks such as illness, unemployment and poverty (Lemke, 2001).

There is then a 'new prudentialism' in education. Prudentialization results when education is addressed to the entrepreneurial self, or the 'responsibilized' self who must make choices regarding his or her own welfare based on actuarial rationality (Peters, 2006). Such prudentialization seeks to 'insure' the individual against risk in a context where the state has transferred risk to the individual. The role of social prudentialism in education has encouraged a shift in forms of social insurance through education from one welfare regime. The promotion of the entrepreneurial self represents a shift away from a rights-based welfare model of the citizen to a citizen-consumer model based on the rejuvenation of *Homo economicus*, where individuals calculate the risks and invest in themselves at critical points in the life cycle.

The key elements of the risk-management program grow out of the shift from the Keynesian welfare state and compulsory social insurance to neoliberalism (or the culture of consumption) and a form of private insurance constructed through choice. Within this new regime (re/de)regulation represents an intensive juridification, a legal liberation and optimism based upon confidence in rules. On this model the well-governed society is committed to the coherence of a framework of rules, a codification, which allows the government to step back more and more from actual involvement in state activities, which now devolve to agencies, institutions, or regions.

Government assumes the metaposition of rule-maker. In this political environment the economic, constitutional, and legal or juridical forms of advanced liberalism overlap to construct the citizen-consumer. Increasingly, alongside the empowerment of consumers – simultaneously their individualization and their responsibilization is a belief in the efficacy of rules and a distrust of professionals. These knowledges and discourses grew up with the welfare state a fact evident in the role of the nineteenth-century census as an instrument of governmentality and came to have an independent existence over time. Understood as a risk-management regime, neoliberalism involves the distrust of expert knowledges, especially those traditionally associated with the welfare state such as the expertise of social workers and teachers. Under neoliberalism the trend has been toward creating a uniform structure of expert knowledges that is based on the calculating sciences of actuarialism and accountancy (thus explaining the label 'the audit society'). 'The social' is promoted as that which is capable of being governed, for example, the regulation of 'the poor'. 'Work' and 'unemployment' have in this way become fundamental modern categories of social regulation. In this sense neoliberalism can be seen as an intensification of moral regulation resulting from the radical withdrawal of government and the responsibilization of individuals through economics. It emerges as an actuarial form of governance that promotes an actuarial rationality through encouraging a political regime of ethical self-constitution as consumer-citizens.

'Responsibilization' refers to modern forms of self-government that require individuals to make choices about lifestyles, their bodies, their education, and their health at critical points in the life cycle, such as giving birth, starting school, going to university, taking a first job, getting married, and retiring. 'Choice' assumes a much wider role under neoliberalism: it is not simply 'consumer sovereignty' but rather a moralization and responsibilization, a regulated transfer of choice-making responsibility from the state to the individual in the social market.

This shift means we have passed from an ontology of the self as producer, which characterized the era of Left politics and the welfare state, to an ontology of *self as consumer*, which now characterizes politics of the Right, the neoliberal market economy, and the provision of public services. This shift can be characterized in terms of a symbolic economy of the self that involves a set of related processes of self-capitalization, self-presentation, self-promotion, self-branding, and self-virtualization as market processes having political, ethical, and aesthetic elements. We might follow Foucault's lead and focus on processes of political, ethical, and aesthetic self-constitution through making choices that involve the purchase of goods and services and, in some cases, longer-term investment decisions.

A genealogy of the entrepreneurial self reveals that it is a relation that one establishes with oneself through forms of personal investment (including education, viewed as an investment) and insurance that become the central ethical and political components of a new individualized, customized, and privatized consumer welfare economy. In this novel form of governance, responsibilized individuals are called upon to apply certain managerial, economic, and actuarial techniques to themselves as citizen-consumer subjects calculating the risks and returns on investment in such areas as education, health, employment, and retirement. This process is both self-constituting and self-consuming. It is self-constituting in the Foucauldian sense that the choices we make shape us as moral, economic, and political agents. It is self-consuming in the sense that the entrepreneurial self creates and constructs him or herself through acts of consumption.

Neoliberalism uses the model of line management to insert a hierarchical mode of authority by which the market and state pressures can be instituted. For teachers this carries with it the effect of de-professionalization, involving a shift from collegial or forms of democratic governance in flat structures, to hierarchical models based on dictated management *specifications* of job performance in chains of command. The implementation of restructuring initiatives in response to market and state demands involves increasing specifications by management over workloads and course content by management. Such hierarchically imposed specifications erode traditional conceptions of professional autonomy over work in relation to both teaching and research. Neoliberalism systematically deconstructs the space in terms of which professional autonomy is exercised.

Traditional conceptions of professionalism involved an ascription of rights and powers over work in line with classical liberal notions of freedom of the individual. Market pressures increasingly encroach and redesign their traditional understandings of rights, so educational institutions must adapt to market trends (for example, just as individual departments and academics are being told of the necessity for acquiring external research grants, so they are also being told they must teach summer schools). The essence of contractual models involves a *specification*, which is fundamentally at odds with the notion of *professionalism*. *Professionalism* conveys the idea of a subject directed power based upon the liberal conceptions of rights, freedom and autonomy. It conveys the idea of a power given to the subject, and of the subject's ability to make decisions in the workplace. No professional, whether doctor, lawyer or teacher, has traditionally wanted to have the terms of their practice and conduct dictated by anyone else but their peers, or determined by groups or structural levers that are outside of their control. As a particular patterning of power, then, professionalism is systematically at odds with neoliberalism, for neoliberals see the professions as self-interested groups who indulge in rent-seeking behaviour. In neoliberalism the patterning of power is established on contract, which in turn is premised upon a need for compliance, monitoring, and accountability organized in a management line and established through a purchase contract based upon measurable outputs.

Like we said in the Introduction, there are four contemporary accontability regimes. There has been an observable tendency in Western liberal states to emphasize both agency and consumer forms at the expense of professional and democratic forms, especially where countries are involved in large-scale shifts from traditional Keynesian welfare state regimes to more market-oriented and consumer-driven systems. indeed, it could be argued that there are natural affinities by way of shared concepts, understandings and operational procedures between these two couplets. One of the main criticisms to have emerged is that the agency/consumer couplet instrumentalizes, individualizes, standardizes, marketizes and externalizes accountability relationships at the expense of democratic values such as participation, self-regulation, collegiality, and collective deliberation that are said to enhance and thicken the relationships involved.

There has been an observable tendency in Western liberal states to emphasize both agency and consumer forms at the expense of professional and democratic forms, especially where countries are involved in large-scale shifts from traditional Keynesian welfare state regimes to more market-oriented and consumer-driven systems. Indeed, it could be argued that there are natural affinities by way of shared concepts, understandings and operational procedures between these two couplets. One of the main criticisms to have emerged is that the agency/consumer couplet instrumentalizes, individualizes, standardizes, marketizes and externalizes accountability relationships at the expense of democratic values such as participation, self-regulation, collegiality, and collective deliberation that are said to enhance and thicken the relationships involved.

We provide here a nuanced and sophisticated reading of forms of 'responsibilization' taking place in education broadly conceived and the manufacture of different forms of subjectivity that are morally selfconstituting through the mechanism of choice within current neoliberal environments. It has to be said that State responsibilization for welfare was a political achievement based on the power of trade unions and working people. It did not 'devolve' all power to the State to encourage an overweening sense of dependency but at its best emphasized a citizen active participation within State provided social and public infrastructures that led to what we might call today the co-creation and co-production of social goods. The dependency story beat-up is part of a neoliberal take that emphasizes the way that the welfare state robbed economic liberalism of it vitality. By substituting the market and employing the moral vocabulary of individual choice-making neoliberals have reinvented subjectivity and the market in moral terms that allows a shrinking state and a kind of parallel privatization that increasingly sees the like of Serco and other private sector companies taking over the responsibility for running what used to be public institutions. The logic of public-private partnerships further drives this strategy more deeply into the social fabric. Yet the basic forms of citizen participation and active co-production at the heart of social democracy remains a clear and viable option for the provision of welfare and social security.

Acknowledgement

This chapter was previously published as Michael A. Peters, 'From State Responsibility for Education and Welfare to Self-Responsibilization in the Market', *Discourse: Studies in the Cultural Politics of Education*, 38(1), 2017, 138–145 and is reprinted here with permission from Taylor & Francis (https://www.tandfonline.com/loi/cdis20).

Note

1 See the recent public uproar at Serco's running of Mt Eden prison in Auckland with $1.5 million in anticipated penalty fines for various offences – http://www.radionz.co.nz/news/political/284397/minster-says-sercos-55breaches-fair. For Serco see https://www.serco.com/ where it advertises its welfare business in education, healthcare, environmental services, justice and immigration, prisons and the like.

References

Foucault, M. (2008). *The birth of biopolitics: Lectures at the Collège de France, 1978–1979* (G. Burchell, Trans.). New York, NY: Palgrave Macmillan.

Hamann, T. (2009). Neoliberalism, governmentality, and ethics. *Foucault Studies*, 6, 37–59. Retrieved from http://rauli.cbs.dk/index.php/foucault-studies/article/view/2471

Keddie, A. (2016). Children of the market: Performativity, neoliberal responsibilisation and the construction of student identities. *Oxford Review of Education*, 42(1), 108–122. doi:10.1080/03054985.2016.1142865

Lemke, T. (2001). The birth of bio-politics: Michel Foucault's lecture at the Collège de France on neo-liberal governmentality. *Economy and Society*, 30(2), 190–207.

O'Malley, P. (1992). Risk, power and crime prevention. *Economy and Society*, 21(3), 252–276.

O'Malley, P. (2009). Responsibilization. In A. Wakefield & J. Flemming (Eds.), *Sage dictionary of policing* (pp. 276–277). London: Sage Publications.

O'Malley, P., & Palmer, D. (1996). Post-Keynesian policing. *Economy and Society, 25*(2), 137–155.

Peters, M. A. (2001). Education, enterprise culture and the entrepreneurial self: A Foucauldian perspective. *Journal of Educational Enquiry, 2*(2), 58–71.

Peters, M. A. (2005). The new prudentialism in education: Actuarial rationality and the entrepreneurial self. *Educational Theory, 55*(2), 123–137.

Shamir, R. (2008). The age of responsibilization: On market-embedded morality. *Economy and Society, 37*(1), 1–19.

CHAPTER 12

Pedagogies of the Walking Dead

Diminishing Responsibility for Social Justice in a Neoliberal World

Introduction: Zombie Theory

> Such behavior [this silencing] is terrorist. ... not content with negative obedience, nor even with the most abject submission. When you do finally surrender to us, it must be of your own free will. (Jean-Francois Lyotard, *The Postmodern Condition*)

This chapter reviews the growth of 'zombie theory' in the West to ask both what it signifies and how it radically departs from the 1960s and 1970s when radical pedagogy based on Paulo Freire and critical thought provided a sense of public hope and agency. The chapter also argues that teachers have been 'responsiblized' and held accountable for all sorts of social outcomes while the state has retreated in terms of support. Ultimately this process has robbed teachers of their confidence and de-professionalized them as mere conduits of neoliberal knowledge and skills.

In popular culture zombies are now suddenly ubiquitous. There are films, TV shows e.g. the National Geographic Channel shows The Truth Behind Zombies, video games, books, pub crawls and organized zombie themed events such as zombie walks', zombie runs, and zombie hunts where people dress up as act as zombies for fun for a short time. 'Even saying you "feel like a zombie" has specific meanings – we conjure images of slovenly or sluggish appearance or behavior' (Cook, 2013, https://contexts.org/articles/the-cultural-life-of-the-living-dead/). Marketing campaigns in USA (Doritos, FedEx, Starburst, Converse, and Chevrolet) picked up the zombie theme and the Centers for Disease Control (CDC)'s tongue-in-cheek disaster preparedness campaign slogan was:

> "If you're ready for a zombie apocalypse, then you're ready for any emergency". ... By the mere creation of the CDC's zombie campaign, the government agency tells audiences that they should prep for a hurricane, too – it's just as likely to turn lives upside down as any zombie invasion. (Cook, 2013, https://contexts.org/articles/the-cultural-life-of-the-living-dead/)

A 'zombie' is from the Haitian French, from Haitian folklore to depict a dead body reanimated through magic, connoting fear, horror and a revulsion toward apathy and sloth. 'Zombie' was first recorded in 1819 in English by a poet in a history of Brazil. Literary antecedents that draw on European folklore of the undead include Mary Shelley's 1818 novel *Frankenstein*. There has been an upsurge of use of the subject in popular culture since the early 20th century such that zombie culture is found in horror and fantasy genres, e.g. a 1932 film directed by Victor Halperin, starring Bela Lugosi, *White Zombie's* plot saw Madeline reuniting with her fiancé Neil on arrival in Haiti. They meet Murder Legendre, a voodoo master. Neil enlists the help of Murder to persuade Madeline to marry him by turning her into a zombie. After the wedding she dies. After pushing Murder off a cliff Madeline is released from her zombie state. A 1968 film, *Night of the Living Dead*, became a cult classic and selected as a film of cultural significance by the National Film Registry. It drew on '*I am Legend*' a 1954 science fiction novel that popularized the idea of apocalypse due to disease. *Thriller*, the 1982 song, album and music video by Michael Jackson was added to the National Film Registry by the Library of Congress in 2009, the first music video ever selected. At fourteen minutes the video is substantially longer than the song. Its narrative featuring Jackson and actress Ola Ray in a setting heavily inspired by horror films of the 1950s features Michael Jackson leading an iconic dance with actors dressed as zombies. Despite some criticism for its occult theme and violent imagery, the video received high critical acclaim and remains immensely popular.

'The Walking Dead' is a U.S. TV series about a central character who awakens from a month's long coma to find an apocalyptic world overrun by flesh-eating zombies. The series is currently in its fifth season and had a strong critical reception and high ratings.[1] Hollywood is overrun by zombies and blood-sucking vampires.[2] One wonders why the U.S. has become a zombie-obsessed vampiric culture. One explanation proffered is that apocalytic fictional narratives like the 'Walking Dead' provide an opportunity to work through the trauma of the breakdown of ethical frameworks that were shattered as a result of World War II, or, perhaps, of the endless appetite for human violence demonstrated in a multipolar world with the rise of the non-state actor.[3] Zombie-ism has also been further titlilated by media stories of gruesome murders involving cannabilism.[4] Some argue these dramas are essentially about ourselves (what isn't?) – the dark side that emphasizes what happens when humanity loses its ethical way. Nicholas Barber (2013) of the BBC explains:

> It's now more than a decade since zombies began their relentless shuffle into the mainstream of popular culture .... By the time Brad Pitt's 'World War Z' was released in June, it seemed it was several years late to the party. Surely there was nothing new to be said about the undead? That tardi-

ness, along with reports of the films troubled production, suggested that 'World War Z' would die a death at the box office. Instead, it went on to rake in $540 m, making it one of 2013s ten biggest blockbusters ....

And zombie fever hasn't been confined to cinemas. A comic-book series with the same grisly antagonists, The 'Walking Dead', was launched in 2003, and was adapted into a television series in 2010 ....

To compare zombies to their rivals in the monster-movie pantheon, vampires and werewolves symbolise the thrill and the romance of having superhuman strength and no conscience – hence the 'Twilight' and 'True Blood' franchises. But there's nothing glamorous about being a zombie. Unlike vampires and werewolves, they're not frightening because of how powerful they are. They're frightening because of how dismal it would be to become one yourself. Another difference is that werewolves and vampires are content to share the planet with the rest of us.

He goes on to speculate:

> It can't be a coincidence, then, that zombies are in vogue during a period when banks are failing, when climate change is playing havoc with weather patterns, and when both terrorist bombers and global corporations seem to be beyond the reach of any country's jurisdiction. It can't be a coincidence, either, that the fourth season of 'The Walking Dead' got off to its hugely successful start just weeks after the United States federal government shut down.[5]

Zombie culture arguably entails a widespread cultural critique. In 'Dead Man Still Walking: Explaining the Zombie Renaissance' (2009), literary and film scholar Kyle Bishop explains how the zombie metaphor reflects consumerism, public health, and politics. He notes how the critique of consumer culture in Romero's *Dawn of the Dead*, zombies try to break down the doors of a mall so they can shop. Cook (2013) notes that

> The indoctrination of youth via the education system is another example of zombism in our society; when young people are taught to memorize facts and prepare so they may perform well on standardized tests, thinking is not required. Like zombies, the students aren't expected to think, just "do".

The figure of the zombie, taken in isolation, thus encapsulates a cultural anxiety of loss. The zombie narrative is striking in how similar it tends to be the mysterious outbreak of a plague (either literal or figurative, but always infectious, and usually transmitted through a bite) that transforms people into the living dead. In the long established tradition of the "zombie apocalypse" in television, novels, and film, a cause is rarely specified, and when it is, it is only as a vague afterthought, lip service to some kind of coherent background narrative. Because really, the audience doesn't need a cause. We feel like we already know it. The cause is us (https://bibliotechne.wordpress.com/2013/09/26/derrida-and-the-zombie-apocalypse/). In transcribing or externalizing too much of ourselves, we are left with a physical form, the form that moves and hungers, that is hollow, its essence transplanted into external technostructures. The zombie plague represents the moment in time (always vaguely situated in the future but never too far removed from the present reality) in which we are confronted by own bodies.

This genre and tradition has reasserted itself as a form of thinking strongly relevant to framing thought concerning philosophy and education in the "end times" - an apocalyptic tradition that is deeply rooted in Judaic and Christian narratives as a source of revelatory literature (Peters, 2011). The current conceptualisation ot the Anthropocene era is one where we are threatened by ecological, nuclear and biological extinction. Without specifying it, the first half of Derrida's "Plato's Pharmacy" a chapter that focuses on the notion that writing is *pharmakon* (a composite of three meanings: remedy, poison, and scapegoat), suggests 'zombies' (Derrida, 1981). Zombies represent in many ways the logical extension of Derrida's discussion of how writing inherently 'infects' and dampens the mind, putting memory to sleep and, by extension, eroding all of our related faculties. Derrida articulates an anxiety that circulates widely in mainstream criticism of new media and technology. This is the idea that we are being hollowed out by our use of technology, externalizing everything essential to our nature, thus effectively severing ourselves from our own humanity (https://bibliotechne.wordpress.com/2013/09/26/derrida-and-the-zombie-apocalypse/).

We use the term 'Pedagogies of the Walking Dead' because the global situation has changed so dramatically since the Brazilian educational philosopher Paulo Freire wrote and published *Pedagogy of the Oppressed*, in Portuguese in 1968, and in English in 1970. Freire's work based itself on phenomenological and existentialist Marxism, essentially a humanist blend of Continental philosophy with an early Marx class orientation. It was imbued with sixties optimism, upbeat with human agency in changing the world for the better and for changing ourselves through the practice of freedom. It emphasized popular education and critical consciousness – the exact opposite of zombie-culture – and teaching for social justice. It spawned 'critical pedagogy' based on educational praxis through critical thinking and critical literacy, of learning to read the word by reading the world. It promised equality and hope.

Today, after thirty-five years of neoliberalism – of the erosion of public education systems, attacks on teachers and public intellectuals, of privatization strategies, and of new national testing and accountability regimes – the fire of pedagogical hope first lit up by Freire and carried forward by a generation of critical educators like Henry Giroux, Peter McLaren, and Joe Kincheloe seems less a raging bonfire than a scramble to keep alive the embers.[6] The fire has not gone out but the public teaching profession is controlled and regulated by State agencies and often vilified by those on the Right, mostly free-marketeers who in a self-serving way want to profit on the misery of the next generation of school children who are now forced to pay their way. They have been cannibalized by a system that feeds on its youth. Currently, U.S. student loans have exceeded $1.2 trillion dollars and become the second largest form of mortgage after housing.[7] Schools have become marketplaces, students have become consumers, curricula have become commodities, as have all the digital software, books, and teaching equipment. Pedagogies are now technical recipes provided by big tech and publishing companies, supplemented by tech-support, MOOCs and other broadcast, one-way media. 'Pedagogy of the Oppressed' has become the 'Pedagogy of the Walking Dead' as teachers are centrally regulated not only in the curriculum and syllabi by having to teach to targets and standards but also prescribed in terms of pedagogy and the style of teaching with little or no opportunity to raise a critical voice.

The journal *Turbulence* makes the case for zombie neoliberalism:

> Neoliberalism is dead but it doesn't seem to realise it. Although the project no longer makes sense, its logic keeps stumbling on, like a zombie in a 1970s splatter movie: ugly, persistent and dangerous. If no new middle ground is able to cohere sufficiently to replace it, this situation could last a while … all the major crises – economic, climate, food, energy – will remain unresolved; stagnation and long-term drift will set in. Such is the 'unlife' of a zombie, a body stripped of its goals, unable to adjust itself to the future, unable to make plans. A zombie can only act habitually, continuing to operate even as it decomposes. Isn't this where we find ourselves today, in the world of zombie-liberalism? The body of neoliberalism staggers on, but without direction or teleology. (http://turbulence.org.uk/turbulence-5/life-in-limbo/)

Chris Harman (2010) in *Zombie Capitalism: Global Crisis and the Relevance of Marx* commented on how the "shadow" banking system based on speculation and unrealistic credit extension wreaked havoc on world markets and left human misery and devastation in its wake. Following the 2008 crisis many commentators talked about 'zombie banks' that were 'undead' in the sense that they were no longer functional or capable of achieving human goals. Harman argues that the whole system has become a zombie system.

Fred Bottling documents the 'Attack of Zombie Debt' that records the return of long term uncollected bad debts that are not written off but return after they are sold as low rates to specialized collection agencies. He writes:

> Zombie debt is another manifestation of an apparently contagious association between finance and the walking dead. Like zombie economics, zombie banks, and zombie capitalism, the phrase seems to follow the logic of Ulrich Beck's 'zombie categories' of modernity, in which old ideas, institutions, or practices persist despite having little currency, relevance, or credibility. The figures return, however, also takes its generic bearings from a longer-standing gothic political-economic lexicon that goes at least as far back as *Capital's* images of industrial monstrosity and dead labor feeding on living, working bodies (Marx 506, 342). At the same time – and with the pop cultural nous of reflexive political media – its sense of a shifting financial mood responds to recent transformations in the political meanings of vampirism: the exciting figure of a voracious consumerist euphoria of unlimited desire (and credit) cedes to depressive stagnation and elegies for neoliberal fiscal strategy.

Michael Sauga (2014) argues that capitalism has gone off the rails and does not service humanity's needs leading to the financial deformation of the system.[8] He echoes the thoughts of many:

> we are, in fact, living through a historic period tied to the image of the zombie because the system which dictates and dominates our globe, from the world-markets to the workplace to the propaganda machines, and I do not hesitate to name it – *capitalism*, has in fact zombified right before our eyes, transforming into a monster that threatens to tear all of our lives apart, unless we can find some way to annihilate the sucker, or at the very least evade it until its virus extinguishes itself in an orgy of self-destruction.[9]

After 35 years of neoliberalism the question is whether there is a space to pursue critical pedagogy? In the neoliberal classroom has pedagogy become sanitized and lifeless – the pedagogy the walking dead? Are schools now only laboratories for producing digital labor in much the same way that industrial schools produced labor for factories? Are we entering a post-pedagogical era? Does neoliberalism leave any room at all for social conscience, for the teachers' voice and, perhaps even more importantly, for the students' voice and for democratic action?

We use the term in a critical way to refer to a system that extracts more from teachers, a system that attempts to responsibilize teachers for student achievement and learning outcomes through new accountability regimes that tries to make teacher assessment dependent on standards and state mandated targets without recognizing structural inequalities. While it is the case that zombie culture might be an appropriate object of popular and critical inquiry and even used to aid critical pedagogy as some scholars claim,[10] we use the term to describe a system that systematically robs teachers of professional autonomy through a variety of strategies: through curricula that specify in ever finer detail expected outcomes, through assessment standards that encourages teaching to the test, and through forms of teacher evaluation that increasingly see pedagogy as a simple banking transaction. The system increase responsibilizes teachers while taking away their professional autonomy.

Responsibilizing Teachers: The International Agencies

The UNESCO Institute for Statistics (2014) indicates that four million teachers will need to be recruited to achieve universal primary education by 2015 including some 1.6 million replacements by those retiring or leaving the occupation. As the UNESCO paper demonstrates there are massive and persistent teacher shortages which have the effect of denying the fundamental right of primary education to millions of children in the coming decades.[11] The *TALIS 2013 Results: An International Perspective on Teaching and Learning*,[12] the largest international survey of teachers, questioned teachers about conditions that lead to best learning environments dispelling some of the myths about the importance of class size and emphasizing the lack of team teaching, management feedback, and significant staffing shortages. Collectively teachers feel undervalued, unsupported and unrecognised. It is reported that in one third of countries less than 75% of teachers are trained.[13] The Draft Declaration of the World Education Forum (WEF) 2015, *Education 2030: Towards Inclusive and Equitable Quality Education and Lifelong Learning for All* (WEF, 2015) articulates anew educational agenda based on the Sustainable Development Goal (SDG) 4 'Ensure inclusive and equitable quality education and promote lifelong learning opportunities for all' emphasizing a framework for action that recognizes gender equality, fosters creativity, focuses on 'functional literacy' for youth while noting 'with serious concern that, today, more than one-third of the worlds out-of-school population lives in conflict-affected areas, and crises, natural disasters and pandemics continue to disrupt education and development globally'.[14]

While the international teacher advocacy groups like the International Taskforce of Teachers for Education for All[15] supported equal rights and equal opportunity the call to support *public education* is muted as is discussion of the privatization of public education. Even in the International Policy Dialogue For a there is no mention of 'neoliberalism' or its policy effect in eroding public education. How is it possible to talk, for instance, of the impact of financial crisis on teachers without mentioning neoliberalism or financial capitalism or financialization? Yes this seems to be precisely what the report *The 2010 Education for All Global Monitoring Report through a Teacher Lens* accomplishes.[16]

In this and subsequent fora there is a distinct reluctance to engage in any critical policy scholarship regarding neoliberalism and its erosion of public education, its effects on standards and assessment, on pedagogy and on the plight of teachers. By contrast the emphasis is on global educational development, on inclusion of the 57.2 million children worldwide not in education, and on the 'management' of teacher education.[17] While the focus on equity, equality and on educational development in post-conflict zones is desirable it is not clear how this target-orientation policy management approach can take place irrespective of the political context and the rise of neoliberalism with its emphasis on market solutions, on private schools, and on parallel policies of privatization in the public sector. In an officially sponsored program with heads of Ministries and other government agencies it is perhaps no surprise that the recognition of public education is occluded, that there is no recognition of the downside and struggles of teachers in the developed world to hold on to their role and status against the ravages of neoliberalism. Why would one even expect the word 'resistance' to figure in such circumstances? One might ask whether there is indeed a practising teacher among these officials, or even an organization that officially registers itself as an advocacy group on behalf of teachers.

It has been remarked that intergovernmental organization actually promote neoliberal education policies as Rutkowski (2008, p. 229) argues: '[International] organizations encourage world change and promote particular ideologies through a set of complex actions and policy recommendations that exploit growing world interconnectedness'. Sarah Brouillette (2014) argues '[s]ince the early 1980s UNESCO has supported the neoliberal image of culture as a politically neutral resource that can be applied to capitalist development goals'.[18]

Moosung Lee and Tom Friedrich (2011) have shown that UNESCO's social democratic liberalism that dominated lifelong learning policy during the period between the 1990s and the early 2000s has been increasingly supplanted by neoliberalism. Michelle Fawcett's (2009) research charts *The market for ethics: Culture and the neoliberal turn at UNESCO*. Her research seeks

> to contextualize and theorize the institutionalization of public-private partnerships at the United Nations Educational, Scientific and Cultural Organization (UNESCO). Once considered a radical organization by the U.S. Government, UNESCO now partners with corporations to launch projects that claim, among other things, to promote cultural diversity, bridge the digital divide or build intellectual property regimes. From peace to development as its institutional goal, from state to market as its mechanism of delivery and from the universal citizen to the local entrepreneur as its subject, UNESCO is undergoing a dramatic shift in organizational focus, one better designed to serve corporate interests than foster public debate about the meanings and uses of culture.[19]

Neoliberalism and Teachers

Lois Weiner, a Professor at New Jersey City University, and Mary Compton, Past President of the U.K. National Union of Teachers, the largest teacher union in Europe, in 'Neoliberalism, Teachers, and Teaching: Understanding the Assault', write (Weiner & Compton, 2009):

> Though the titles and acronyms of policies differ from one country to another, the basics of the assault are the same: undercut the publicly-supported, publicly-controlled system of education, teachers' professionalism, and teacher unions as organizations. The very nature of education is being contested: the Fourth World Congress of the international organization of teacher unions, Education International (EI), held in Brazil, explored the theme 'Education: Public Service or Commodity'? Over the last couple of decades a new global consensus about reshaping economies and schools has emerged among the politicians and the powerful of the world. Whereas in the past governments – preferably democratically elected – have assumed the responsibility to ensure that all children are educated, schools and universities are now regarded as a potential market. In these educational markets, entrepreneurs set up schools and determine what is taught and how it is taught in order to make a profit.

The assumption that schooling is a 'public good' is under the most severe attack it has ever endured. Teacher trade unionists are grappling with the increasing privatization of education services, the introduction of business 'quality control' measures into education, and the requirement that education produce the kind of minimally-trained and flexible workforce that corporations require to maximize their profits. Among scholars and global justice activists, these reforms being made to the economy and education are often called "neoliberal.[20]

We have examined some of these broader themes in a number of related publications. In *Poststructuralism, Marxism, and Neoliberalism: Between Theory and Politics* (Peters, 2001) focused on two interrelated themes: the culture of Western Marxism and contemporary neoliberal capitalism in order to argue that poststructuralism is not a form of anti-Marxism. Poststructural philosophers view themselves in some kind of relationship to the legacy of Marx: either they have been Marxist or still view themselves as Marxist. In a post-Marxist era these philosophers have invented new ways of reading and writing Marx. We engage neoliberalism as a political project that is committed to the revitalization of *homo economicus* and neoclassical economics and provide a deconstruction of neoliberalism, considered as a world-historical political project aimed at a form of globalization.[21] The aim was to show that among poststructuralist philosophers all entertained a historical relationship to Marx and Marxism and some like Deleuze and Guattari regarded themselves as Marxist. This then was an argument for an understanding and analysis of neoliberalism by poststructuralist Marxist philosophers that emphasized human subjectivity even while problematising aspects of an essentialist humanism.

Neoliberalism is anti-teacher and anti-union. In many countries around the world neoliberal policies have tried to limit the power of the teacher collective, to criticize teacher education programs, to institute new forms of training that put graduates in front of children without appropriate experience of reflection.

Neoliberalism and After? Education, Social Policy, and the Crisis of Western Capitalism, Peters (2011) examined the era that began with the election of the Thatcher and Reagan governments, an era dominated by contemporary forms of neoliberalism-based market fundamentalism, globalization as world economic integration and the ideology of 'free trade', and an attack on 'big' government and social welfare. The book provided a historical and theoretical investigation of contemporary neoliberalism in relation to education policy and its rollback of the Keynesian welfare state. It argued that education is the basis of an open society and is a social welfare right in the emerging knowledge economy. Drawing on the theoretical lens of Michel Foucault's work on governmentality understood as a form of radical political economy, the book explored and critiqued neoliberalism as the ruling consensus.[22]

Education, Cognitive Capitalism, and Digital Labor (Peters & Bulut, 2011) focused on the attempt to understand neoliberalism in the epoch of digital reason, including fundamental changes to the nature of capitalism and new forms of educational capitalism centered around the question of digital labor.[23]

One of the pressing questions surrounds the nexus among the forces of neoliberalism, globalization and finance capitalism especially in terms of new forms of educational capitalism that erodes the public sector and turns the sector over to for-profit capitalists either in the form of charter schools or whole system providers.

We conclude by returning to the zombie metaphor, summing up the links between pedagogy, politics, neoliberalism, corporatisation and capitalism. In *Zombie Politics & Culture in the Age of Casino Capitalism* (Giroux, 2011). Giroux uses it to examine and argue that the current political and pedagogical conditions that have produced a 'growing culture of sadism, cruelty, disposability, and death in America'. In a TV interview with Bill Moyers on *Moyers & Company*, he explains that the US now has

> "machinery of social and civil death" that chills "any vestige of a robust democracy". Giroux explains that such a machine turns "people who are basically so caught up with surviving that they become like the walking dead – they lose their sense of agency, they lose their homes, they lose their jobs". What's more, Giroux points out, the system that creates this vacuum has little to do with expanding the meaning and the substance of democracy itself. Under "casino capitalism," the goal is to get a quick return, taking advantage of a kind of logic in which the only thing that drives us is to put as much money as we can into a slot machine and hope we walk out with our wallets overflowing". (2013, https://billmoyers.com/segment/henry-giroux-on-zombie-politics/)

The zombie metaphor not only suggests a zombie-like symbolic face of an authoritarian power in politics, but also a right-wing teaching system, a mechanization via the use of IT, testing, standardization and technologies of power have emerged in education. With a growing politics of disposability, an uncaring disposition of cruelty, this exacerbates the 'ongoing war being waged on young people, especially on youth of color'. It is a bleak message that applies to a major sector of American society – its youth and minorities who are increasingly marginalized with little voice in contemporary life and politics.

However, the crisis is not just in schools but in higher education. Whelan, Walker and Moore's 2013 edited collection, *Zombies in the Academy: Living Death in Higher Education* argues that the increasing corporatization is creating a crisis in higher education best understood through the language of zombie culture – the undead, contagion, and plague, among others. They highlight an environment that emphasizing publication (often acknowledging only those published in specific citation journals), narrow research topics, and the vulnerability of many academics now that fewer people are considered for the tenure system and more are on short term contracts. There are many other publications now on these topics, but with both these books being published in 2011 and 2013, well before the Trump era it seems remarkably prescient and the use of the zombie metaphor even more relevant.

Acknowledgement

This chapter was substantially revised in 2018, from an article, Michael A. Peters and Tina Besley, 'Pedagogies of the Walking Dead: Diminishing Responsibility for Social Justice in a Neoliberal World', *Artículo de Reflexión Pedagogía y Saberes* No. 43 Universidad Pedagógica Nacional Facultad de Educación, 2015, pp. 49–57.

Notes

1 See the official website at http://www.amc.com/shows/the-walking-dead
2 See the Twilight series at http://www.thetwilightsaga.com/. Some critics argue that this follows the Harry Potter saga, basically in part also a story about the Christian prohibition against sex before marriage i.e., pro-chastity and pro-life – https://spesunica.wordpress.com/2008/12/01/is-twilight-anti-christian-yes/
3 See e.g., http://www.livescience.com/27287-zombie-apocalypse-world-war-ii.html and http://news.stanford.edu/news/2013/february/why-zombie-fascination-022013.html
4 See e.g., http://www.alternet.org/story/155783/what_does_our_obsession_with_zombie_stories_tell_us_about_our_politics
5 See http://www.bbc.com/culture/story/20131025-zombie-nation
6 See the recent *Paulo Freire: The Global Legacy* (Peters & Besley, 2015).
7 See https://studentloanreduction.com/student-loan-debt-reaches-record-1-2-trillion/

8 See *The Zombie System: How Capitalism Has Gone Off the Rails* at http://www.spiegel.de/international/business/capitalism-in-crisis-amid-slow-growth-and-growing-inequality-a-998598.html
9 See http://endofcapitalism.com/2012/11/27/the-arrival-of-zombie-capitalism/
10 See e.g., http://www.slideshare.net/jessestommel/zombie-pedagogies-embodied-learning-in-the-digital-age
11 See also the UNESCO eAtlas of Teachers at http://tellmaps.com/uis/teachers/
12 See http://www.oecd.org/edu/school/talis-2013-results.htm
13 http://www.teachersforefa.unesco.org/v2/index.php/en/
14 See http://en.unesco.org/world-education-forum-2015/
15 See http://www.teachersforefa.unesco.org/v2/index.php/en/about-us/our-mission/our-mission
16 http://www.teachersforefa.unesco.org/v2/phocadownload/Publications/2010_synthesisgmr_english.pdf
17 The full list of policy fora is:
   1. "Teachers, the financial crisis, and the EFA challenge of reaching the marginalized" Addis-Ababa (Ethiopia, 22-23 February 2010)
   2. "Providing teachers for E FA : quality matters" Amman (Jordan, 6-7 July 2010)
   3. "Ensuring Equity in Country Policies and Practices for Providing Quality Teachers toward Achieving the E FA Goals by 2015" Bali (Indonesia, 13-15 September 2011)
   4. "Teachers' challenges for E FA in India" (with global perspectives) New Delhi (India, 29-30 May 2012) 5. "Three Years of Global Partnership to Address the Teacher Challenge – Three Years from the 2015 E FA Benchmark: Achievements and Perspectives") Windhoek (Namibia, 28-29 November 2012).
18 See UNESCO's Neoliberalism at http://www.buffalo.edu/calendar/calendar?action=describe&which=06386FF2-69C4-11E4-8B B E -B78C2C3EEDE4
19 See http://www.nyu.edu/projects/cinema.resources/dissertationsSite/indices/phd_graduates/fawcett_michelle.php
20 http://newpol.org/content/neoliberalism-teachers-and-teaching-understanding-assault
21 See the review, Ulf Schulenberg, *Amerikastudien/American Studies*, Vol. 47, No. 3, Vladimir Nabokov at 100 (2002), pp. 430–432.
22 See the following reviews: Darko Štrajn, *International Review of Education*, August 2012, Volume 58, Issue 4, pp 585–587; Ellison, Scott (2013). Transformational Crisis? Thinking within and beyond the Limits of Neoliberal Education Policy, *International Education*, Vol. 42 Issue (2). Retrieved from: http://trace.tennessee.edu/internationaleducation/vol42/iss2/7
23 See "Control and becoming in the neoliberal teaching machine," Amit S. Rai, review of Michael Peters and Ergin Bulut (2011) Cognitive capitalism, education, and digital labor. http://www.ephemerajournal.org/contribution/control-and-becoming-neoliberal-teaching-machine

References

Bishop, K. (2009). Dead man still walking: Explaining the Zombie renaissance. *Journal of Popular Film and Television, 37*(1), 16–25.

Cook, D. N. (2013, November 16). The cultural life of the living dead. *Contexts: Understanding People in Their Social Worlds*. Retrieved November 6, 2018, from https://contexts.org/articles/the-cultural-life-of-the-living-dead/

Derrida, J. (1981). Plato's pharmacy. In B. Johnson (Trans.), *Dissemination* (pp. 63–171). Chicago, IL: University of Chicago Press. Retrieved from http://www.occt.ox.ac.uk/sites/default/files/derrida_platos_pharmacy.pdf

Derrida, J. (1982). Of an apocalyptic tone recently adopted in philosophy (J. P. Leavcy, Trans.). *Semeia, 23*, 63–97.

Derrida, J. (1984). No apocalypse, not now (Full speed ahead, seven missiles, seven missives) (C. Porter & P. Lewis, Trans.). *Diacritics, 14.2*, 20–31.

Giroux, H. (2011). *Zombie politics & culture in the age of casino capitalism*. New York, NY: Peter Lang.

Giroux, H. (2013, November 22). Segment: Henry Giroux on Zombie politics. *Moyers & Company*. Retrieved November 6, 2018, from https://billmoyers.com/segment/henry-giroux-on-zombie-politics/

Northcote, G., Rabindranath, L., & Trothen, S. D., & The Zombie Apocalypse. *Biotechné*. Retrieved November 6, 2018, from https://bibliotechne.wordpress.com/2013/09/26/derrida-and-the-zombie-apocalypse/

OECD. (2013). *TALIS 2013 results: An international perspective on teaching and learning*. Paris: OECD Publishing.

Peters, M. A. (2011). *Neoliberalism and after? Education, social policy, and the crisis of western capitalism*. New York, NY: Peter Lang.

Rutkowski, D. (2007). Converging us softly: How intergovernmental organizations promote neoliberal educational policy. *Critical Studies in Education, 48*(2), 229–247.

UNESCO Institute for Statistics. (2014). *Wanted: Trained teachers to ensure every childs right to primary education*. Retrieved from http://www.uis.unesco.org/Education/Documents/fs30-teachers-en.pdf

WEF. (2015). *Education 2030: Towards inclusive and equitable quality education and lifelong learning for all*. Geneva: WEF.

Whelan, A., Walker, R., & Moore, C. (Eds.). (2013). *Zombies in the academy*. Chicago, IL: University of Chicago Press.

CONCLUSION

Education for Ecological Democracy

> We have every reason to think that whatever changes may take place in existing democratic machinery, they will be of a sort to make the interest of the public a more supreme guide and criterion of governmental activity, and to enable the public to form and manifest its purposes still more authoritatively. In this sense the cure for the ailments of democracy is more democracy.
> JOHN DEWEY, (1927), 121

∴

> Environmental ecology, as it exists today, has barely begun to prefigure the generalised ecology that I advocate here, the aim of which will be to radically decentre social struggles and ways of coming into ones own psyche ... Ecology must stop being associated with the image of a small nature-loving minority. Ecology in my sense questions the whole of subjectivity and capitalistic power formations.
> FELIX GUATTARI (2000), 2

∴

Democracy, Yet Again

This brief chapter makes an argument for a concept of 'ecological democracy' and for an education that is based upon it. It traces the development of the it and canvases educational possibilities for its instantiation by utilizing the work of Dewey and Guattari.

Donald Trump's decision to quit the UNFCCC Paris Agreement, a contemptible decision that does the U.S. no good in term of moral leadership and one almost universally condemned by world leaders, raises the question about the structural capacity of democracy at the extra-state level to reach consensus or indeed to action decisions at a global level. Under the circumstances one wonders whether democracy is able to deliver ecological outcomes or whether in the standoff between democracy and oil and gas capitalism that it has the power to harness and transform the energy sector. The fact is that modern representative democracy was never designed to handle environmental challenges and many scholars now seek the establishment of new global institutions that carries the mantle for intergenerational environmental problems based on evidence-based sustainability science. One set of anxieties revolve around whether democratic institutions based on deliberative forms of government have the power to set new environmental norms, to curb the transnational energy multinationals, or to institute change quickly enough in order to avert environmental collapse.

There is some evidence that democratic values increasingly operate now at the global level and multi-stakeholder dialogues between civil society, NGOs, governments and world agencies are now more common, yet some critics doubt whether concepts of world democracy will ever be strong enough to reconcile either radical participatory politics and the world's energy multinationals, or the climate deniers and the scientific mainstream consensus. Some scientists despair that green diplomacy perhaps best represented in the Paris Agreement, where the French hosts acting in concert with many agencies engineered an agreement with 195 countries, can ever protect itself and its environmental policy decisions against the actions of authoritarian thumb-nosing and outright grand-standing on the basis of flimsy 'America first' sloganizing.

Yet others talk of the longer-term transformation of democratic culture aimed at producing green citizens committed to the principles of bioregionalism on the one hand and to principles of discursive democracy on the other, steadfast in their belief that deliberation is the appropriate space in which to change people's habits, beliefs and actions.

Ecological Democracy

The term 'ecological democracy' (ED) has been established in the literature for a couple of decades (Dryzek, 1992, 1997; Morrison, 1995; Faber, 1998; Ungaro, 2005), if not always in an explicit conceptual formulation. It is slowly evolving as a liberal notion that presupposes a link between democracy and ecology, sometimes cashed out in terms of 'sustainable development' or 'green capitalism' ('green consumerism') while emphasizing that ED requires a form of grass roots participation by citizens both individually and collectively. The exact nature of the link and the success and results of ED have been up for on-going scrutiny and political scepticism. Both 'ecology' and 'democracy' are expansive concepts that have been refined and developed over the last couple of decades so it is not surprising that the links between these and cognates concepts are hard to pin down.

There has been a peak in the use of the concept with applications in a variety of settings. For example, an online journal based in India established in 2013 has adopted the name (http://ecologicaldemocracy.net) which it introduces in the following way:

> The last century has seen many national movements successfully liberating countries from colonial rule. But since the last quarter of the twentieth century, we have witnessed world-wide schizophrenia in our development policies. Global players like the U.S. and European Union and arms of their economic hegemonies such as the World Bank and I.M.F. have forced governments to adopt policies which are resulted in a serious all round crisis, including an ecological crisis. On the other hand there is a multitude of UN Conferences on various dimensions of the ecological crisis. To understand this schizophrenia and to evolve policy frameworks to respond to this crisis from the ecological swaraaj perspective is the need of the hour. Our online journal www.ecologicaldemocracy. net is an effort to bring cohesion to the efforts of all who believe in the idea of ecological swaraaj [self-governance in Hindi].

The term 'radical' ecological democracy (RED) stands for *degrowth* policies, grassroots participation and has been used to demonstrate problems for existing democratic structures (Kotari, 2014; Rose, 2006). RED contributes to the search 'for sustainable and equitable alternatives to the dominant economic development model' that pursues the 'goals of direct democracy, local and bioregional economies, cultural diversity, human well-being, and ecological resilience at the core of its vision' (Kotari, 2014, p. 57). RED also maps on to the concept of 'radical democracy' developed by post-Marxist thinkers Ernesto Laclau and Chantal Mouffe starting in the early 1990s (Laclau, 1990; Laclau & Mouffe, 2001). One line of thought, which I support, has begun to map notions of 'radical' and 'open' on to overlapping concepts of democracy and environment through notion of collective subjectivity (Peters, 2002, 2013).

Randolph Hester (2010), in another example, outlines new principles for urban design that he calls *Design for Ecological Democracy* emphasizing how 'responsible freedom' rests on respect and acknowledgement of an interconnectivity with all living things. Finally, an example based workshop entitled Ecological Democracy that was held at the University of Sydney 20–21 February 2017 advertises itself in the following terms:

> The role of democracy in the face of global environmental threats has been subject to intense scholarly debate over the past four decades. At times, ecological democracy has had a bright future ahead of it. Yet the ideal of ecological democracy continually faces challenges both to its conceptual foundations and to its practical realization on national and global scales. This workshop will seek to focus on new considerations and directions for ecological democracy, while looking back to examine the impact and viability of its founding texts as well as empirical studies of the relationship between democracy and sustainability. (http://sydney.edu.au/environment-institute/wp-content/uploads/2016/11/EcologicalDemocracy_Draft-programme.pdf)

The wide-ranging workshop included sessions on: Foundations of Ecological Democracy; Rights, Institutions, and Deliberation; Democracy and the Non-human; Culture & Ecological Citizenship; Diversity, Culture and Democracy; Ecological Democracy and Indigenous Peoples; Resources, Democracy and the Local. A panel discussion 'Ecological Democracy – Looking Back, Looking Forward' chaired by David Schlosberg with Robyn Eckersley, Karin Bäckstrand and John Dryzek as discussants, examine the attempts at reconciliation between democracy and sustainability within environmental political thought including problems of 'the representation of the nonhuman, the relationship between democracy and ecological limits, and the design of green states'. The note continues:

> Since this first wave of scholarship [in 1980s and 1990s] on ecological democracy, there have been numerous crucial developments that pose a range of challenges. On the environmental side, we have seen the acceleration of climate change, arguments for setting planetary boundaries around humanitys environmental impacts, and widespread acknowledgement that the Earth has entered a new epoch: the Anthropocene. On the political side, we have had the growth of environmental and climate justice movements, the proliferation of institutions for global environmental governance, and the anti-environmental and post-truth era.

In short, the second wave of ecological democracy concerns the growth of political movements broadly embracing the concept of environmental justice in an attempt to counteract and address backsliding anti-environmentalism. The third wave of ecological democracy (ED) takes place in relation to President Trump's anti-environmentalism, his withdrawal from the Paris Agreement, his championing of world oil and gas, and cuts to the jurisdiction and budget of the Environmental Protection Agency (EPA). In this political environment, the future of environmental sustainability depends upon more radical forms of ecological democracy tied to notions of citizen science and forms of learning as activism.

Origins and Possibilities

The concept and practices of ED have developed as part of a broader theoretical re-examination and conceptual development of 'participatory', 'strong', 'discursive', 'inclusive', 'deliberative' and 'radical' democracy (Barber, 1984; Dryzek, 2010; Ester, 1988; Gutman & Thompson, 2002; Laclau Mouffe, 1985; Young, 2000, 2001). These diverse threads spring in part from attempts to revisit democracy after the rise of neoliberalism in the age of globalization that hastened the decline of social democracy. Social democracy as part of the Keynesian postwar consensus developed an ideology based on the compromise between market and State that supported the mixed economy and capitalism as the means of wealth generation and distribution that necessitated State intervention based on rights and equality of opportunity to correct the defective tendencies of the market toward increasing poverty and growing inequalities.

In effect, it was largely this attempted compromise that led to the first green social democracies and red-green coalitions in Germany under Gerhard Schroder (1998–2005), the 'plural Left' coalition in France (2012–2014), Lipponen's first and second cabinet in Finland that included socialist and green members (1995–2002), Norways Red-Green coalition (2003–2013), with similar developments in Iceland, Italy, Denmark, Sweden and Portugal. Radical red-green alliances formed in the Netherlands' (GreenLeft), Denmark (Unity List), Norway (Green Left Alliance), Italy (Left Ecology Freedom), and Greece (SYRIZA). There are also red/green political alliances and/or electoral agreements between social-democratic or liberal parties with green parties such as the Red-Green Alliance in Canada, Sweden and Italy.

After the demise of the Keynesian-based and the empirically discredited neoliberal variant of capitalism, the goal of transcending global capitalism seems far-fetched, and Left parties – Far-Left and centrist socialist – began to question the basis for renewed social democratic appeal. Under the Third Way, social democracy capitulated to neoliberalism and thus compromised the green market solution and no growth policies. Under the rise of authoritarian populism in its first phase with Thatcher-Reagan and then most recently under Trump, working class voters have been easily captured by anti-immigration far-right parties that promise to bring back industrial jobs at home.

The origins of green parties begin in the 1970s first in Australia and then Germany. By the 1980s and especially after *Green Politics: The Global Promise* (Spretnak & Capra, 1984) green agendas became more progressively tied to policy issues outside immediate ecological considerations.[1] As Silke Mende (2015) the West German Green Party 'founded in opposition to the guiding principles of the West German postwar consensus' and their entrance into the Bundestag in 1983 marked a turning point in German parliamentary history but soon also reverted to traditions of political liberalization with a mixture of classical elements of conservativism over conservation of resources. Stewart Jackson (2012, p. 593) suggests the Australian Greens, as a political organization, are possibly following the transformation of European green parties moving from 'a movement based party to a pragmatic parliamentary party'. The question is where do green parties go after the Trump retrenchment of global oil and gas? Is there any legitimate resistance against neoliberalism and authoritarian populism that draws off the working-class vote?

Education for Ecological Democracy

Education has the possibility of bringing together two powerful concepts and international movements of ecology and local democracy that are needed to bring about the transformation of grassroots civil society. This combination of 'ecological democracy' that rests on two fundamental principles – the freedom to participate in local society and our growing awareness of the interconnectedness of all living things. It also draws and encourage the development of new forms of green identity and citizenship.

Peters and González-Gaudiano (2008) observed the evolution of environmental education (EE) over three decades toward a new relation to identity struggle, new social movements and green citizenship.

> During its thirty years of existence, despite having faced problems and diverse challenges from country to country, environmental education (EE) has acquired a certain influence over the design of educational and environmental public policies on an international level. Throughout these three decades, environmental education has contributed to the configuration of new ontological and epistemological proposals, as well as introducing practices that have become well-established and have made significant contributions to the strengthening of not only the environmental education field but educational processes in general. However, as EE became established a great variety of viewpoints were taken

into account and elements incorporated not only from the widest variety of theoretical approaches and philosophical currents, but also from very different schools of thought and action, which established important articulations with complex social movements such as feminism, multiculturalism, peace, democracy, health, consumerism and human rights to mention but a few.

One definition of ecological democracy emphasizes *sustainability in action* by emphasizing a relationship between biological processes and political subjectivities of participatory democracy considered as a co-evolutionary strategy. *Education for Ecological Democracy* is based an alternative democratic model that strives to educate students about the norms and values of democracy-in-action and eventually incorporate them as interested citizens into environmental decision-making and collective action. 'Ecological democracy' is still a concept in the formative stage. In its radical form 'it places the goals of direct democracy, local and bioregional economies, cultural diversity, human well-being, and ecological resilience at the core of its vision' (Kothari, 2014). In educational theory and practice it is closely associated with the notion of *deliberation* that is considered central to consensus decisionmaking and majority rule. The principles of deliberative democracy are embraced for their educative power and pedagogical force in teaching secondary school students to reason in democratic fora about ecological issues. The deliberative nature of ecological democracy has a strong base in grassroots participation within civil society. In philosophical terms, it is indebted to John Dewey's (1916) *Education and Democracy* and more recently to Jürgen Habermas' (1984) theory of communicative rationality that proposes the ideal of a self-organizing community of free and equal citizens, coordinating their collective affairs through their common reason. Free and open debate is a necessary condition for the legitimacy of democratic political decisions based on the exercise of 'public reason' rather than simply the aggregation of citizen preferences as with representative or direct democracy.

From its development in the 1980s and 1990s Green Political Theory (GPT) or ecopolitics founded on the work of John Dryzek (1987), Robyn Eckersley (1992), Val Plumwood (1993) and Andrew Dobson (1980), participatory democracy has been viewed as a central pillar and key value, often associated with descriptions of decentralization, grassroots political decision-making and citizen participation, 'strong democracy' (Barber, 1997) and increasingly with conceptions of deliberative democracy. The value of participatory or grassroots democracy also seemed to gel with a new ecological awareness, non-violence and the concern for social justice. Green politics favoured participatory and more recently deliberative democracy because it provided a model for open debate, direct citizen involvement and emphasized grassroots action over electoral politics.

Local government is often more democratic than any other level of government. At the same time it provides education for the practice of political education instructing children and others people in the art if decision-making that is sensitive to opinions based on local knowledge and on the representation of diverse political groupings and sub-state actors. It is especially appropriate in mobilizing community to gain local support for ecological projects ensuring that power is widely dispersed while also encouraging people to rebuild democracy at the local level moving toward forms of self-organization that can collect, analyse and monitor ecological data on the local environment while hooking up to larger global concerns.

In an era of authoritarian populism based on the echo-chamber of Twitter politics the only sure answer to Trump's arrogance and world selfishness is to organise, to educate and to motivate the younger generation to take matters into their own hands, combining forms of learning with activism.

Acknowledgement

This chapter was previously published as Michael A. Peters, 'Education for Ecological Democracy', *Educational Philosophy and Theory*, 49(10), 2017, 941–945 and is reprinted here with permission from Taylor & Francis.

Note

1   The Origins of Green Parties In Global Perspective, at http://www.ghi-dc.org/fileadmin/user_upload/GHI_Washington/Publications/Bulletin35/35.179.pdf

References

Barber, B. (1984). *Strong democracy: Participatory politics for a new age*. Berkeley, CA: University of California Press.

Dewey, J. (1916). *Democracy and education: An introduction to the philosophy of education*. New York, NY: Palgrave Macmillan.

Dewey, J. (1927). *The public and its problems: An essay in political inquiry*. University Park, PA: Pennsylvania State Press.

Doherty, B., & de Geus, M. (Eds.). (1996). *Democracy and green political thought: Sustainability, rights and citizenship*. London: Routledge.

Dryzek, J. S. (1992). Ecology and discursive democracy: Beyond liberal capitalism and the administrative state. *Capitalism, Nature, Socialism, 3*(2), 18–42.

Dryzek, J. S. (1997). *The politics of the earth*. Oxford: Oxford University Press.

Dryzek, J. S. (2010). *Foundations and frontiers of deliberative governance*. Oxford: Oxford University Press.

Ester, J. (Ed.). (1998). *Deliberative democracy*. Cambridge: Cambridge University Press.

Faber, D. (1998). *The struggle for ecological democracy: Environmental justice movements in the United States*. New York, NY: Guilford.

Guattari, F. (2000). *The three ecologies* (I. Pindar & P. Sutton, Trans.). London: The Athlone Press. Retrieved from https://monoskop.org/images/4/44/Guattari_Felix_The_Three_Ecologies.pdf

Gutmann, A., & Thompson, D. (2002). *Why deliberative democracy?* Princeton, NJ: Princeton University Press.

Habermas, J. (1984). *The theory of communicative action: Reason and the rationalization of society* (T. McCarthy, Trans.). Boston, MA: Beacon Press.

Hester, R. (2010). *Design for ecological democracy*. Retrieved from http://www.radicaldemocracy.org/

Jackson, S. (2012). Thinking activists: Australian greens party activists and their responses to leadership. *Australian Journal of Political Science, 47*(4), 593–607.

Kothari, A. (2014). Radical ecological democracy: A path forward for India and beyond. *Development, 57*(1), 36–45. doi:10.1057/dev.2014.43

Laclau, E. (1990). *New reflections on the revolution of our times*. London: Verso Books.

Laclau, E., & Mouffe, C. (1985). *Hegemony and socialist strategy: Towards a radical democratic politics*. London: Verso Books.

Laclau, E., & Mouffe, C. (2001). *Hegemony and socialist strategy: Towards a radical democratic politics* (2nd ed.). London: Verso Books.

Mason, M. (1999). *Environmental democracy*. London: Earthscan.

Mendes, S. (2015). Enemies at the gate: The West German greens and their arrival at the Bundestag – Between old ideals and new challenges. *German Politics and Society, 33*(4), 66–79.

Minteer, B. A., & Taylor, B. P. (Eds.). (2002). *Democracy and the claims of nature: Critical perspectives for a new century*. Lanham, MD: Rowman & Littlefield.

Mitchell, R. (2006). Building an empirical case for ecological democracy. *Nature and Culture, 1*(2), 149–156.

Morrison, R. (1995). *Ecological democracy*. Boston, MA: South End Press.

Mouffe, C. (1999). Deliberative democracy or agnostic pluralism. *Social Research, 66*, 745–758.

Peters, M. A. (2002). Anti-globalization and guattaris: The three ecologies. In M. A. Peters, M. Olssen, & C. Lankshear (Eds.), *Futures of critical theory: Dreams of difference.* Lanham, MD: Rowman & Littlefield.

Peters, M. A. (2013). Institutions, semiotics and the politics of subjectivity. In B. Dillet, R. Porter, & I. Mackenzie (Eds.), *The Edinburgh companion to poststructuralism* (pp. 368–383). Edinburgh: University of Edinburgh Press.

Peters, M. A., & González-Gaudiano, E. (2008). Introduction. In E. González-Gaudiano & M. A. Peters (Eds.), *Environmental education: Identity, politics and citizenship.* Rotterdam, The Netherlands: Sense Publishers.

Putnam, R. D. (1993). *Making democracy work: Civic traditions in modern Italy.* Princeton, NJ: Princeton University Press.

Smith, A. M. (1998). *Laclau and Mouffe: The radical democratic imaginary.* London: Routledge.

Smith, G. (2003). *Deliberative democracy and the environment.* London: Routledge.

Spretnak, C., & Capra, F. (1984). *Green politics: The global promise.* New York, NY: Paladin.

Ungaro, D. (2005). Ecological democracy: The environment and the crisis of the liberal institutions. *International Review of Sociology, 15*(2), 293–303.

Young, I. M. (2000). *Inclusion and democracy.* Oxford: Oxford University Press.

Young, I. M. (2001). Activist challenges to deliberative democracy. *Political Theory, 29*(5), 670–691.

POSTSCRIPT

The End of Neoliberal Globalization and the Rise of Authoritarian Populism

Scanning the headlines a day or so after the surprise of the Brexit on 23rd June with 52% voting to leave the E.U. a number of commentators examined its loaded significance for the neoliberal ideal of globalization. One such commentator writing for the *Economic Times* suggested:

> Brexit heralds not just Britain's exit from the European Union but the decline and maybe fall of the twentieth century ideal of a liberal, globalised world. It heralds a twenty-first century ethos based on ultranationalism and racist xenophobia, blaming foreigners and minorities for all ills, and claiming against all logic and humanism that turning your back on the world will somehow bring back a golden past.[1]

Another writing for the *Sydney Morning Herald* followed with a similar theme:

> The economic story of the past quarter century was the rapid advance of globalization, the unleashing of trade and commerce among countries rich and poor – a McDonalds in every European capital, 'Made in China' labels throughout Toys R Us. The Brexit vote on Thursday ends that story, at least in its current volume.[2]

Jim Tankersley registers a peak in anti-globalization sentiment that follows a slowdown in trade growth, the stand-off on trade agreements, the growth of anti-immigration among an anxious working-class, the rise of a populist xenophobia in parties of the Right and endlessly exploited by Donald Trump as presumptive Republican nominee. By reference to the IMF's Deputy Managing Director David Lipton in a paper 'Can Globalization Still Deliver?,' Tankersley raises the question of whether globalization can show positive results for working-class people.[3] The more pressing issue is whether this is a harbinger for Trump taking the White House. As Stephen Collinson puts it:

> The referendum campaign – just like the U.S. election – has boiled with populist anger, fear-mongering by politicians, hostility towards distant political elites and resurgent nationalism, and exposed a visceral feeling in the electorate that ordinary voters have lost control of the politics that

shape their own lives. Its success raises the question of whether those forces will exert a similar in uence in America in November.[4]

With uncanny timing Jonathan D. Ostry, Prakash Loungani, and Davide Furceri (2016), all from IMF's Research Department, enquire whether neoliberalism has been over sold. That the IMF should use this term, once considered notionally abusive and avoided by most economists, neoliberalism has broken new ground. Ostry et al. (2016) recount the alleged beneefits of neoliberalism thus:

> The expansion of global trade has rescued millions from abject poverty. Foreign direct investment has often been a way to transfer technology and know-how to developing economies. Privatization of state-owned enterprises has in many instances led to more efficient provision of services and lowered the fiscal burden on governments. (p. 38)

They turn their attention to areas where expected benefits have not materialised:

> Our assessment of the agenda is confined to the effects of two policies: removing restrictions on the movement of capital across a country's borders (so-called capital account liberalization); and fiscal consolidation, sometimes called "austerity," which is shorthand for policies to reduce fiscal deficits and debt levels. An assessment of these *specific* policies (rather than the broad neoliberal agenda) reaches three disquieting conclusions:

– The benefits in terms of increased growth seem fairly diffcult to establish when looking at a broad group of countries.
– The costs in terms of increased inequality are prominent. Such costs epitomise the trade-off between the growth and equity effects of some aspects of the neoliberal agenda.
– Increased inequality in turn hurts the level and sustainability of growth. Even if growth is the sole or main purpose of the neoliberal agenda, advocates of that agenda still need to pay attention to the distributional effects (pp. 38–39).

Capital account liberalization has revealed uncertain growth benefits with increasing bouts of economic volatility and crisis frequency. The capital inflow surges – some 150 since 1980 – have led to financial crises in 20% of cases and a boom-bust cycle. Ostry et al. (2016) directly question the high cost-to-benefit ratio of capital account openness and they also question austerity as a means of curbing and paying down public debt. Both openness and austerity are associated with increasing income inequality that may also undercut growth prospects.

Inequalities had been further exacerbated by privatization policies and governmental load-shedding so that now social provision has been whittled away and consumerised. Thomas Piketty (2013) in an academic blockbuster argued that that inequality is not an accident but rather an endemic feature of capitalism that can be reversed only through state intervention and will threaten the democratic order unless capitalism is reformed. *Capital in the Twenty-First Century* analysed economic data sets to develop his formula explaining economic inequality: $r > g$ (meaning that return on capital is generally higher than economic growth). Economic inequality is not new, but it is getting worse, with possible radical impacts.[5]

Neoliberal globalization – the target of so much Left critique over the Reagan-Thatcher, Bush-Blair, and some would say, Obama-Cameron, years – seems now on the back foot, both in the U.S. under Trump, and also in Europe with the emergence of the Alt-right and the likes of Marie Le Pen, leader of the National Front in France, Geert Wilders in the Netherlands, Nigel Farage and the U.K. Independence Party, Heinz-Christian Strache in Austria and the Vlaams Belang Party in Belgium, to name a few. Right-wing populism is on the rise. It is fiercely anti-immigration and anti-integration, often associated with neo-Nazis and white supremacist groups. It commonly assumes a kind of authoritarianism and anti-liberal stance towards rights, and while it appeals to the common man (*sic*) – sometimes explicitly anti-women and anti-feminist – it paradoxically nevertheless does not subscribe to the notion and practice of equality. The far-right is anti-pluralist and anti-democratic believing in the strong state and an authoritarian populism. Right-wing populism has strong links with elements of the far-right not only in terms of ethnocentrism, xenophobia and anti-immigration stance but also over traditional and social conservative values concerning heterosexuality, the patriarchical family, the subordination of women and cultural minorities, often combined with fundamentalist Christian values. Economically, as is evidence in the raft of Trump's executive orders, there is a strong tendency toward protectionism and an isolationism in foreign policy.

Trump's election has unleased a new offensive against academia[6] and universities are already feeling the effects of Trump's travel ban on their application numbers. Even with a new policy on travel ban placed on six countries, mostly Muslim, it seems clear that international students in U.S. universities will be severely curtailed. Many U.S. universities and universities around the world have been outspoken against the discrimination of Trump's immigration and travel-ban policies.

Trump's ascendancy is also bad news for U.S. and world science with the disappearance of governmental science websites such as the White House pages on climate change and the likely curtailment for alternative energy science funding.[7] Various publications have complained that the president's view on science are shockingly ignorant.[8]

At the level of schooling Trump is on record saying he may cut the Department of Education[9] and his appointment of Betsy DeVos[10] indicates an education agenda that will boost Charter schools, defend the ideology of school choice, support the radical Christian orthodoxy to advance private religious schools, and rethink the necessity of the Common Core. Other elements on the agenda include vouchers, greater teacher accountability, more student debt, and an attack on America's public schooling system with a commensurate downsizing of the Department of Education. Many educators are worried about the future of liberal arts colleges and STEM education, and the undermining of teaching about evolution and climate change.[11] CBS reports Trump as saying: As your president, I will be the biggest cheer-leader for school choice you've ever seen, he said, promising that in his White House parents can home school their children.[12] We face the end of the liberal era of schooling – the end of educational equality – and a reassertion, especially as Trump's presidency unfolds, of less government involvement and the endorsement of socially conservative values.

Acknowledgement

This chapter was previously published as Michael A. Peters, 'The End of Neoliberal Globalization and the Rise of Authoritarian Populism', *Educational Philosophy and Theory*, 50, 2018, 323–325 and is reprinted here with permission from the copyright holder (Michael A. Peters).

Notes

1 See Swaminathan S Anklesaria Aiyar http://economictimes.indiatimes.com/news/international/world-news/brexit-may-mean-end-of-globalisation-as-we-know-itstormy-days-lie-ahead/articleshow/52909952.cms

2 See Jim Tankersley, http://www.smh.com.au/world/us-election/britains-brexitjust-killed-globalisation-as-we-know-it-20160626-gpsojs.html

3 For other similar accounts see Don Lee http://www.latimes.com/business/la-brexit-globalisation-future-20160624-snap-story.html; Larry Elliott who writes: The age of globalization began on the day the Berlin Wall came down. From that moment in 1989,

the trends evident in the late 1970s and throughout the 1980s accelerated: the free movement of capital, people and goods; trickle-down economics; a much diminished role for nation states; and a belief that market forces, now unleashed, were unstoppable. He argues that Britain rejection of the E.U. is a protest against the economic model that has been in place for the past three decades https://www.theguardian.com/business/2016/jun/26/brexit-is-the-rejectionof-globalisation; Joseph Murray talks of Ebd of New World Order http://www.breitbart.com/london/2016/06/23/brexit-signals-end-new-worldorder/; Nelson D. Swartz and Patricia Cohen head their joint piece Brexit in America: A Warning Shot Against Globalisation http://www.nytimes.com/2016/06/26/business/economy/for-america-brexit-may-be-a-warning-of-globalizationslimits.html?_r=0; Vassilis K. Fouskas writing for Open Democracy before the vote suggests: British voters on June 23 may also decide the future of globalization/nancialization. If Britain votes to leave the E.U., globalization may be over, and with it an era in history https://www.opendemocracy.net/can-europe-make-it/vassilis-k-fouskas/brexit-real-threat-to-globalisation

4   See http://edition.cnn.com/2016/06/24/politics/us-election-brexit-donald-trumphillary-clinton/
5   See http://ideas.ted.com/thomas-pikettys-capital-in-the-twenty-rst-centuryex-plained/ and https://www.ted.com/talks/thomas_piketty_new_thoughts_on_capital_in_the_twenty_rst_century?language=en
6   See http://www.universityworldnews.com/article.php?story=20170113164552838
7   See https://arstechnica.com/science/2017/01/have-politics-trumped-science/
8   E.g. https://www.scienti camerican.com/article/trump-comments-on-science-are-shockingly-ignorant/
9   https://qz.com/898530/in-just-one-week-as-president-donald-trump-has-wreake-dunparalleled-havoc-on-american-education/
10 See Secretary DeVos at 2017 Conservative Political Action Conference, C-Span https://www.c-span.org/video/?424394-101/betsy-devos-delivers-remarks-cpac
11 https://www.scienti camerican.com/article/trumps-rst-100-days-science-educatio-nand-schools/
12 http://www.cbsnews.com/news/where-donald-trump-stands-on-education/

References

Ostry, J., Loungani, P., & Furceri, D. (2016). Neoliberalism: Oversold? *Finance and Development, 53*(2). Retrieved from http://www.imf.org/external/pubs/ft/fandd/2016/06/ ostry.htm
Piketty, T. (2013). *Capital in the twenty-first century* (A. Goldhammer, Trans.). Cambridge, MA: Harvard University Press.